MELTING
POTHEAD

MELTING POTHEAD

By SIDDY SHIVDASANI

White Falcon Publishing

www.whitefalconpublishing.com

Melting Pothead
Siddy Shivdasani

www.whitefalconpublishing.com

All rights reserved
First Edition, 2020
© Siddy Shivdasani, 2020
Cover design © White Falcon Publishing, 2020
Cover image © Siddy Shivdasani

The contents of this book have been certified and
timestamped on the POA Network blockchain as a
permanent proof of existence. Scan the QR code or
visit the URL given on the back cover to verify
the blockchain certification for this book.

Requests for permission should be addressed to
meltingpotheadsiddy@gmail.com

ISBN - 978-93-89932-50-8

Contents

Acknowledgements

Thank you Deborah for inspiring, Nad for believing, Nicole for understanding, Sunita for supporting, David for honesty, Marc for those kicks up the arse, Audrey for expert proofreading, Andy for being a good nephew, my dad for good material, and my mum and Ice-T for bringing me up.

I'd also like to thank the dozens of people from all walks of life who gave me great feedback, encouragement, financial backing and marks to the manuscript.

I wouldn't have been able to do it without you.

Preface

"You half-caste cunt" is undoubtedly the most shameful thing I have ever said to a fellow human being. I would totally understand if you stopped reading this book now. Put the book down. Step away from the book.

It was a particularly absurd thing to say considering that I am mixed race. If you want to know why I wanted to hurt this person so badly then you'll have to read on, quite a bit. I'll tell you this much now, though: I was 14 and his racial background had nothing to do with why I hated him. It's the only time in my life that I've used a racist expletive in anger. And I apologised to 'Morgan' in my suicide note.

This is not an autobiography, it's the stories of a journalist's life, forever embedded in conflict situations. I don't offer a linear narrative, it's snapshots of my life: Memoir, anecdotes, reportage and opinions. I apologise in advance for throwing you readers around...life has kinda thrown me around.

I was born in Kingston upon Thames, Greater London, on May 9, 1972. My mum is white-English and my dad was brown-Indian. I grew up in the black capital of Europe, Brixton, south London. On Railton Road: The Frontline.

Part I: The Frontline

1. Sectioned

*'It is no measure of health to be well
adjusted to a profoundly sick society'*

We were piling out of the canteen as the sun bore down on
us through the open windows when a small, brown bird
flew in and perched itself on the back of a chair. I stuck out
my left index finger a few inches away and it hopped on.
Everyone turned around to look in astonishment. I calmly
walked over to the object of my desire carrying my new,
little friend, which was surprisingly heavy. Annoyingly,
another mental patient shrieked "boo!" and it flew away
before I reached 'Maddy'. It was the closest I'd ever come
to putting a wild bird at ease.

That was the high point of my time at Goodmayes
(psychiatric) Hospital in east London, near my home at
the time and where former world heavyweight boxing
champion Frank Bruno had been incarcerated several
years earlier. I'd like to compare notes with him one day
about how many cops it took to restrain him when *he* was
sectioned. Bruno pops up so many times in my story.

Just weeks before I befell the same fate as him, I'd
returned to my spiritual home — The Frontline — for
more weed. I ended up spending three days and two nights
in nearby Brockwell Park, revisiting my childhood years
and dreaming of a new world order. I didn't sleep. It was
summer but felt freezing at night. I saw monsters howling
in the leaves of the trees as I froze, wearing just a T-shirt,
thin gilet and shorts. Barefoot after discarding my sandals.
I saw ghosts in the sky during the days. I ate what was left
of my dope when I'd run out of tobacco.

My "mission from God" was to create a living hell,
one in which lesser souls would perish. I was some sort

of highly-trained operative, working for the world. The days were fine, despite the ghosts. I twirled like a Sufi on the grass during the sunny, breezy hours to get closer to God. On the third day, I stepped out of the park's Tulse Hill gate and twirled on the road. A white Mercedes stopped, the driver put his window down and shouted: "What are you doing?"

I told him to "fuck off" and banged on a rear window as he sped off. Moments later, I heard sirens approaching. Three male police officers cornered me outside the entrance to an estate and — deja vu — the short arse one in the middle bawled: "What are you doing?"

I took a step forward and bawled back: "Are you calling me out?"

I can't remember the words he used to signal their attack but they pounced on me instantaneously and simultaneously. Then began a protracted wrestling match on the floor as van loads of more cops arrived. I think it's fair to say it was more protracted than the agitator-in-chief anticipated. He screamed "aaaaaaaargggggghhhhhh" as I sunk my teeth into one of his calves as we grappled. He fucking deserved it. Wanker. I wasn't committing a crime when they approached me.

One quarter of troublesome offenders police deal with on the streets have mental health issues. He was aggressive and ignorant. I don't know how many it took to subdue me in the end, around a dozen. I wasn't taking notes.

I could still hear sirens approaching.

My wrists were bleeding and bruised because the handcuffs were gripping so tightly. There was a blonde, female PC grinning broadly at me as I was eventually spirited into a cage at the back of a Transit van. I wasn't scared, just wired and annoyed about the tight cuffs.

A young, white, male PC was looking at me from the back seat of the van. Even though I was seated, caged and cuffed, his eyes were bursting with fear — to a level I've never seen before or since in another human being. He looked away when I caught those eyes. I wanted to tell him: "Relax, the show's over."

It wasn't.

After the short journey to Brixton Police Station, they had a special technique for getting me from the van to a cell. Six of them sort of cradled me with linked arms, almost like pall bearers, as we moved inside. Then they poured me into a cell and mercifully removed my cuffs. I started doing yoga postures as soon as the door lock clunked shut.

Eventually, an officer opened a hatch and told me that my mum had turned up. Apparently, some of my other immediate family were upstairs. My mum had been waiting for me in the doctor's room. It was nice to see her. I had calmed down a lot and we chatted casually while my wrists were being examined by the doctor. She seemed relatively calm herself, which isn't usually her style.

Soon after, I was transferred to a secure unit at Maudsley (psychiatric) Hospital in nearby Camberwell. I don't know at what point it registered but back at secondary school, pupils used to joke about "ending up at Maudsley", although that was never directed at me. I didn't even know what it meant at the time, so I guess the joke was on me in the end.

It was a mad few days inside that place and I'd say that I was the most aggressive 'inmate'. It was similar to how I imagine prison. Not a bad prison but a prison nonetheless.

I later discovered I had only spent a few days in there but my recollection was a few weeks. I twirled in my room throughout the first night, occasionally threatening to lose my balance and breath. I don't know why I did it, something about Sufis again. I'd become very fit over the previous few weeks because I had been walking so much.

The days were mainly spent in the smoking room. It was pretty hardcore. Forget One Flew Over the Cuckoo's Nest, this was on a whole different level of insanity. It seemed like everyone related to a person I knew on the outside, somehow. For instance, I thought my dad had possessed one of the other patients. I had no fear, I was incredibly manic. The consultant who saw me one-on-one was scared. Even in that state, it wasn't lost on me that he should have been hardened to aggressive patients.

The next day, I was taken to a room and when I entered there were a dozen or so mental healthcare professionals standing there, staring at me. The consultant sat in the middle at the front and started asking me questions. I verbally abused them and, with an escort, stormed out. It was like having two brains. One was crazy, the other was saying: "Obviously, having a dozen people staring at me isn't going to put me at ease."

At one point, a small, see-through plastic bag with my personal effects from the police was handed to me. I think a lens from my sunglasses was in it. But one thing gave me the creeps: A Bounty bar wrapper. I took it to mean there was a bounty on my head. I hadn't eaten a Bounty and, even if I had, why would they give me the wrapper? I guess I'll never know. Maybe hope I never know.

There was a tall, white, middle class patient who I felt comfortable with and after we'd struck up a rapport, he started slamming doors. I asked him why he was doing it and he said: "It's *the work*."

I didn't know what he meant but I started doing it, too, for hours on end. Anything that would slam. The closest to logic I can muster is we were trying to affect sound waves.

What brought me to that point in the summer of 2008? I suppose my mental illness, bipolar disorder, had been bubbling away inside me all my life. Looking back, I had been in episodes before being sectioned.

Bipolar is a mood disorder, not a personality disorder. There is a mood scale of zero (suicidal) to ten (feeling like a god). Symptoms manifest themselves at each point of the spectrum. I've experienced the lot and, therefore, have bipolar 1. The trick is to try and stay in the middle sections. I assess myself every day. For the last few years, I've mainly managed to stay between the start of four and the end of six. How my moods manifest themselves is a long story. But it's fair to say I've been a victim of my own success in masking symptoms, including by self-medicating with cannabis, booze and cigarettes.

I have faced a lot of prejudice in my life but the stigma and ignorance over my mental illness trumps everything. I describe that 2008 episode as "my personal 9/11", it is amazing that I lived to tell the tale.

I do believe I have have this 'insight' in *and* out of manic episodes, on a slightly different wavelength, like on a mind-altering drug. It's important to make a distinction between a manic episode and a depressive one. For me, a manic episode feels like I am consciously operating in the unconscious world. I miss what everybody else sees but pick up on things no one else sees. I still believe that to be true but who knows? I feel it is also tied up with my inner conflict of having a mixed race, mixed culture, mixed class background. In Britain, I'm a nutter but on the streets of Mumbai — or "Bombay" as my Indian family will always know it — I'm just part of the general jamboree.

Being depressed is more self explanatory but if I'm psychotic as well then paranoia and suicidal thoughts kick in. It's unbearable. Several years before my 9/11, I got stoned and, for some reason, looked up "bipolar" in a health encyclopaedia. I had the symptoms but didn't want to give up dope and take the drugs I'd be prescribed. Then I buried that self-diagnosis deep in my mind with another joint.

Part of me doesn't regret being told I have a mental illness so late on, in my mid-30s. It might have held me back from achieving all I did as a journalist if I'd known earlier. I'm glad I have my diagnosis these days, though. I self-police and am firmly in charge of my own destiny now I'm single. My daughter is the most precious thing in my life and I'm determined to do everything in my power to stay sane so I can continue to play an important part in her upbringing.

A big chance to diagnose me was missed back in 2002. I had a "nervous breakdown", which I now know was a psychotic episode. I had an appointment with a consultant psychiatrist while being signed off work at The Sun for a month. But I found her arrogant and, consequently, wasn't open with her.

She said I was a social "chameleon", my personality "hadn't fully formed" and I was "allergic" to cannabis. She told me to pay for therapy but I couldn't afford to, so I was given sessions for a year with a student therapist. The consultant had assumed I could afford to go private because I was working for The Sun. But I had a big mortgage with my now ex and things were tight. It's a measure of the consultant's failure that she didn't even think I should be given therapy with a fully-trained professional.

...

Before I started to unravel after taking redundancy from The Sun in 2007, I felt great. I got seriously into yoga and loved practising it in the garden of our idyllic home in the Goodmayes bungalow estate, which is a conservation area. But then I started getting back into cannabis. Initially, it took my yoga practice to a higher level.

My plan was to open a pizzeria in Goa. It wasn't just a pipe dream: I had trained at a pizza school in Naples and researched extensively. Also, I have Overseas Citizen rights in India. But my now ex didn't *really* want to go, despite being a second generation Indian. And we'd made a bad investment in a Docklands development not long before the credit crunch hit.

Eventually, I had to start shifting again on various newspapers. One of the places I ended up was the Evening Standard. With the benefit of hindsight, it was a huge mistake. I'd been conditioned over many years to start work in the afternoon and finish late at The Sun. But I had to be at the Standard, across town just off High Street Kensington, at 7am. Sleep deprivation is bipolar sufferers' number one trigger for psychotic episodes.

It was fine to start with at the Standard but I wanted to be in Goa having a cool breeze blowing through my hair as I sped around the countryside on a moped. And the investment situation was eating away at me. It was a major factor in my deterioration.

I was psychotic when I was going through this but I remember when I was starting to lose it. There was a bit in stupid US TV series Lost when one of the characters says: "I think I'm going mad."

His friend replies something like: "If you think you're going mad, you're not. You're going mad when you think you are seeing things the way they really are for the first time."

That's what it felt like.

One of the confusing aspects of my manic bipolar episodes is that I can be quite creative and intelligent when in them. For instance, I had only ever played the board game Risk once with people. But I liked the concept and bought a version for my PlayStation 2. I must have only had ten games. Then, as I was totally losing the plot, I put it on the hardest level against the PS2…and won. I had no conscious strategy. I was heavily stoned and didn't even know I was in a good position until it flashed up that I had conquered the planet.

A total blur.

Though one thing I do remember thinking after winning is: "Now I'm ready."

My deterioration was gradual but my now ex finally left our bungalow. She was puzzled as to how I could carry on working while I was so obviously going nuts.

But I wrote a few barnstorming headlines, which the Editor made a point of praising. That shows mental dexterity because writing a headline for The Sun is quite different to the Standard. The Editor particularly liked one about ongoing issues at then new Heathrow Terminal 5: "Fasten your seatbelts for T5 summer of hell."

One which didn't make it on the foreign page lead story was about a UN report into Israeli-occupied land: "Occupied territories in their worst state since 1967."

When the colleague in charge of the page read it, he exclaimed: "Siddy!"

I can only speculate about his reaction but my sentiment was extremely off-message for the Standard and it got changed to something about UK charities giving record amounts of money to Palestinian NGOs.

I started coming in later and later and didn't give a shit. I used to mumble something about "engineering works at Stratford". Near the end, I was sleeping in my clothes and getting stoned before setting off for work. I got more and more agitated in the office. I had a few flare-ups and was taken aside by the Chief Sub-editor, who voiced his concerns.

Amid the walls closing in on me, there was a gorgeous white girl in the office. I couldn't keep my eyes off her. She had a certain poise that made her compelling viewing. Just before I was about to go down the escalator in that building for the last time (although I didn't know then that it would be the last time), she was at the top to my right and gave me a huge smile. I still don't know why she smiled (even though I got in contact with her many years later and we are now friends).

...

Like I say, a lot of the chronology is a bit mixed up in my head but before I went totally off the rails, I was also doing shifts at national Sunday paper The People at 1 Canada Square, Canary Wharf. It's a weird place to work, a bit like how I imagine it to be living in The Matrix. One Saturday evening, all the shops were closed when I went down for a cigarette. It was desolate. But somehow, I got chatting to this South American-looking guy who was wearing a crumpled, brown leather jacket and a colourful, cotton scarf. He was sitting outside a "Tumi" luggage store. He stood up and started telling me he was disgusted with the chainstore because the company's name was nicked from an ancient type of Peruvian ceremonial dagger. For him, it was a clearcut case of cultural appropriation. The conversation was brief but as I turned and walked off, he said: "You can sue them."

It was an odd thing to say but things were kinda going that way. When I got upstairs, I immediately googled "Tumi". I got the point. As a Shiv*dasani*, the UK launch of Coca-Cola's "Dasani" water in 2004 pissed me off. Make up your own fucking names, don't steal them. I mean, there was a guy I studied with back in college whose *full surname* was "Dasani". Fortunately, and hilariously, the launch became a fiasco when it emerged that the product was tap water. It was quickly withdrawn from UK shelves.

I'd deteriorated further the following week at The People. I set out for work listening to my old school portable CD player. But instead of going by public transport, I decided that, as 1 Canada Square was the tallest building in the country, at the time, I'd navigate my way there on foot. Somehow, I managed to get into a fight in a quiet part of Docklands. There was this man in his 30s dragging two boys, aged around seven or eight, by the arms about 50 yards from me. Rightly or wrongly, my perception was that the boys looked distressed and, with my headphones still plugged in, I shouted: "Fucking paedophile."

I don't know why I said it. I kept going but for some reason, I turned around to look back a few moments later and he was just two feet from me and about to pounce. I don't know what would've happened if I hadn't turned around. But I quickly and easily used a judo move to throw him to the ground and get on top of him without sustaining any injuries to myself or him. As I prepared to launch my right fist into his face, I looked into his eyes and calmly said: "I'm going to kill you."

But after a few seconds, something started pumping through my veins and I let him go. He was in tears and asked: "Why did you say that?"

I assumed he was referring to the accusation rather than the death threat. He gathered up my CD player and headphones, which were partially broken, and gratefully gave them back to me before running away. It was a horrible, horrible experience, knowing that, for a moment, I was about to try and kill someone.

But I do find it bizarre that you can say the maddest thing and people take it to heart. You wouldn't last long in Brixton with that mentality. And as far as that guy is concerned, did I touch a nerve? I'm not saying he was a "paedophile" but I did get the sense that he was mistreating those boys. I can't fully rationalise my behaviour and perceptions due to my state of mind. Maybe he had a mental health issue, too. I can't imagine a sane me leaving my daughter unattended to get into a fight with a nutter over anything he or she said.

Anything.

This was on the path that led me to Goodmayes Hospital. And Maddy…

I was transferred from Maudsley in an ambulance in the evening and I was wrapped in a blanket. My now ex was in the back with me but we didn't speak. I was deliberately trying to zone out and all I can remember is seeing the nightlights through the cabin front window. Maddy was there at Goodmayes Hospital with a female pal waiting to see who the next 'inmate' would be. She was slim and had sparkly, brown eyes. The first thing she said to me was: "Are you ready to dance into the future and never look back?"

I smiled and said: "Yeah."

Maddy had an intoxicating aura. In that moment, I felt like she was the girl of my dreams. She told my now former partner: "You're beautiful."

It felt like a handover.

I was quite happy to be there, like paradise compared to men-only Maudsley. So cool being on a mixed-gender ward, especially because Maddy was so gorgeous and lovely. That first evening was spent in the smoking room. It was like a house party, music blaring out of a little ghetto blaster in the corner. I told Maddy we had been separated by the forces of evil. She smiled at me in wonderment.

A few days later, I thought she was trying to escape. I chased after her down the stairs and into the car park, pursued by four or five male nurses. A cab was waiting, in my mind, for me. I jumped in the back and clambered out the other side. I could see her walking off with tears running down the cheeks of her round face but I was surrounded and twirled around again before being captured.

She was to escape again. This time she took heroin. I understood the desire to escape your own head. The only thing stopping me from trying to get hold of my own poison was knowing the pain would be worse later, as it was for her.

She sang, she danced, she cried, she shouted. Her many moods were disturbing yet alluring. One time I emerged from my room after having my one and only wank during my time there, walked into the canteen and, smiling up at me, she said: "Temptation will always be there."

How did she know? (No smart answers).

We'd already shared a memorable kiss. We were in the smoking room — the platform for our affection — and she suddenly had this glint in her almost Far Eastern eyes. She smiled, paced across towards me as I sat, leant down and delicately placed her tongue in my mouth. It only lasted several seconds but I didn't resist and I didn't try for more. A moment of bliss amongst the monotony. A few days later, I slipped my now ex's wedding ring, which I'd been wearing on my little finger, into Maddy's boot when she wasn't looking. The next day I felt guilty because I knew I'd have to ask for it back. But she was so delighted with the gesture that she offered it up.

Even — especially — in our maddest moments, we romanced on a mental ward.

After a couple of weeks, I was released. But I became excruciatingly paranoid. I thought the radio was talking to me. It was the hardest two weeks of my life. I spent every waking moment planning my own suicide. But I didn't want my now ex to be the one to find me hanged. Actually, for anyone to see that.

Eventually, I got up one morning and drank bleach. I went into the garden and tried to have a fag. But I quickly changed my mind about ending my life yet didn't have the wherewithal to make myself gag. Eventually, I did throw up. My ex emerged from the bedroom panicking and dialled 999.

The paramedics got me to drink some milk and took me to nearby King George Hospital's A&E unit. They didn't sound the siren and didn't seem bothered. They had probably dealt with hundreds of similar incidents.

The mental health team decided not to readmit me to Goodmayes Hospital but I was sectioned again a few weeks later over the paranoia. On the night I was readmitted, I made another suicide attempt. I wrote a note apologising to everyone I could think of who I had wronged over the years, including Morgan, the guy I racially abused. Then I tried to hang myself using my belt attached to a shower rail in my ensuite bathroom. But the rail couldn't take my weight and the whole thing collapsed.

All ligatures were confiscated and I was placed on suicide watch, which involved African, male nurses taking turns sitting on a chair with the door open all night. They weren't chatty. I was a broken man. I'd gone from being on top of the world, a revolutionary, Romeo demi-god, to a pathetic, skinny, suicidal nerd.

Maddy — who also has bipolar — wasn't there and another female patient told me: "She thought you were engaged."

As I remembered the ring, she added: "You were just flirting, that's okay."

Maddy had been away on a female-only ward, no doubt to protect her from the clutches and gazes of lusty men such as myself. But one day she came back to be discharged. She looked sparkly and blousy, although, without being drugged up, the magical glaze was missing from those eyes.

She was still the centre of attention, though, sitting on a packed table in the canteen, happily chatting away and giggling with her old mates. I was the bore, the sick one, sitting all alone. She was ignoring me and I felt abandoned. I was desperate to find out if I'd meant anything to her. I sloped up behind her when she was outside the office and said: "You're looking good."

"So are you," she replied. But there was embarrassment in those eyes, which had once promised to deliver me to a whole new world. My mum revealed how she recognised her beauty. But she also said that Maddy lost something without the medication, which had given her, in my mum's words, "heroin chic".

I had consumed so much cannabis before being sectioned the first time that it was still in my blood three months later. But the medics suspected I'd taken more between stays. I hadn't. My now former partner then came with some south Indian food — masala dosa — which

I love. But I was so paranoid that it had been laced with dope that I got her to eat a bit for every bit I ate. She was a powerful advocate for me in the NHS system. And she used to come with a picnic for us to eat in the grounds during sunny days.

She was not my only ally.

My weight fluctuates wildly depending on my state of mind and I had wasted away since being arrested. Inside a few months, I went from needing a dozen cops to subdue me to struggling to walk for more than five minutes. Some of the staff were total arseholes and some of them were wonderful. There seemed to be little in between at Goodmayes. However, one nurse will always stick out in my mind. He was the lowest in the hierarchy and had been in the job for decades but his kind soul motivated me to build up my strength with short walks, increasing bit by bit.

This middle-aged man never made a show of that kindness but I owe him a great debt. I don't know what his racial background was but I'd say maybe Algerian or Moroccan. I'd like to thank him to his face one day.

I returned to Brixton Police Station many months after being released from Goodmayes to fight a potential prosecution. I didn't know what the specific charges were but I was scared shitless. My immediate family turned up in support and I wore a suit and tie. I was taken down to the cells on my own to be formally rearrested, as a matter of procedure. I recognised the female officer on the desk and told her I was "sorry". She said: "You've got nothing to be sorry about, you weren't yourself."

But the cops I'd fought with wanted me prosecuted. Fortunately, my psychiatrist wrote them a letter to say I was in a severe psychotic episode at the time and their senior officer consequently canned the case.

Bipolar is apparently "trendy" these days. Be careful what you wish for, it's not for the faint-hearted. I had to rebuild my reality from scratch. However, I've retained some of the "truths" I became aware of during episodes. Bipolar is part of who I am and I've learned to live with the idea that I can't separate it from the rest of me.

My favourite philosopher is Krishnamurti. One of his quotes sustains me each and every day: "It is no measure of health to be well adjusted to a profoundly sick society."

2. Fair cop

'Bloodclaat, rasclaat, bumbaclaat!'

I finally lost patience with the teacher talking back to me, burst into tears, ran up to him, grabbed hold of his right leg as tightly as my little arms could around his knee and kicked his shin as hard and as often as my eight-year-old frame would allow. He eventually prised me off his leg after about a minute. I was immediately escorted to the headmaster's office. I can't remember who took me.

Up to that year, my education had been going quite well at Henry Fawcett School in Kennington, south London, a few miles from Brixton. The teachers seemed to love me. The previous one, Ms Bowyer (she made a point of being a "Ms"), thought the sun shone out of my arse. In those days, the whole class of say 30 kids would just get on a regular double decker Routemaster for school trips. She sat next to me one time and, in hushed tones, said: "I haven't told anyone else in the class yet…I'm pregnant."

I felt so honoured that she shared her news with me first. She was lovely and her classes and approach were inspirational. Then came Mr Fair, who looked like a Nazi from a WW2 flick — or a Bond villain — with his slicked-back blonde hair, short beard and thick-lensed spectacles. Mr Fair.

My first impression of his classroom was that it was devoid of colour, as was he in his thick, heavy-looking, dull brown, pinstriped suit (which, it later occurred to me, he wore every day). And he kept a cane on top of his blackboard, even though corporal punishment would then have, presumably, been unthinkable at that school (it was officially outlawed nationally in 1986). But it didn't bode well.

Our first morning with Mr Fair started with us all poised at our desks, waiting for him to get things under way. But he just sat there, stone-faced, behind his desk. After about five minutes, we started whispering to each other. The volume increased bit by bit over the next few minutes. Then he stood up and announced something like: "One hundred lines each, 'I will not talk in class.'"

That school year turned out to be a battle of wills between the two of us. I would give him backchat every day, every single day. Sometimes all day. He would retaliate by giving me lines. They got scruffier and scruffier. For instance, lines would start with the letter "I", so I would just crudely draw a straight line from the top of the page to the bottom. And I'd do this in full view. I wanted him to know that I wasn't going to yield.

He used to send me to the next door classroom for the Deputy Head, Mr Jackson, to inspect my lines. The thing is, Mr Jackson was great. He was this kindly, middle-aged guy with a down-to-earth, working class vibe. We would often sit next to each other on the 2B bus home and happily chat away. He knew I was a good kid.

There were three tutor groups in my year and the disruption my battle with Mr Fair caused led to many of my classmates' parents moving them to the other two groups. Eventually, my class lost between a third and half its numbers and I asked my mum if I could follow suit. I was miserable. So she met with the headmaster, Mr Curle (me and my mum used to call him "Curly-whirly, spotty botty"), and asked him if I could switch as well. He said: "If Siddy wants to move class, he's going to have to move school."

When my mum got home, she dropped this bombshell on me and asked if I wanted to move school. I immediately dismissed the idea, looked up at her, smiled and said: "No, I'm going to fight him."

It was a self-fulfilling prophecy and the day came when I literally, physically, fought him. I was talking back to him and he said: "One hundred lines."

I knew what to write at that point, he didn't even have the creativity to mix up the lines. You know, keep things fresh. It was something banal like: "I will not misbehave in class."

I can't remember exactly, it was a long time ago. Anyway, I just kept talking back to him.

"Two hundred lines."

Backchat.

"Three hundred lines."

Backchat.

"Five hundred lines."

Backchat.

The era of civil disobedience finally ended at "a thousand lines". I snapped and attacked him. I reckon I punched above my weight. Well, kicked.

The epilogue is that what was left of my tutor group got divided between the other two the following school year. As for Mr Fair, he was effectively demoted to being a teacher's assistant…for Mr Jackson's tutor group. Ha. Mr Fair was, inadvertently, one of the biggest influences on my life.

It has taken me this long to contemplate why Mr Curle wouldn't let me switch class. I suppose even more of the other children would have followed me. I don't recall anyone giving me any verbal support during my 'mission' but I assume the other kids were on my side. And I'm sure some of the teachers must also have been with me in the David and Goliath battle. I honestly don't know whether

Mr Curle was a good guy or not. I'd say, though, that he was upper middle class and I was conscious of that at the time because so is my mum.

Looking back at pictures of myself at that age, I was so innocent-looking, a pretty boy. I wasn't particularly physically big or strong. And you'd think that the kids from the tough council estate encircling the school would be the ones causing the disruption. But no, it was the pretty boy with the posh mum. If I write this seemingly in the third person, I suppose I was quite detached from the situation even at the time. I had no plan. I was just reacting to what I saw as injustice.

I had placed my trust in teachers up to that point. I would report things to them, before and after that year. A grass. But never to Mr Fair. I hated him from day one and I let him know. But I didn't dehumanise him. One day, I was on my way to school with a friend and his mum and we spotted Mr Fair on the walk in, chatting to a female teacher. In a patronising way, we sort of pitied him and hoped this woman would have a positive effect.

I don't know if he was a monster but he was totally in the wrong job. He didn't get on with kids. He should have been an accountant or a solicitor, something in that area.

Where did my rebellious attitude came from? Probably my dad, even though he only played a tiny part in my upbringing. He's in my genes. My mum was disowned by her well-to-do English family when she ran off with an Indian. My parents were living in Holland when I was a baby. But my mum, understandably, left him when I was about six months old. She fled to London.

My life at Henry Fawcett didn't get off to a bad start in the nursery but I was a squatter in Brixton at the time and I witnessed council workers on my road smashing up a house on the inside to deter us. The next day I started smashing up the nursery.

Monkey see, monkey do.

I can still vividly remember being in a class of crying kids with their mums there when we moved from the nursery into the classroom next door for first year infants. I was fine but was thinking: "We've only moved next door, why are they crying? What are they going to do to us?"

As an adult looking back, it is obvious that the kids didn't want their mums to leave. Anyway, the calling of the register became a character-building exercise for me throughout my entire school career. My full first name is "Siddartha" but I'd always been called "Siddy", so I didn't respond when my name was called out and they had to tell me that I was "Siddartha". After my mum picked me up from school, we were holding hands walking down the street and I looked up to her and said: "Mum, my name's not 'Disaster' Shivdasani."

I quickly settled in and my *real*, alternative, education started, aged five. I was always aware of my Eastern heritage. I wore Indian clothes from the day I could walk and they accounted for half of my dressing up box. I fantasised about being a warrior prince. My Indian side is actually warrior caste, *Kshatriya*.

One day in class, I was reading a textbook which was describing a battle between the British and Indian rebels. The thrust of the story was that a few hundred Brits had bravely defeated thousands of savages. I was impressed. But then I noticed that the accompanying picture showed that the Brits had guns and the Indians didn't. Like shooting fish in a barrel, although that particular phrase didn't come to mind at the time. Suddenly, I wasn't so impressed. These are the sort of things that crop up from time to time when you are mixed race — and have the journalism gene.

My first real experience of being exposed to racial tensions was on a warm summer's day in Kennington Park when I was seven. I was playing with a white friend my age when a white boy a few years older approached us and started telling us that "black people are bad". I tried to persuade him that there are good people and bad people, full stop. My friend got the heebie-jeebies and promptly left after trying to persuade me to come with him. I stayed to argue the case. I told him "I'm half Indian" and [for the purposes of this discussion] "*I'm* black".

He said: "Come with me."

I followed him to a secluded skateboard area in the park. As soon as I entered, I was surrounded by a group of maybe 20 black boys aged between about nine to 12. One, who was clearly the leader, emerged from the crowd and the white kid who'd brought me told him: "He says he's black!"

The leader asked me: "Are you black?"

It seemed like a Catch 22 situation but I got the feeling I needed to make a quick decision so I piped up: "Yeah."

The leader said: "Let him go."

All I knew at the time was that I'd had a close shave. But it later occurred to me that I'd had an insight into a world that I hadn't previously known existed. The white kid who'd led me there must have been luring racists into a trap. I wonder what happened to those who took the bait? Quite sophisticated in its own way. Police in east London started using a similar tactic decades later to snare violent racists. Presumably, the offenders just got arrested and prosecuted.

My second exposure to racism came when my form group went on a school journey to the Isle of Wight the same time. 'Trevor' was a black kid I didn't like. He was strange. He looked and dressed like a miniature old man. He had droopy eyes. Trevor once creeped me out when he gleefully told me: "Your mum smells of milk."

I bleated: "No she doesn't!"

I don't know why I was so upset about it. Anyway, I shared a room with him and two white boys on the holiday. As soon as it was just the four us in the room, the white boys told Trevor: "You're a nigger."

I wasn't familiar with the word but I knew it was bad and that it related to his race. It was weird. Where were these boys getting this from? They knew they were being nasty but getting off on it. Trevor didn't respond. He wasn't angry, just sad. He swallowed his pain. I felt his pain. I stayed out of it but I avoided those white boys for the rest of my time at Henry Fawcett. They were both brilliant footballers and I'd previously thought they were pretty cool. Maybe I should have stood up for Trevor. Being called a "nigger" is certainly a lot worse than being told "your mum smells of milk". That situation, to me, illustrates the power dynamic of racism.

. . .

My white half brother (who has a different dad, Rob) was born in 1979, two days before my seventh birthday and taking me to school evidently became too difficult for my mum. So the day came when she walked me to the bus stop on Brixton Road. I had played on the streets pretty much from the age I could walk but I can remember thinking at the time, when I realised what was happening: "You've gotta be kidding!"

She gave me my bus fare and sent me on my way. I'd adjusted to my new reality by the time it was my stop. But can you imagine that today? My daughter is seven at the time of writing and the idea of sending her out to pasture in the morning, hoping she'd make her own way back in the evening, is insane.

I did get into trouble a few times, like one day me and an older, white friend went to a West Indian gambling den just off The Frontline around that time. We were fearless. My mum hit the roof when she found out we'd been there and eventually banned me from having contact with that boy. She also freaked out when I took myself swimming without telling her. I must have packed my towel and trunks before leaving for school in the morning, not knowing it would be an issue. Aged seven.

And if you think that's mad, there was this black girl in the year *below* me and she used to take her *little sister* from nursery at Henry Fawcett to Brixton. She was perfectly charming and friendly to me. I liked Dionne a lot. The funny thing is that she refused to pay her fare (kids were meant to fork out half back then). The (mostly black) conductors would do everything in their power to make her pay up or get off. But she did neither.

She would be all sweetness and light with me one second and then instantaneously turn into a ferocious, sharp-tonged firecracker when the conductors deigned to bother her. She would swat them like flies and then get back to being lovely to me in a heartbeat. She was six. Formidable…scary.

Those were happy days on the whole. I wasn't a bully and I wasn't bullied. Some of the black kids were rough but some of the white kids were, too. There weren't many Indian subcontinent Asians but one that I was friends with,

'Vijay', was very sweet, despite living on the rough estate around Henry Fawcett.

Looking back, I must have been troubled on some level, even before the Mr Fair year. My mum starting to take me to judo lessons when I was about seven. It was good, although I got a bit frustrated about not having stripes on my belt, so one day I drew some on. Judo, as I understood it at the time, was a form of physical combat which involved restraining an attacker in self defence without injuring them.

But once, I just started fighting, unrestrained, in a lesson. I didn't go back after that because I was afraid of the repercussions. Something must have seeped in because I have employed judo moves a few times as an adult in real situations without thinking about it.

Like most kids, I was a sponge.

I also started picking up the West Indian swearwords in the playground at a tender age. When the black kids cottoned on to this, I used to draw a crowd. I would say: "You bloodclaat, rasclaat, bumbaclaat!"

I had no idea of what any of it meant but I did the full-on Jamaican accent and my audience was on the floor. It was a nice feeling making them laugh. It must have sounded hilarious coming out of my mouth.

Ironically, I don't think I'd have been accepted by black kids when I was growing up if I'd acted black. The idea of it simply never crossed my mind. I picked up my south London accent from kids of all colours. Nowadays, white and Asian kids act black and I think it's pathetic. A certain type of cultural appropriation. The black kids didn't act black in Brixton, they just were. I know I'm not racially black, "wiggers ("white-niggers" who act black) really piss me off. I even cringe when *black* people 'act' black.

My best friends in Brixton around that time were two black brothers around my age, Peter and Clive. We mainly played football on the street with their friends and cousins, occasionally, accidentally, breaking windows. We also used to climb fences at the back of the terrace gardens and this elderly, black woman used to invite us in for biscuits. She was the classic 'Big Momma' stereotype. She had next to nothing, not even a sofa or a TV. But she gave us what she did have and seemed to enjoy our fleeting company as she sat at her kitchen table. Her then council townhouse must be worth millions now.

The thing some may find surprising is that the 'gang' in the area was a pretty even mix of black and white. They were three or four years older than us and used to pick on us a bit. Aside from the issues of behaviour (they once made a tramp drink piss in front of us), gang culture seems to be much more racially-defined these days.

However, I was the only non-black member of our 'gang' and one of the brothers' cousins was nicknamed "Rubber Lips". He did have big lips and seemingly didn't give a shit about it. I called him "Rubber Lips" around the black kids and he wasn't fussed. But one day, I was walking along the street with a white woman who lived in our council house. I saw him and innocently asked: "All right, Rubber Lips?"

He gave me an icy stare and didn't respond. I was totally confused, especially when the woman I was with took me to task over it. Ironically, everybody seems to want big lips these days.

I lost touch with the brothers after I moved to a different part of Brixton. But years later, aged 16, I was working in Brixton's Ritzy cinema as an usher. Clive came in and tried to sell me a secondhand Walkman. I was polite about it but I told him I wasn't interested. I didn't acknowledge I knew him. I still feel guilty about that.

Where did he get the Walkman from? I don't know. But they were good kids, genuine, with warm hearts. I wonder how life worked out for them.

I was trying to better myself and there was something in me that was determined to use every advantage I had to move forward with my life. Only now that I'm in my mid-40s am I looking back and re-engaging with some of the people from my past.

. . .

I had the vague idea from quite a young age that the police were out of control in and around Brixton. This personally impacted on me when my (white) stepdad, Rob, got caught up in a violent incident outside Henry Fawcett minutes before I was about to perform in the school play one evening when I was eight.

He parked up with my mum and, as they walked up to the school gates, they spotted a group of white men kicking the shit out of a black youth on the floor. Imagine a Rodney King-style beating but with no one there to film it. Rob, ironically a filmmaker, tried to intervene and said: "Stop it! What are you doing?"

But they turned on him and Rob recalled: "They told me to go away because they are the police and I said, 'Well, you're not behaving like the police.'"

Rob began to swear at them and told them to "leave the boy alone". By this point, a crowd was gathering and a van carrying uniformed officers turned up. Rob described the victim as being "little and not aggressive", adding: "He was probably a teenager but he looked like a child to me."

They were bundled into the vehicle and Rob took a beating in the back. He recalled: "I was still being stroppy, I was so angry. I can remember one of them, a nasty piece of work. He kept laughing at me. I was so struck by their arrogance, like they knew they were going to get away with it."

Loads of kids came up to me before the show, telling me what had happened. I couldn't quite believe it, the versions of events varied wildly. I recall being up on stage, spotting my mum in the audience but realising Rob wasn't there, wondering what the fuck had actually gone down.

I still vividly remember picking him up from the local police station that night. Rob's ear was ripped during the altercation and he had to have stitches. The incident was the talk of the school the next day and Rob was a hero among the kids. I asked for my mum's recollection of the incident and she described it as an "eye-opener".

"I was brought up on Dixon of Dock Green," she said, referencing a fictional, kindly 'bobby on the beat' in a BBC TV show which ran for 20 years from the mid-Fifties. The incident was a reality check and she remembered thinking: "Ah, so *this* is how the police *really* operate."

They later met up with the boy and tried to persuade him to get proper legal representation. But he was resigned to his fate and said: "They're the police and I'm black."

Both the boy and Rob were charged with assaulting the police officers and were tried together. Fortunately for Rob, he had a good barrister, was treated as a reliable witness and got off. But the youngster was convicted and, according to Rob's recollection, got a jail sentence. This (and many similar incidents, no doubt) was the context leading up to the first major Brixton riot, in 1981.

An amended Race Relations Act had become law in 1976 but police forces were exempt. Many young black men believed officers discriminated against them, particularly by using the notorious "sus law", under which anybody could be stopped and searched if cops merely suspected you might be planning to carry out a crime.

In early April, 1981, the police's Operation Swamp was launched in a bid to cut street crime in Brixton. More than 1,000 people were stopped and searched in six days and it's a massive understatement to say that it heightened tensions. The thing is that The Frontline had been the one place in Brixton where the police were a bit stand-offish. It had been a safe haven and, to tell the truth, as a child with a Mediterranean appearance, I had no idea that it was a tough area. It was the norm for me. I'm certain that, because I grew up there, the locals regarded me as part of the community and that insulated me from problems 'outsiders' might have encountered.

It's worth pointing out that the local population as a whole treated the operation as an invasion, many of the rioters were white. And Rob was stopped "four to five times" under the "sus law". He had starting getting involved in making controversial, anti-Establishment films about Northern Ireland at the time and he said an Irish republican friend of his compared Brixton to "occupied west Belfast" during the height of The Troubles.

Thankfully, I wasn't in Brixton when the first riot broke out on April 10, 1981. My then council home was 50 yards from the epicentre of the conflict. My mum said it was surreal watching it on the TV in Leicester, where we were staying with Rob's parents. I think I'd be a slightly different person now if I had been there. I'm glad I was shielded from that.

I watched a documentary about it several years ago and it turned out that many house parties were held when things died down and lots of people turned up wearing new clothes and jewellery acquired during the looting. And there was even a song to mark the occasion: "Brixton riot a murder, police couldn't push it lickle furder."

What would have happened if the police had, indeed, pushed things a little further?

I found the Brixton riots quite inspiring as I was growing up. That people would fight back, refuse to accept oppression, harassment and being constantly violated. What would have happened if there were no riots? Would the police brutality have just carried on? I think so.

I might not have been there for the 1981 Brixton riot but I did get caught in the middle of another riot.

Rob took me to watch Arsenal for the first time when I was seven on November 2, 1979. We stood on the terraces and saw Arsenal beat Brighton 3-0. I was totally hooked. It was so exciting to actually go to games, as well as being a nice thing for me and Rob to do together. But unfortunately, it was the era of regular, hardcore football hooliganism. Me and Rob were in Arsenal's Highbury stadium's famous North Bank terrace, albeit to the side, to see them play West Ham on May 1, 1982, when I was nine. Among the Hammers' supporters was the most notorious mob in the country at the time: "The Inter City Firm."

They were named that because of their MO of travelling to matches first class by InterCity train. About ten minutes into the game, around 500 ICF hooligans invaded the North Bank. I had been sitting on one of the bars with Rob holding me in place. When the invasion started I just fell back into his arms. There were red smoke bombs going off and dozens of punch-ups. The players were quickly led off the pitch as Arsenal fans poured onto it. My abiding memory is of an Arsenal fan staggering around ten feet from us with a massive head wound. It was like part of his head was bursting through his skull. A huge, bloody boil on one side of his forehead.

I can't say I was afraid, I didn't, as a child, feel personally threatened. I didn't find it *seductive*, either, I was there for the football and the atmosphere. But it wasn't lost on me that it was like being in a theatre of war. The cops gradually started taking control of the situation and things began dying down after about ten minutes. The ICF members were shepherded by the police, for their own protection, into a side section of the terrace with their West Ham scarves on. Then the players came back on and the game restarted. I do remember glancing over to the ICF hooligans and taking note of the fact that they eventually became engrossed in the game. Weird scene.

There are three epilogues to this story. Firstly, I later learned that an Arsenal fan had been murdered. My first thought was the guy with the head wound. But actually, the victim was stabbed to death outside the ground.

Secondly, three or four years later, I did a fictionalised story of the riot in my English class, imagining things from the ICF point of view as they prepared to invade. But my teacher (we had a love-hate relationship) thought it was unrealistic that the game would have restarted.

Oh, and Arsenal won 2-0.

3. Extra gear

'Black people don't bruise'

The sky was lit up by flames on the evening of the 1985 Brixton riot. It had all died down the next morning and I walked with Rob through a ghost town of burned out, overturned cars and smashed-in shopfronts. It was like being on a huge film set.

I was at Pimlico comprehensive in Westminster at the time, then the most multi-cultural school in the country. You might think it was posh because of its location but actually the pupils were almost exclusively drawn from the sprawling council block estate next door and rough areas south of the river. The first day back after the riot, everyone was talking about it. How the police had shot a black woman — Cherry Groce — in her home because she was suspected of harbouring her son who was wanted over firearms offences. He wasn't there.

The whole year of boys went to have PE at one point during the day and our teacher, 'Mr Hunk', looked agitated. I'd always liked him. He was a tall, white, muscular, blonde, handsome, charismatic guy. Sort of like He-Man.

But what happened next was a bit weird. Instead of letting us get changed, he marched us into the gym and ordered us to sit down on the benches and listen. It seemed like he was angry with *us*. He then proceeded to give a lecture on how the police were just doing their jobs and that the woman who got shot — and paralysed from the waist down — was harbouring a bank robber. He seethed: "Do you know what a sawn-off shotgun can do? It can take out a whole car."

There was a deathly silence.

There was no time left for our lesson so we never did get changed and no one talked about 'the speech' afterwards.

I thought it was a demonstration of breathtaking arrogance by Mr Hunk. I knew through personal experiences that the police often behaved like a gang of racists in my area. And I'm quite sure that many of my fellow pupils would have been aware of that themselves, often through their personal experiences or those of people close to them. What Mr Hunk did was inappropriate and unprofessional. I knew it then as a 13 year old and I know it now. Surely, there would or should have been guidelines about that sort of thing.

Many years later, mother of six Mrs Groce received £500,000 in compensation from the Metropolitan Police, with no admission of liability. The officer who shot her — Detective Inspector Douglas Lovelock — was prosecuted for malicious wounding but acquitted.

Let's talk again about firearms offences.

Mrs Groce died in 2011 aged 63 and a 2014 inquest ruled there was a causal link between the shooting and her death. In the same year, an inquest jury concluded that eight separate police failures had contributed to it. The Met eventually apologised for the wrongful shooting of Mrs Groce.

Her son, Michael, got a three-year suspended sentence for illegal possession of a sawn-off shotgun but was never charged with any offence related to armed robbery or the riots. He insisted he had taken possession of the weapon because he feared for his life.

What do you say now, Mr Hunk?

One thing I *would* say for him is that he did save an old woman's life. She was about to jump to her death from a third floor window which looked down on one of the submerged playgrounds at Pimlico. A few of the pupils playing football at lunchtime looked up, spotted her and started shrieking: "Don't do it!"

She did jump but miraculously, survived. What actually happened is that one of her calves got impaled on an iron railing on the way down. A million to one shot. Mr Hunk was the first one on the scene and rushed to hold her in place until the fire brigade arrived. The whole school turned out to watch. But I decided, after hearing what had happened, that I would avert my eyes from the gruesome display.

My other abiding memory of Mr Hunk, apart from chatting up admiring female teachers, is taking us for sprinting during PE. Pimlico School is on a sort of island surrounded by roads and our running track was the narrow pavement around the grounds. We were doing the 100 metres sprints in pairs with two teachers, one at each end. Mr Hunk was at the start. I hated running because I was always slow. Before my turn, this tall, blonde, nice guy put his head down and ran his socks off. Unfortunately for him, towards the end of the 100 metres, he ran into a lamppost face first, with such impact that he bounced five foot from where he'd just come from and landed flat out on his back. He was motionless.

The boys at my end were in fits of laughter. Some were on the floor. I could see the funny side but didn't want to laugh until I knew the boy was okay. Mr Hunk went ballistic at the laughers. What did he expect? We were a bunch of ghetto-hardened kids. Some would have laughed even if the boy had died. Some *especially* if he'd died. That's the reality.

To illustrate the kind of thing that went down at Pimlico, a friend of mine was nearly murdered playing at lunchtime. Growing up, there was this playground game called "Stingball". The idea was to throw a tennis ball at someone so hard that it would hurt. Being slow, I never played it. One summer, a more vicious version of the game — "Beats" — became all the rage. And when I say rage...

The idea was that when someone was hit, the victim had to escape from the playground as everyone tried to punch and kick him. One day after lunch, I was in a design and technology class and, before the lesson began, all the boys were talking about how Beats had got out of hand. The boys were kinda excited that a boy had been beaten to a pulp.

Then the Deputy Head, a handsome and charismatic (more so than Mr Hunk on both counts) Asian man called Mr Singh, came in and spelled out the gravity of the situation — with considerable drama. The victim was not a close friend but a friend nonetheless, a decent guy. He, incidentally, had the same racial make-up as me. Mr Singh said the paramedics had to use special lifting equipment to scrape him off the floor, so as not to damage his spine. He added that the boy was fighting for his life and talked about "murder charges". Suddenly, the excitement was gone. Now it was about fear.

What actually happened is that the victim *had* managed to escape the playground but the pack continued chasing after him anyway. He was knocked unconscious as he fell when his head hit a steel bar which was part of the school's electronic, outer blind system. The story is that the last assailant jumped on the boy's head. Fortunately, for all involved, the victim escaped with some broken ribs and made a full recovery. But I found him to be a slightly different person after that.

I was never the type to get involved with a game like Beats, even had I been fast. But I was quite badly behaved in my own way, especially from the age of about

13. I barely did a jot of homework during my whole time at Pimlico. I was the class clown and would frequently be sent out for being disruptive.

...

Back in my early days at Pimlico, aged 11, I was on my way home and these two older, black boys cornered me after I got off the Tube at Brixton. They told me to come with them and we ended up on this secluded, open staircase just off the high street. It was horrible. I didn't know what they wanted from me but I was scared.

Eventually, after coming to the conclusion I had little to take other than a few coins, they let me go. I ran a mile or so home in tears and my mum called the police. This white detective turned up at our home, asked me what had happened and for descriptions. I told him that the older, taller, darker one had "a lot of facial bruising". The detective said: "Black people don't bruise."

I was totally speechless. Shocked. I was thinking: "Hang on a minute here."

HE HAD BRUISES.

It was a chilling moment. My best friend at that time — 'Ralph' — was black and he was a gentle giant. A real softie, much more so than me. We were inseparable. The point being that the boys being black was not my issue. The detective drove me to the scene and I was sitting in the back of the car feeling almost as nervous and bewildered as when I had been with the two boys.

Part of me had always wanted to believe that my fears and the stories about cops weren't *really* true, despite the incident outside Henry Fawcett School with Rob years previously and the 1981 riot. It woke me up a bit. That cop knew black people bruise. Apart from anything, I simply couldn't believe it at the level of an adult openly talking shit, especially to a child.

In that first year at Pimlico, a black boy in the fifth year tried to "drapse" my watch, which had the then new feature of being both digital and analogue, a bit James Bond. "Drapsing" is kind of like a mild form of mugging. It usually equated to older kids taking stuff off younger kids, knowing they would never report it. Drapsing could involve a physical element but not necessarily. My scene happened on a platform bench inside Pimlico Tube station. He was a big guy, a six-footer. He was all over me. We were both gripping the watch and I just held onto it for as long as I could, as tightly as I could. I might have let go if he'd hit me. But he didn't and, eventually, he gave up, saying something like: "This kid's got spirit."

You're damned right.

My Sony headphones once got drapsed. They were taken by a black kid outside my form classroom before afternoon register. The annoying thing is that this big, white guy, 'Martin', assured me he'd get them back for me. But possession is nine tenths of the law and he knew it. He should have stopped them from being taken there and then or stayed out of it.

Martin saw himself as a hardman but the truth was that he was afraid of certain black boys. I did, miraculously, manage to get the headphones back a few weeks later but no thanks to Martin. I was in a playground with him once and he told me he was going to hit me round the head with the cricket bat he was holding. I said: "No, you're not."

I was wrong. Martin became a lawyer.

...

Despite Pimlico's shortcomings, there were some good teachers, especially my form tutor, Mr Nicholls. He genuinely cared about us during my time there and he was extremely patient. He once invited an Auschwitz survivor to talk to us. Everybody was incredibly respectful. I can't speak for the others but that experience had a huge impact on me. I simply could not comprehend the evil of the Holocaust, that people would do that to their fellow human beings on such a massive scale.

My tutor group was a mixture of white (including Jewish), black and Asian. We mainly got along, although there was a lot of piss-taking about our racial backgrounds which, occasionally, boiled over. But I noticed, when I was around 13, some of the boys were organising themselves into racially-defined gangs.

One morning break time, I was playing football and this boy from the year below, who happened to be black, kept fouling me. Bearing in mind there was no referee and it could get a bit rough, I finally snapped, grabbed him by the arms, pinned him up against a wall and delivered a few, ineffective, punches. I was wearing woollen gloves.

I'd forgotten the incident by lunchtime until the boy I'd hit came into the playground with an older, mixed race boy who used to wander round the school grounds carrying a rounders bat, without ever being challenged by the teachers. I recall that he had actually left the school but still hung around. He was aged around 16.

They took me to another playground area and there was a multi-racial, multi-age gang waiting for me. I was encircled and they were starting to give me little digs.

I was resigned to taking the beating of my life. I feared for my life. But then the black gang from my year, led by Colin, a boy I'd been friends with before he got all militant, emerged from the distance to retrieve me, followed by most of the rest of the boys from my year. It was like something out of a movie. Robert, who was white and one of my best friends, had alerted Colin.

...

I have faced racism from Asian people, though not nearly as much as from white people. But I've had virtually no racism from black people. One of the few times I did was from a girl in my form early on at Pimlico. 'Denice' was of Jamaican extraction and lived in the infamous Stockwell Park Estate in Brixton. I feared that place and I'd had run-ins in the past with boys from there. Some of them, black boys, played in my Brockwell Park Saturday morning football league and they didn't give a fuck. I don't remember anything specific, I just knew that was somewhere I didn't want to go for fear of being mugged or attacked. I lived on The Frontline but I was a familiar face there.

Me and Denice, who was in my tutor group, had an on-off friendship over the years. We once had an altercation after she accidentally ripped my new jacket. I pushed her away, unfortunately with more force than I'd intended. She went flying against a desk, then came for me and scratched my face to ribbons.

I digress.

One day, my dad — universally known as "Peso" — picked me up from Pimlico when I was about 13. It was one of the happiest moments of my life. I can see still see him walking up to the school gates with a big smile on his face. I hadn't been picked up by anyone pretty much since I was seven, so to be picked up by *my dad*, who lived in India,

was a special occasion. And I wanted to say to all my school
friends: "You see, my *Indian* dad does actually exist."

The next day, Denice being Denice saw this as an
opportunity to tease me and took great delight in comparing
my dad to "a monkey". Looking back, it probably just
tickled her that I'd be so hurt by an insult usually aimed
at black people. I got quite tearful about it and somehow
ended up in an office with the Deputy Head of Year. She
was Greek and told me she used to get teased about being
a "bubble and squeak" (which is not quite the same) and
I should just shrug it off, which I did. It's quite amusing
in a way.

Not that it was specifically directed at me but I do also
recall a black kid — who went on to become a professional
footballer — repeatedly using the word "Paki". We were
getting changed after PE and he was talking to someone
about why there were no Asian professional footballers in
Britain. I can still remember how angry I was when he
asked everyone: "Why are there no professional Pakis?"

I just wish he hadn't used that word. Things would
have kicked off if I had talked about "niggers". My other
abiding memory of him wasn't good either. I got into some
stupid row with an on-off white friend, 'Graham', as we
were leaving school at the end of the day. I was holding
a football and I told him to "shut the fuck up or I'll blast
you in the face". He challenged me to try. I wasn't a great
footballer and had no genuine belief I'd hit the target
but — Sod's Law — I nearly took his head off. I felt a
bit of pride. But Graham was essentially a nice guy going
through a devastatingly difficult period of his life. He
challenged me to a fight a few days later.

Dozens of boys gathered round us but neither of us
would throw the first punch. My rationale was that he had

challenged me, so why should I throw the first punch? The footballer held me by one of my wrists and tried to get me to punch Graham. Fighting 'duels' were great entertainment back then but I'd managed to dodge being one of the leading men over the years, and did so with Graham, who I was not afraid of. It was just him trying to boost his street cred, which was a bit pathetic.

Misbehaviour was such a big issue that, halfway through my time at Pimlico, they created a tutor group full of the most disruptive boys in the year. Graham was put in there. I thought it was pretty harsh and, having met him years later, I think it sent him down a horrific path...to jail. But he was his own worst enemy in a way, he was so desperate to be in with the 'cool' kids. I heard that one of them once poured the contents of an ashtray over his head and he burst into tears. He was an arse-kisser, all for the sake of being 'cool', which was never going to happen.

But there were certainly worse-behaved boys in my class, especially 'Kelvin', my day-to-day nemesis at Pimlico. He was a black kid with a Jamaican background. I got a bad first impression of him. He was also from Stockwell Park Estate and mates with Denice. I would not submit to his will, not even parting with my coppers so he could play a game called "penny up". Kelvin was actually not that big or strong but he was a force of nature, charismatic in his own way but essentially, a bully. He had two, white sidekicks who hung around him because they thought it made them 'cool'. I nearly came to blows with him a few times but I was scared of his two, older sisters. They were fearsome, like I'd imagine they would *literally* scratch your eyes out.

One of the few times my mum drove me to Pimlico was because I was going on a school journey and had luggage. As we were driving through Stockwell, I saw Kelvin on the street struggling to the bus stop with his suitcase. He was running late and I think it was the first time that I ever recognised he was vulnerable. There was something in his body language that made me realise he wanted just to be a normal kid. When I look back, it seems obvious he'd been brutalised.

You have to bear in mind that we were sworn enemies but without hesitation, I told my mum to pull over. I put his suitcase in the boot and got him in the car. Kelvin turned to me and gave me a huge smile. He never gave me a problem again after that. That was when we were around 13 and a few years later he was living on his own in a hotel room near the school. He used a crowbar to prise open parking meters for pocket money. And I realised more and more that, whatever was going on in my life, his must have been tougher than I could possibly comprehend.

I mean, this guy went to a parents' evening on his own. I rated him for turning up under those circumstances. And he did make a go of things in the later years, especially in maths, which was taught by Mr Nicholls. But he should, in all fairness, have been in the naughty boys' class, not Graham. And let's not be sentimental about Kelvin: At times, he displayed an almost murderous streak.

The epilogue to that story is that I ran into him in the street during my early 20s when I was doing a journalism course in Vauxhall, south London. We had a little chat as we walked along and he seemed happy. I will always remember him telling me: "I never forget my friends."

My actual best friend for most of my time at Pimlico also had a Jamaican background but he was a different kettle of fish all together. Ralph was very straight in many ways, he didn't get into dope like me and a few others at 15, for starters. He had a great sense of humour, though. He was warm and sensitive. A lot of his character can be explained by knowing his domineering mother, who brought him up single-handedly. I reckon she thought I was a bad influence on Ralph. Maybe I was.

I used to call him "Timothy" in reference to Ronnie Corbett sit-com, Sorry. In it, Corbett played a middle-aged man who is still living with his mum because she won't extract her claws from him. She sabotages all his potential escape routes, romantically and otherwise. It was cringemaking. It's funny because 'my' "Timothy" was a tall black guy (6ft 5ins, eventually), while Sorry Timothy was 5ft 1ins and white. The only physical thing they had in common (presumably) was that they both wore glasses. I once sent him a postcard from Greece — Ralph not Ronnie — and in it I called him a "bloodclaat". I phoned him up when I got back and his mum came on and gave me an ear-bashing about using that swearword.

"Language, Timothy!"

I wanted to tell her that I had sent the postcard to Ralph not her and that it was none of her business. But she scared the shit out of me. I lived quite close to Ralph so we would travel home together most days. He did listen to me but I think, in the end, he hated me. He was seriously into this blonde girl in his area and struck up a friendship with her. I don't know whether he was in love with her but he certainly talked about her a lot. Eventually, he wanted to show her off to me and we met. Okay, so you've guessed what happened next...

Yes, horny me got together with her for a while. My rationale was that if anything was going to happen between them it would have already occurred. I was a 15 year old virgin. It's a shame, though. Ralph and I were close. I suppose it would have been tremendously hurtful if the tables had been turned. But frankly, I wouldn't have showed her off before she was in the bag. Okay, I'm trying to justify my actions. I can't. It was a betrayal and it cost me a great friendship. Would I do it again as a randy, 15 year old boy? Probably.

. . .

I lived and breathed football for much of the early part of my life. I would have loved to have been a pro and, specifically, played for Arsenal. I had this recurring dream about coming on as a substitute at their old Highbury ground. But the only thing I had in my favour was a good footballing brain.

Most of the Saturday morning league boys in Brockwell Park weren't quite good enough for their school teams, although it probably helped to give a few of them a nudge in that direction (including Ralph). Anyway, one time, I was playing right back in a match and was getting murdered by the opposition left winger. He was a fast, tall, strong, black guy. Definitely school team potential. Lightning quick.

We all had full kits, shirts, shorts and stockings but this kid was wearing grey tracksuit bottoms. As an aside, I sort of felt that it diminished the standing of the league that he wasn't wearing the proper kit. Anyway, as he was about to fly past me for the umpteenth time, I conducted an *experiment*: I deliberately tripped him up. He went flying, landing in a heap on the floor. After a few moments, he turned in my direction while still down and looked at me daggers. Then he got to his feet before pulling a spanner out of one of his tracksuit bottom pockets! I turned around and ran as fast I could in the general direction of my home. As I said, I was slow but boy, I found an extra gear that day. When I finally looked behind me, I couldn't see him and I stopped running. I'm sure he felt like he'd made his point…and I then understood why he was wearing tracksuit bottoms.

Nothing was said about it the following week. I still occasionally see "Spanner Lad" around my area and it always sends a chill down my spine.

As well as playing regularly, from the age of 13, I used to go to most Arsenal home games with my mates, unaccompanied by an adult. And we'd go to other games in London, such as at Chelsea or even QPR, if Arsenal were playing in a different part of the country. It was a great outlet for me. The atmosphere back in the Eighties was pretty electric (there was actually an electric fence at Chelsea but it was never turned on).

I was quite resourceful when I think about it. I used to spend a week painting Arsenal's old ground during my summer holidays in return for a season ticket. I'm sure I won't get sued for this because they're probably all dead by now but the painters on the payroll were basically a small bunch of elderly, somewhat kindly, drunks. Can you imagine anything like all of that happening now? These days, painting Arsenal's Emirates Stadium *probably* involves a contract that gets put out to tender and various multi-national corporations vie for it. That's *probably* an exaggeration.

Arsenal playing legend George Graham took over as manager in 1986 and we won the League Cup in his first season. When we were painting the stadium during our summer holiday, me and my mate, 'Gary', were once taking a break in the iconic East Stand where fans were having their pictures taken with the Cup. The funny thing is that they just left it behind on its own for an hour when the photographer went to lunch. Anyone could have just walked in off the street and taken it. *We* could have taken it.

My other abiding memory of growing up with Arsenal was me and Gary eventually having the balls to stand in the epicentre of the North Bank terrace, where all the singing emanated from. There used to be this young lady who would often position herself behind one of the bars in the most tightly-packed section. Women hardly went to football in those days, let alone placed themselves in that area of the ground. AND she was gorgeous. This is a bit pervy but we (I mean all the males in that particular section) used to take turns lining up behind her, hoping Arsenal would score so we'd get squeezed against her gorgeous behind in the melee. She definitely got off on it, as did we! Talk about up the Arsenal! I suppose she must have been some sort of exhibitionist.

My career as a journalist had its roots in my obsession with football. I used to buy weekly football magazines, such as Match and Shoot, from the age of 11. Then I started buying The Daily Mirror for its football coverage. I was not a good student at Pimlico but I must have absorbed a lot by reading red-top tabloids. I was learning unconsciously.

For the entirety of my six years at Pimlico, I caught the Tube from Brixton. There was a newsstand outside the station where I would buy my magazines and papers. The funny thing is that the (white) woman who usually served me always gave me the wrong change. Too much! Sometimes she would give me more than I gave her in the first place. Like maybe 50p more.

This 'arrangement' was unspoken. Looking back, I find myself speculating whether she thought that my preoccupation with words would lead me into some sort of worthwhile career. I guess I'll never know but I'm sure she wasn't giving the wrong change to everyone. That little bit of money that I saved or accrued did make a difference. I wasn't a squatter at that point but things were still pretty tight. I may not have made it as a journalist if it hadn't been for the newsstand woman.

The Mirror was an assertion of my "lefty" background and identity. A black classmate used to buy The Sun and we were like two Jedis with our lightsabers. He laughed and laughed many years later when he heard that I was working for The Sun. Leroy wasn't a tall guy but he was big and strong. It was bizarre that he was so right-wing. I couldn't understand it but we had fun. Everyone referred to him in a deep, booming voice as "Leeeroooy", even the black boys, especially the black boys. It was related to his stereotypical image as the big, strong black guy. He was infamous for his "nipple twists". If you'd done something to piss him off then he'd grab hold of your nipples, twist them and lift you off the ground by them. Agony. But he was protective of his friends, especially us in his tutor group. He'd walk the walk rather than just talk the talk when it came to standing up to anyone in the school. He had a particularly strong personal identity, especially as he had St Lucian heritage rather than Jamaican. Leeeroooy was a one-man band and did not affiliate himself to any gang.

We weren't close friends but we used to have "cussing matches", which would often draw a crowd. "Cussing" is West Indian for "cursing", essentially taking the piss out of each other. I used to pick on parts of his body, clothes and shoes. He was more old school, mainly cussing my mum. A crowd of up to a dozen kids from all races used to witness these clashes as we'd walk the couple of miles from Pimlico, over Vauxhall Bridge and to Stockwell, where he lived. If you landed a decent verbal blow then everyone would laugh and shout: "Cuss! Cuss!"

...

As I came towards the end of my time at Pimlico, dope started to become an important part of my life. I had my first joint when I was 15 and smoked it on and off until I was first sectioned in 2008. I haven't touched it since. I miss it. I regularly dream about it. It's still part of who I am. But it's not really compatible with bipolar disorder. I have a great long-term memory but my short-term memory is poor. I don't know if there is a link.

Me and my friend Robert (who tragically died in his early 30s of a rare disease not long after we'd reconnected many years later) used to get stoned at lunchtime when we were in the sixth form at Pimlico. It was fun. We got into some really hilarious debates during government and politics, and sociology lessons.

I don't know if the teachers knew we were stoned but they didn't give us any obvious indication that they were pissed off about it. I do believe dope can open up the doors of perception. But I have also learned to my cost that it can close them pretty abruptly as well. I used to think it should be legalised. I don't anymore, although I think it should be decriminalised, along with other recreational drugs.

One of my worst stoned memories was in a park in west London with Robert and a Jewish friend. We were sitting in a playground getting blasted during school hours and this little white kid — around five years old — came up and started talking to us. He heard me being called "Siddy" and started calling me a "Paki". It was such a frustrating situation because I couldn't do anything about it. So many levels of frustration. This obnoxious child was so cocky and eventually told us: "My dad's a policeman."

I thought: "That figures."

4. The Pimlico Strangler

'He was looking at me funny'

His mammoth hands were gripping my throat and he was squeezing harder and harder. Everything in my head started going grey and fuzzy. I had gone beyond the point of resisting. He had it in his heart to kill me there and then.

Moments earlier, I had Morgan in a headlock a few yards outside the school gates in the middle of a quiet road on a hot day. I can't remember what the beef was about but I promised to let go if he calmed down. He said he would, so I freed him. Suddenly, as I was walking away, I felt his hands grip around my neck. He'd come at me from behind, which was his MO. Fortunately, I was with a handful of classmates who, eventually, managed to loosen his grip and pull him off me.

I was no match for him physically but I was still prepared to fight him. He had the heart of lion...from The Wizard of Oz. I was more wary of Kelvin than Morgan at the time. Kelvin was short and not particularly physically strong. But he had a strong mind, like me. And he had those sisters. Morgan was a colossus physically but his mind was feeble. He was a boy in a man's body. A powerful body. A weird boy. Looking back, I shrugged off my battles with him but my mum told me years later that she feared he would end up killing me. She even arranged a meeting with the school and Morgan's (obnoxious, white) mum, who shrugged: "What do you expect me to do about it?"

We had a long history. I can't remember the chronology of a lot of this but I think my mum has photos of us together when we were still crawling. I never liked him, though. He threw a marble at my face, chipping one of my adult front teeth when we were quite young.

Then, when we were about eight, he stole his Jamaican dad's pay packet and bought my friendship for a day. He took me for McDonald's and bought a flash gaming machine, akin to having a handheld Space Invaders console. He acted strangely that day, didn't say much. I didn't know where the money had come from but I could tell he'd done something bad to get it. I wasn't complaining and I wasn't judging, especially because a Big Mac and fries was a real treat for a "dirty squatter" like me back then. When I found out how he'd got the money, it all made sense. I felt a bit guilty. A bit.

A few years later, somehow, he joined me and my stepdad, Rob, when we cycled up the hill to Crystal Palace, which is no mean feat. It was fine. I reckon his home life must have been shit and he enjoyed himself. We bonded a little that day. A little. I'm not saying I was an angel. I definitely was hanging out with him on the 'pay packet day' because he had money and I did something in the Mr Fair era which he hated me for.

There was this sweet, little Mexican kid called Carlos who joined our class that year in Henry Fawcett. We hit it off straight away. Anyway, once when I was leaving Mr Fair's class after another tiring day of lines and backchat, my new, green parka jacket had gone. I went into an instant panic. After about five minutes, Carlos appeared, smiling, with my jacket. It was his idea of a practical joke. But I didn't see the funny side. I had been dreading having to tell my mum that I'd lost my jacket. We were so poor that I'd probably have had to go back to wearing the one that had to be replaced in the first place. But after the relief of getting it back, I started rifling through my pockets and couldn't find a £1 note I'd put in there.

That was a lot of money for me back then. I think I told my mum when I got home and somehow we ended up in

Mr Curle's office with Carlos and his mum. He vehemently denied taking the note and I didn't know what to say. All I knew was that my £1 note was gone. Morgan was quite protective of Carlos and got in my face about it. I was so sad I'd lost the lovely, little Mexican as a friend, he was the sweetest guy in the world with his big, round, reddish-brown face, sparkling brown eyes and winning smile.

About two weeks later, I was in my bedroom and I noticed a bulge in the tiny pocket of my jeans. I put my right index finger in and pulled out a crumpled £1 note. I was standing and my knees nearly buckled, my face hotted up and my head went into a spin. But with everything happening with Mr Fair, I just didn't have it in me to clear Carlos's name. I was already in so much trouble.

Sorry, Carlos.

Obviously, that was a shame but I was always interested in meeting kids from other countries. Everyone was excited when a "Vietnamese boat person" joined our class in my last year at Henry Fawcett. It was amazing how seamlessly she fitted into that kaleidoscope of colours. It was a good school for what it was.

Years before, a boy called Roger from Jamaica joined my class. I was fascinated to learn that he did actually get the cane over there. He was so different from the often abrasive British-Jamaican kids I was so familiar with. He didn't have the tough, ghetto mentality. He was a nice lad, a softie. Our families became friends for a few years. They were lovely people.

When I was 13, I was on a bus going from Kennington to Brixton. Halfway there, I spotted Roger, got off and ran after him. He remembered me and we had a little chat. But he seemed broken. Like he had become just another ghetto kid. He didn't seem pleased to see me at all. I didn't know whether to take it personally. But my instinct was that he'd have been far happier if he'd stayed in Jamaica. It was sad to see, he was so vibrant when he was seven.

· · ·

My first physical confrontation with Morgan came during my final year at Henry Fawcett when I was ten and reasonably settled after the Mr Fair era. Admittedly, I was the one who came up from behind that time. All the boys played football every break and lunchtime with no monitoring. I can still vividly remember the moment that Morgan made a horrendous tackle on 'Vijay', my diminutive, Indian friend. It was a violent act. Vijay flew into the air and landed in a crumpled heap on the floor. A straight red card in today's Premier League — and we were playing on tarmac.

Morgan was the biggest, strongest kid in the school and Vijay was the smallest in our year. I can't remember who was on whose side in the game but my gut reaction was to jump onto Morgan's back. It wasn't really a fight, my actions were more symbolic of my outrage than anything else. The other boys quickly broke it up.

When I was leaving the playground after the bell went, my bag was missing. My obvious suspicion was that Morgan had taken it. I don't know how, maybe someone tipped me off but I found it hanging from a cistern over a toilet bowl in the boys' loos. I reported this relatively trivial matter to a teacher and Mr Curle took me to my classroom and, with a smirk, he pointed to Morgan and said: "Is that him?"

I said: "Yeah, the fat one."

My classmates burst out laughing but Mr Curle snapped: "Oi, there's no need for that."

The next year we both went to Pimlico and all the new kids were in the main hall as a teacher read out the names of who'd be in whose tutor group. My heart sank when it was announced I would be with Morgan — for five fucking years.

I don't think he had a mental illness. I don't have a clue what his problem was. I'm sure his life outside school wasn't great but the same could be said for most of us in that tutor group.

Morgan had a sense of entitlement, which I assume he got from his mum. When he did badly on the "11-plus" equivalent, she blamed the system. He *was* fucking stupid. Stupid because he would never take responsibility for his actions. Always quick with an excuse. No work ethic. No sense of responsibility when it came to being physically strong, unlike Leeeroooy. I don't know what the deal was with his father. I mean, I knew his parents weren't together. I'm not even sure they ever were. Maybe getting a sense of who his dad was might have given me a better idea of why Morgan was such a fuck-up.

There was nothing 'black' about him, apart from the way he looked, like he didn't even have an ounce of the cool part. His presence was huge, he could have used that to be a respected figure but his character, boy, I wouldn't be surprised if he turned up on the news.

Looking back, Morgan was my real nemesis, not Kelvin. Most of the time, I cut Morgan with my mind. He was huge and strong but I didn't fear him.

Once, I was sitting down in an English class, I looked up and caught his eye. Bearing in mind that there were long periods of normality between the violent incidents, I half smiled at him. I thought nothing of it but as I walked out at the end of the lesson, he was waiting for me and punched me in the face. Totally blindsided me. I mean, I didn't know there was a problem and, as some of you may know, being hit in the face when you're not physically prepared for it is a lot worse than when you are. His explanation to the teacher: "He was looking at me funny."

The strange thing is that I wouldn't say he was a bully, not in the classic sense. He wouldn't throw his weight around, no direct threats. Yet his solution to every perceived problem was violence. And he was cowardly about it, like blindsiding and "jumping" people he thought had wronged him. There were times I felt sorry for him. He tried to make friends but somehow seemed to always get it wrong. So wrong. Like he thought that if he just smiled then everybody would like him and when that didn't work, the red mist immediately descended.

I'm not saying I was the good guy and he was the bad guy. I was arrogant. I did and still do tend to bring out strong emotions in people, one way or the other. But I was popular in my own way and he wasn't. There was a gang of us in my tutor group and he was at the periphery of it. Especially in the summer, my mates would make the relatively long journey to my house and play football over the fence in Brockwell Park.

We played in a Saturday morning league and I ended up being the manager: Washing the kit and picking the team, even though I was a pretty average player. Morgan wasn't part of it because he wasn't good enough AND because I didn't want him around. Everyone needs to find their role in a gang. The only thing he had to offer was brute strength and he was more liable to attack one of us (especially me) rather than defend one of us, so he was out. And when I say "gang", we didn't get up to anything particularly bad, we just hung out together.

I have to point out that I was quite forgiving of Morgan, up to a point, giving him lots of chances. One time, for whatever reason, he followed me down into Pimlico Tube station after school and onto a train. I can still see him marching towards me, cornering me and then punching me to the ground. I didn't report it.

"Cussing" and piss-taking were a huge part of school life — no one was spared. But he used to react violently, often without giving any notice that he was about to explode. Another time, I was walking away from the school with him and a few others and he took offence to something I said and ended up assaulting me, smashing me against metal railings. Two policemen on the other side of the road witnessed the attack and rushed directly over, ready to arrest Morgan. But in pain, I assured them I was okay and, eventually, they went on their way.

There was this especially pretty white girl in our class who I chased after for a while, all the boys in my year fancied her. Morgan tried a joke to make her laugh but again, got it wrong. She was so outraged that she called him a "mongrel". It was a horrible moment. I felt for him — and myself. I had never considered her to be racist and she seemed to be quite interested in me (a "mongrel") at one stage. I suppose it was a pre-cursor to my own racist outburst at Morgan…

It was a music lesson and the teacher hadn't arrived. My tutor group was sitting around the room on chairs in a circle. Me and Morgan had a row, I don't remember what it was about, nothing major. But something in *my* head snapped. I was just so fed up with this guy. To tell the truth, I thought he gave mixed race people a bad name. I hated him so much. We both wanted the other to be non-existent.

I growled at him: "You half-caste cunt."

He called me a "Paki", which didn't bother me coming from him. But I got up out of my chair, walked towards him, grabbed hold of him around the neck and wrestled him to the floor, judo-style. Then it got a bit weird. You have to remember his size — we are talking heavyweight boxing legend George Foreman. Somehow I managed to wrestle him on top of me. But rather than seizing on his advantage, he just lay on me like a dead weight. Our classmates eventually lifted him off. I don't know why he reacted in that way. He was unpredictable. I was kind of embarrassed, the way I lost control. At that point, the teacher came in and tried to get to the bottom of what had happened. Morgan bleated: "He called me a 50-50."

He actually couldn't bring himself to repeat what I had called him. He should have, then I probably would have been in big trouble. And rightfully so. But that was the difference between us and that was the end of the matter, as far as the teacher was concerned. I'm honestly not sure whether that incident happened before or after he tried to strangle me.

I'm trying to remember how, as a child, I had come to have so much contempt for him. Even though he wasn't a bully, he was conscious of his huge physical presence, as was everyone else. Maybe he'd have developed a personality if he wasn't so big and strong. He was a parasite, the way I saw it. He never initiated anything good, he would just try and muscle in on other people's fun and didn't see a problem with that.

I should point out a few things. Firstly, my 2008 attempt to end my own life in Goodmayes Hospital, as mentioned in the preface, was not directly related to my vile, racist insult to Morgan 22 years previously. It just popped into my head when I was writing to a long list of people I had wronged in my suicide note before trying to hang myself while in a psychotic episode. I genuinely felt bad about it then and still do now. It was totally out of character but he was so vicious to me. Also, in my defence, at that time, "half-caste" was how most mixed race people were described at Pimlico. That's even how I described myself. The point was that I wanted to hurt him. I should have called him a "fat cunt", not that I've used the C-word in anger many times in my life and never to a woman.

The police did finally get involved after the last time he assaulted me. I was 15 and was due to play my regular Tuesday evening game of football at Brixton Leisure Centre. I phoned up a friend in Victoria and invited him to play but he said he didn't have any money. I offered to go to his place and give him some. There was a subtext. Morgan used to take my friend — a half Japanese guy — hostage in his own flat. His Japanese single mum used to ask me how she could get rid of Morgan. The best I could suggest was some sort of restraining order.

Anyway, I knew Morgan would be there and it was part of my motivation for going. He was in the flat with Graham, who I was on-off friends with, when I arrived. As the other two boys were coming with me to Brixton, it was obvious that Morgan had to vacate. I waited in the hallway for them to get their stuff together.

As Morgan walked past me, I bowed my head a little so I didn't have to make eye contact. Next thing I knew, the back of my head cracked against the wall behind me and my nose felt like it had been plastered all over my face. He had blindsided me again and landed a haymaker flush on my nose as his parting shot. I should have known. Blood spurted out, it went fucking everywhere. I rushed over to the kitchen sink to chuck as much cold water over the affected area as possible to cool the pain.

After about five minutes, the blood flow eased, I got myself together and headed off to Brixton with my two friends to play football. I have a high pain threshold. When I got home, I told my mum: "I think my nose is broken."

She rushed me to A&E immediately. I don't know at what point the cops became involved. I suppose my mum must have informed them. I made a statement at a police station in Victoria a few days later. I think Morgan got off with a caution. I was teased a bit at school for involving the cops. But looking back, I can understand my mum's fear that he would have ended up killing me if nothing was done.

I was not the only one Morgan had it in for. He once jumped a black kid but that victim and his brother jumped him in retaliation and kicked seven shades of shit out of him. Good. He did make friends with a small, white boy near the end of his time at Pimlico. It was like they were in love at one point and it was genuinely nice to see. More importantly, for me, it meant he was off my back. But I heard that friendship ended in tears.

Some time later, through my mum, I applied to the Criminal Injuries Compensation Board over my broken nose. Morgan wasn't at the hearing. I was brought into a smallish room and there were three people sitting behind a table. It felt a bit like a kangaroo court. They asked me to give my account of the incident, which I did. Then someone started to read out Morgan's police statement. Again, the phrase "he was looking at me funny" popped up. After a few minutes of this, the chairwoman snapped: "Stop! I think we've heard enough."

I got around £550 compensation, enough to buy myself a motorbike, which I was old enough to ride by that point.

Actually, because I was still growing, my hooter didn't end up too badly. I could have had a nose job on the NHS but the consultant told me they would effectively have to break it again to do the surgery and that didn't appeal.

Morgan used to turn up for the infamous all-nighters at The Ritzy cinema in Brixton a few years later when I was working behind the coffee bar. I did reluctantly serve him when there was a crowd. But in my head, it was like: "Will you ever just fuck off out of my life?"

One time, though, he came out of the auditorium while a film was on in the early hours and it was just me, him and the cinema owner's wife in the foyer. I said to him, point blank: "I don't want to serve you."

He looked forlorn, hurt and timid. The puzzled owner's wife asked: "Why don't you want to serve him?"

I was thinking: "Where do you want to fucking start?"

She said: "I'll serve him."

That was fine by me, I just had to let Morgan know that I was still defiant. That I would still fight him, knowing I would lose. The last I heard of Morgan was a few years later. Ralph ran into him in Brixton and asked what he was up to. Morgan said: "Oh, a bit of this and that."

5. Muggers' Mile

'Can you tell the manager?'

We'd travelled half the country (to Liverpool, Manchester or Coventry, I can't remember) when I was 19 to watch our beloved Arsenal, in my second generation Jamaican friend's black, Nissan 280Z sports car, which looked like the Batmobile (I was definitely Robin). After that exhausting, long journey, just 50 yards from his Brixton council flat on the way back, we were stopped by the police, in a Transit van.

They ordered 'Mr. T' — as he wants to be known as in this book — to get out. He did and then turned his back on them and placed his hands on the car roof while they frisked him (they didn't ask to frisk *me* or even ask me to get out of the car, although I did). They told him that it was unnecessary to adopt that posture. Mr. T told them: "I want to."

They had no basis to stop us. What happened next was something I will never forget and I don't think those cops will, either. Mr. T waited and waited for them to pull off, which they did, eventually, reluctantly, slowly. Then he overtook them at breakneck speed and took a sharp right. For several minutes, Mr. T put his foot to the floor as we weaved our way through a labyrinth of back streets before he finally got out of the car, stood up, casually leant his left elbow on the roof and, in that moment, waved to the officers as they went the wrong way past us. They wanted to tail us but Mr. T — a council worker who moonlighted as a bouncer — wasn't having it. And he did that without breaking any laws. That's called a "fuck you" attitude.

Like it.

Love it.

Another black bouncer, who lived on the same estate, told me he drove his little, white van around because he got sick of getting stopped by the police in his BMW. Sometimes, you have to ask yourself: "Who's committing the crimes here?"

That was just the tip of the iceberg and I was getting off lightly, I totally recognise that. I'm not black. Another black Ritzy bouncer spent six months in jail for verbally abusing white, undercover cops. He didn't do it. The screws repeatedly told him: "They all say that."

It was occupied territory in a two-mile radius of Brixton Police Station at that time. On reflection, I think it's worth pointing out that race was all-pervading in that area in my life those days, so excuse me for making constant reference to it. It's there for context, not division. I recently saw some footage of a group of black guys being interviewed in the aftermath of the 1981 Brixton riot. They were at pains to point out that, *for them*, it was not a race issue which underpinned those troubled times but police brutality and harassment, generally.

...

In those days when I started going to watch Arsenal aged 13 without being with an adult, there was a multi-racial group of us Junior Gunners who made our way to north London from the Brixton area. We weren't exceptions, lots of kids younger than us used to turn up unaccompanied, too. There was a special standing enclosure for us but you could go to all parts of the standing areas of the ground, obviously aside from the away fans' area.

Many of my classmates were jealous that I'd actually gone to the games and got the inside track on stuff they'd only seen on Match of the Day.

A stone's throw from Highbury stadium was a fish and chip shop run by a Chinese family. Whoever I went to games with, we always ended up there and it was mega busy. But these people were so efficient that they quickly dealt with the long queues before things ever got out of hand. The waiting was never an issue, their work rate was prodigious.

But there was a horrible side to it. There was one (white) guy who used to buy a bag of chips and then sit down on a chair and spend the whole time being threatening towards the staff, making racist remarks and generally being a total wanker.

After every single home game.

It was disgraceful. Looking back, I think it is equally disgraceful that no one ever intervened. I would have done so if I had been an adult at the time. I actually think most of the customers disapproved of this arsehole's behaviour but kept quiet. The whole thing was a cloud which hung over the staff there. It left a bitter taste. Those Chinese people stayed silent. And looked so unhappy. The racist wanker eventually got a job as a football steward for home games, so he stopped coming to the chippy. Thank God.

Arsenal was one of the few bright spots of my life at that time but I started smoking cannabis a few years later and it grabbed me by the bollocks. It's one thing having the odd joint here and there but I lived for getting stoned when I was still a kid. For those of you who don't know, it knocks the ambition out of you. Paradoxically, life feels empty and boring without it. In later years, my Irish flatmate, 'Brian', laughingly dubbed us the "go-getters" as we wiled away the hours, days, weeks, months and years getting wasted in my tiny flat he dubbed "the cell", listening to Pink Floyd and talking endlessly about women. Brian once commented on the picture of Battersea Power Station on the cover of Pink

Floyd album Animals. He asked: "Wouldn't it be amazing if
that building actually existed?"

I ushered him towards the window and said: "Look,
you can see it in the distance."

A nice, stoned moment.

I miss getting high, having not had a joint for over ten
years at the time of writing. It's like dope introduces you to
a whole new world. At certain points of my life, I've been
totally hooked. When my half brother started smoking it
aged 16, I was in my early 20s and I told him that he could
smoke with me but I wouldn't buy it for him, facilitate
his habit. As it turned out, he got into much stronger stuff
without any help from me.

Personally, I always preferred getting stoned to
drinking, or any other recreational drug. I did ecstasy once
and had a great, slightly surreal night at a house party.
But I lost my personality for two weeks after that and
vowed to never do it again, even though I'd been fine on
it a few times previously. And cocaine…I absolutely loved
it but was never a habitual user because I immediately
recognised how *moreish* it was. Instant confidence.

Dope, on the other hand, made me feel like it was
giving me a special insight into the world. Getting stoned
was like taking a break from reality and I now recognise
that using it in the context of bipolar was "self-medicating".
Dope didn't make me bipolar but during an episode, it was
like pouring petrol on an already raging fire.

When I was 16, I took a summer job at the KFC on
Baker Street, central London, with two of my best (white)
friends. We had such a great time, earning proper money
for the first time and feeling like we were adults with
the whole world as our playground, although we chose
to spend most of our time off getting stoned in various

bedrooms. It was a comparatively big store back then and we got on with most of the people of all different colours we worked with. But there was a white football hooligan, a notorious "Chelsea Headhunter", whose Irish girlfriend was an assistant manager. He didn't like me, thought I was gobby.

I used to mainly work on the tills while he was at the back in the kitchen with his girlfriend. I did make a few cheeky comments but one time I asked an innocent question of her about when the next tray of chicken was up and he thought I'd made a disparaging remark. He went mad and tried to get to me in the service area. But these two, young, black women intercepted him and pushed him to the floor as he was grappling with them. I was in a bit of a state of shock. The incident made me feel like a kid again. I mean, he was out to harm me. But I tell you this, I'd be more afraid to go up against that pair of Jamaican women than a pair of Chelsea Headhunters like him. He wasn't popular and they would have battered him given the chance. I was quite touched by their instantaneous, protective instincts towards me.

It was a great summer in KFC but the years after leaving full-time education were extremely depressing and I would have been lost without The Ritzy cinema in Brixton. The sad thing being that it was what Pink Floyd might describe as "cold comfort". Not for the only time in my life, my mum gave me a much-needed kick up the arse, when I was 17, after I stayed on in the sixth form at Pimlico to get decent enough GCSEs to qualify to do A-levels. As September approached, I was an usher at The Ritzy but somehow I didn't have the heart to return to Pimlico. My mum gave me a cutting of an ad for Merton College, which is situated way to the south and west of Brixton.

Thankfully, it was quite a mixed race institution, although not in the same league as Pimlico. One of of our government and politics teachers, who was well meaning (and wore noteworthily rubbish clothes), showed us this incredible TV series about fitting into British society. The first episode started with a young man with dreadlocks being caught shoplifting at a local grocery store. By the end of the series, he'd shed his dreads and was working there as a security guard. Happily ever after. We were meant to swallow this shit whole.

Staggering.

This would have been around 1991. I know that Rastas being encouraged to lose their dreads or Sikhs having to cut their hair and lose their turbans to get jobs left many of them bitter and resentful: *Less* willing to *assimilate* into society than they might otherwise have been. Personally, I believe in integration rather than assimilation. Multiculturalism is one of the things I love most about Britain, if not *the* most.

Looking back at that period, I was quite a tough kid with a semi-criminal mindset. I never tried to be 'cool' or celebrate being a ghetto boy but I was largely a product of my environment outside of my middle class home, where my mum and siblings had little concept of what I was up against. I find it frustrating to this day how my life experience, compared to theirs, was not even acknowledged, let alone dealt with.

Pimlico was a pretty tough school when I was there and I went on to become part of the tapestry of Brixton. I shudder to think how close I came to becoming embroiled in that world for the rest of my life. I can just see myself in that little flat, smoking my brains out, being a gamer and just drifting. I mean, it was ever decreasing circles. An interesting time but mostly for the wrong reasons.

Again, not to be cool, I was a regular fare-dodger through much of my teens. It started in earnest when I turned 16. I used to buy child travelcards and it nearly backfired a few times. Once, I was on the Victoria Line, sitting in a half-empty carriage when two burly ticket inspectors got on board at Oxford Circus. I was caught in about seven different minds but I still can't think of a way out of my predicament other than the option I chose...

Instinctively, with them ten feet away and about to start their checks, I waited for the sound of a click to signal that the doors were about to close. Then I rapidly made my move, just about managing to squeeze out before they shut. A split second thing. The inspectors had immediately gone after me but they were were trapped inside, their angry faces pushed up against the doors as the train pulled away. Mission Impossible: Successful (that's Peso's line). I didn't rub it in as they grimaced. Instead, I moved away down a pedestrian tunnel connecting to another platform and spent a few moments regaining my composure. It was a horrible feeling, knowing how close I came to being caught. Equally, it was a huge relief to have pulled it off.

These days, I don't think fare-dodgers are high on the list of priorities in London. It's more a case of collateral damage in the drive to increase profits. In other words, the operators would make less money if they sincerely tried to catch all the fare-dodgers. But it wasn't like that for me. Maybe the money I saved on travelcards was the difference between being able to go to matches and not.

Another time, I arrived at Brixton station and there was a queue of passengers from the "excess fare" window down to the bottom of the stairs. Excess fare windows were, in theory, for people to buy a ticket if they had been unable to do so at their point of departure (or effectively "own up").

There was maybe 50 policemen holding a line, no one was getting out of the station without coughing up. That was one time when I wasn't fare-dodging but it stuck in my mind because the police eventually turned around to leave and — in that exact moment — the dozens of people queueing all the way from the window to the bottom of the stairs poured through the barriers. Climbing, running, pushing. *That* is Brixton.

I don't know if it's still the case but at the time, it had more people flowing through it than any other Tube station in London not linked to one of the capital's major rail network terminals. Despite this, there were times when it only had a little booth for people to hand their tickets in. What used to happen was that cheeky passengers used to slam down a 50p coin and move on. The cheekier ones, like me, would slam a coin down but keep hold of it.

One time, I slammed a 10p coin down but as I withdrew my right arm, the woman inside the booth grabbed me by it. She was very persistent, holding onto me for dear life to give her colleagues time to intercept me. I punched her arm and she let go. I ran as fast as I could and got away with it.

Around that time, I used to have a two-to-three zone travelcard. For some reason, I was once getting out at Walthamstow, north east London. The thing is that I had traveled from zone two Brixton through zone one, which is not allowed without topping up. But a team of inspectors were checking *everybody* at Walthamstow. Unbeknown to me, my travelcard indicated that it had been issued in Brixton. I told him that I had come from zone two Finsbury Park, north London, where I had stayed the night with my French girlfriend (I got the idea because I had previously gone on one date to see the Four Tops with a beautiful French girl, who lived there. Sadly, I never did get to spend the night with her).

The inspector asked me: "Does Finsbury Park Tube Station have escalators or lifts?"

The thing is, I used to get off at Finsbury Park to watch my beloved Arsenal. My answer: "Neither, it has stairs."

Keyser Soze, eat your heart out.

The irony of my fare-dodging is that the guy who used to run my Saturday morning football league, Charlie North, had worked on the railways all his life and his last assignment before retirement was at West Dulwich Train Station, which was my point of departure for Merton. I'd been late to most things my whole life and I used to cut it pretty fine, sometimes missing my train. But on one occasion, the train had actually been cancelled. So, I turned up late to my English class and told my teacher about the cancellation, i.e. the one time it wasn't my fault. Understandably, she didn't believe me but I managed to manoeuvre her to say: "I suppose you've got a note from British Rail."

Me: "Well, actually…"

I reached inside my pocket and produced a British Rail-headed note (penned by Charlie) explaining my tardiness. Everybody cracked up, including my teacher, who was a lovely woman. A big fan of my work. I can't clearly remember doing fare-dodging as a fully-fledged adult but I do vaguely recall a handful of times I've fought my way through Tube barriers while blind drunk.

. . .

I started work at The Ritzy aged 14 as an usher and eventually became a projectionist around the age of 18. I was the youngest in London. The Evening Standard even did a feature on me.

Funny that I ended up working for them many years later. I had keys to the cinema and, being the responsible young man I was, I used to get my mates in after closing time. We'd have the run of the place, getting stoned, watching horror movies and thrillers, stuffing ourselves full of popcorn and ice creams. Cola floats were a particularly big hit.

The Ritzy was a bit of a flea pit at that time but being held together by Sellotape and elastic bands was part of its charm. One day, I came in early and there was a closed doors, media event going on in the auditorium. It turned out to be a shift of mixed fortunes for me. The event was a memorial for an author who'd recently died. There were a few celebrities in the foyer, including renowned jazz singer George Melly and feminist author Germaine Greer. It was a surreal moment when, as she headed to the ladies' loo, she told him: "I'm Germaine Greer."

But the punchline is that Satanic Verses author Salman Rushdie was there, a few years after he'd been issued a "fatwa" for blasphemy by Iran's Supreme Leader, Ayatollah Khomeini. I watched from the projectionist's room as Rushdie spoke on the stage. Many years later, when I was working for a British-Asian tabloid, the Editor said it would be easy to track down Rushdie for any would-be assassins — just throw a luvvies' do and he's bound to turn up.

Anyway, I'd happily downed quite a bit of the free Champagne on offer and, by the time the event was over, I was pissed. I was doing fine lacing up the film into the projector but there was a knack to starting it. They were old projectors and the huge spools were on towers. You had to ease the bottom one in to keep the film tight, otherwise it would jerk back the film too quickly, then slow down, creating a looseness. When it snapped back tight, the film would break apart. It must have taken me four or five attempts to get the film going and the full-house, 400-strong audience were in tears of laughter as this pantomime played out. I didn't see the funny side of it at the time. I just wanted to sober up, which is unusual for me.

Lots of crazy things happened at The Ritzy. I once prevented a rape just outside. It was all a bit farcical. I was 19 and was inside on a sunny afternoon before the cinema opened its doors. I noticed at some point that there was this black man wrestling with this white woman on the floor and I rushed out to intervene. I grabbed hold of him, dragged him off her and got a tight grip as I pinned him down. He had his bits out. My initial instinct was to punch him in the face to subdue him. But he wasn't putting up a fight. I just wanted someone to call the police.

I recognised him as a regular who kept himself to himself and always did seem a bit odd, very quiet. I also recognised his victim. She used to go around Brixton collecting used drink cans and was holding two full bags. People were walking quite nearby but no one got involved. I'm sure those passersby were totally bemused as to what was actually going on.

The next bit is when it descended into *total* farce. I decided to release him and go for help in the cinema. But the woman was still on the floor because her bags of cans were weighing her down. And as soon as I turned my back, he got back on top of her. I was caught in two minds but I decided to bang on the cinema doors and then go and drag him off again, which I did. Eventually, a colleague came out and I told him what had happened, while I was holding the guy down. He called the police but the woman had run off by that point, leaving her cans behind. It was a surreal situation. We let the guy get to his feet and button up and let him know that we'd keep him there until the police arrived. He said: "I want them to arrest me."

I have to say, I felt quite sorry for him. He wasn't right in the head. Later that day, it emerged that he had told another member of staff he was a virgin (he looked around aged 30) but "that's going to change today".

That sort of thing was par for the course at The Ritzy...

A few years earlier, when I was an usher, I was sitting on a chair in the corner of the lobby reading a football magazine and this ashen-faced blonde woman in her mid-20s came up to me, crouched down a little and quietly told me: "I have stabbed my boyfriend in the stomach. He is lying on the kitchen floor and he's not moving."

My response: "Can you tell the manager?"

I understood the enormity of the situation, I wasn't being callous or dismissive. But being so young, I didn't want to get involved. I already had enough on my plate and I'm not a drama queen.

...

Cops' presence makes me feel uneasy most of the time, not safe. But there have been exceptions. There was this horrible man with dreads — although not a proper Rasta — in his 40s who used to occasionally make a point of walking through the front doors and straight into the auditorium without paying, just to show he could do it. He never stayed more than five to ten minutes. It was just pissing in corners, often showing off to bewildered, white girlfriends.

A few of the staff, including me, eventually got sick of this charade one evening and I phoned Brixton Police Station. They weren't interested. This guy was trespassing and that's against the law, so me and a female colleague decided to find a cop on the streets. We did find a young, white officer and he was only too happy to help. As he entered the cinema, the troublemaker was leaving. He never did it again.

I'm all for *good* cops.

Another evening, the Lambeth "poll tax" rate was due to be announced at the borough's town hall, just across the street from The Ritzy. There was a bit of a commotion at one point as riot police tried to disrupt things but they ended up getting encircled by protesters, who subsequently became rioters, lobbing all manner of missiles onto the would-be aggressors. It was quite a dramatic turn of events. I knew this would be big news, even though it was nothing like on the scale of two of Brixton's major riots back in 1981 and 1985.

As this scene played out, we were only letting people out of the cinema, the plan being to shut the place down after the current film was over. But there was this very persistent man banging on the glass doors, shouting: "I've come to see the film."

The bouncer — Mr. T — was like: "Yeah but they're *rioting* out there!"

A reporter from The Sun rang up The Ritzy to get the scoop and I put the phone down on him. He phoned back to ask why I'd hung-up on him. I can't remember what I said but again, it's ironic that I ended up working for them. Also noteworthy is that we witnessed plain-clothes policemen parking outside of The Ritzy in a green Astra (giveaway) and shoving truncheons up their sleeves. I recall a documentary about the 1981 riot when similar tactics were employed. Back then, a reporter pointed out to a uniformed officer what was happening, not realising the aggressors were police. The officer reassured the reporter: "It's okay, they're *our* thugs."

. . .

I moved into my own, tiny, one-bedroom flat on Railton Road — The Frontline — when I was 19. I felt like I'd *arrived*, what with having my own place. I went to have a look the day before I got the keys and was presented with a bizarre scene. This young, white couple were running down the street towards me with a group of about half a dozen black men chasing after them. I recognised the leader, he was a regular troublemaker at The Ritzy and was riding a BMX even though he must have been well into his 50s. The hippyish-looking couple stormed into a community centre and the gang stopped in their tracks. I had no idea what was going on and still don't have a clue. But it was an interesting reintroduction to life on The Frontline.

That stretch of the road was known as "Muggers' Mile" because it had the highest mugging rate in the country at one point. I had few problems there but you had to have your wits about you. Many years later in Beirut, I told this to my white, English, elfin-figure Editor, who had spent time in Brixton and found it terrifying: Not in a racist way but in a tough neighbourhood way. He said: "Yeah but you're built like a light-heavyweight boxer."

That's probably true, to an extent. Also, my mentality growing up there was that "you better have a knife" and "even if you beat me up, I will hurt you on the way down". I had no idea how aggressive I was. I'm still coming to terms with that now. It helped that I was a familiar face but that also only occurred to me many years later.

I was once getting my sweat on in the men's sauna at Brixton Leisure Centre in my early 20s and all the other occupants, six or so, older black guys, were talking about Railton Road. I was curious about their conversation. The bit that stuck with me was one who (not to me) said:

"When you are on The Frontline, don't walk with your head up and don't walk with your head down."

I thought that was brilliant advice. I'd been doing that for most of my life but until then, I'd never heard anyone sum it up so succinctly. People were always bugging for change or pulling low-level scams on The Frontline. One was second-rate hustlers asking if you had change for £2 in £1 coins. I reached inside my pocket, handed over the change but the hustler closed both hands, walked away and said: "Bad luck, mate."

I only fell for this once but a handful of different blokes tried it on me. I think that particular scam only lasted one summer on Railton Road. Another of the few times I got done was being offered weed on Muggers' Mile (this was not my normal dope MO, I had my suppliers, often white and often outside of Brixton). The guy only wanted £2 for what looked like a tenner's worth so, speculatively, I gave it a whirl. Turns out it was dry tea leaves. Talk about "tea leaf" (Cockney rhyming slang for "thief").

I got a sixth sense for who was dangerous in Brixton, mainly outsiders: Junkies looking to raise funds to score or simply wired. It wasn't about race. One day a black man was tapping me up for change and I wasn't interested. When I didn't comply, he told me: "I've been to jail, you know."

I asked him why he'd been to jail and he almost burst into tears before telling me the story, which I've forgotten. The point being that I don't generally find West Indian men scary, which seems to put me in a minority. I assess each person individually, irrespective of colour. One of the scariest men I came across in Brixton was a white man who used to come into The Ritzy and cause trouble. He wasn't big and he wasn't strong-looking but he was dripping with evil (whatever that is). His eyes were blank.

The thing that frightened me most about him the most was that he seemed to have no self-regard. That's what made him dangerous. Like he had some sort of death wish.

These instincts are developed over many years and sadly, to a large degree, shut you off from being in touch with more subtle instincts about the people you allow into your life. Basically, if someone doesn't pose any immediate physical danger, then they are kinda "all right". I thought I was a softie but maybe that's not the case.

"Fronting" is a major element in ghetto life throughout the world, I would imagine. It's about performing a role as someone you don't want to fuck with. It's similar to how many people describe prison life. Predators are all around and they seize on anything they perceive as weakness: Kindness, generosity, empathy etc. But one incident superseded all of that. I was in The Ritzy in the evening and a friend had his massive, BMW touring motorbike parked outside. A huge black man in his 30s, maybe 6ft 7ins, ran towards the bike and kicked it over. My friend rushed out and shrieked: "Oi!"

But the aggressor tore himself away from smashing up chained push bikes and ran towards my friend, who hotfooted it inside, getting the manager to rapidly lock the doors. The aggressor picked up a small glass bottle and threw it at the wired window doors with such force that it seemed like the bottle had actually passed through because glass hit the coffee bar 15ft back. It was the wired glass that hit the coffee bar. Then this hulk ran across the road into a shop. Within minutes, dozens of riot cops started piling into the store. They just seemed to keep coming and coming. I guess the guy was an escaped mental patient.

I still get tapped up for change and cigarettes in my everyday life and I mostly refuse. If I do hand over something then it's because I read the person asking as potentially dangerous or if I'm feeling well-disposed to a tramp down on his luck. And I'm always more prepared to hand over a cigarette to a tramp than change because I know they will enjoy it and won't spend the cash on scoring smack or crack.

I was rarely an "outsider" in Brixton from a racial point of view. But there were a few occasions. I felt unwelcome in West Indian take-aways, for instance. It's still an issue for me. So much of black culture has been appropriated that West Indians, at some level, must be wary that their cuisine is also going to be appropriated. I can just envisage the "McJerkchicken burger". I wrote the previous sentence a few weeks ago but the funny thing is that I've just watched a TV ad about McDonald's new "The Jamaican" chicken burger, which has a "sweet and spicy jerk sauce". I kid you not.

One time I walked into a West Indian off licence on Railton Road near my flat and felt like the American Werewolf in London protagonist who walked into a pub on the Yorkshire Moors — it went silent and everyone turned around and looked at me. My usual place was closed and I only wanted some Rizla.

Around that time, I was living with Brian. The day he told a black man to "fuck off" on The Frontline was the day I thought he'd shed a lot of his racial prejudices. He was being hassled for change day in and day out and finally snapped. New faces tended to get targeted more than most for a while. The black guy was starting to get aggressive, banking on the white boy to be intimidated. But it didn't work out that way.

One evening, we were walking down Muggers' Mile when a police car pulled up next to us. A tiny male cop

and a tiny female cop got out and ordered us to stop, which
we did. They told us that they had seen one of us slip the
other one a £10 note, which was true (although perfectly
innocently), and that they were going to search us, which
they did. Those two were like a tourist couple on safari
in Africa from the moment they nervously stepped out
of their vehicle. They were so jittery but you could also
sense that they were getting a thrill from the experience.
A white knuckle ride.

We had nothing to hide, so thought it was kinda funny.
A nice story to tell the next day. They were perfectly civil
and I reckon they just wanted to have it on some report
that they had executed a stop and search on The Frontline,
so they singled out two white-looking men. The thing is,
though, we were on our way to score some hash, so they
would have got two arrests if they'd stopped us on the
way back.

The late, black broadcaster and campaigner Darcus
Howe, who lived in Brixton for much of his life, did a
TV documentary series where he toured Britain. His
conclusion was: "Brixton is a cocoon from racism."

That may seem absurd but it's well observed. Apart
from all the byproducts of being a poor area, we all got
along. Brixton accepted all the people rejected elsewhere
at the time: West Indians, Africans, Asians, the Irish, gays,
lesbians and so on. Pretty much everyone was aware of
and united against police misbehaviour. I'm glad I got out
of Brixton, in my late 20s, though. I was sick of all the
car and house alarms and the gentrification creeping up
on us. But I still feel like it's home when I go back, which
I regularly do.

I only found out recently why there are so many
black people are in Brixton: Because there was a Labour

exchange there when the Windrush generation came over from the West Indies. So much for "lazy niggers".

. . .

After I got fired as a projectionist from The Ritzy aged 19 over a personality clash with one of the owners, I looked around for a week and got a job minding a snooker hall in Kennington. It was located under arches supporting a rail track. The whole place would shake a little every time a train passed over. Apart from the trains, it was a quiet place. I don't know how they survived.

I was doing shifts for a young, white boy on his days off. It was cash in hand and I thought I could at least improve my snooker skills. The business next door was a car wash and it was owned by the same people. On my second day, this white woman from there came to hang out with the white boy...and me.

Somehow, the conversation got on to Frank Bruno and another white boy chipped in saying what a phoney the boxer is "because I saw him being all black in Brixton". I had the happy image in my mind of Bruno lapping up all the attention walking down Railton Road in a snappy suit, waving and smiling. The context is that the boxer had a big white following from his early days all the way to the end of his career. And his relationship with veteran, white BBC boxing commentator Harry Carpenter was seared into the national consciousness. Catchphrase: "Ya naaat I mean, 'Arry..?"

Also, Bruno married a white woman and, consequently, was branded an "Uncle Tom" by some black people. Anyway, I made it obvious that I'm not a racist and this ugly expression swept over the woman's rapidly-reddening face. I didn't know it then but my days were numbered there. I'm still crap at snooker. The next day I turned up at work to be told that I was late, which I wasn't. The boy I was alternating shifts with started bawling at me about my tardiness. I pointed to my watch and calmly told him: "I'm not late."

He responded by pointing to the hall's tacky pool ball clock and shrieked: "That's the clock that counts!"

I quipped: "What am I supposed to do, carry it around with me?"

Facetious, I know. Habit of a lifetime. Then he started bawling at me about £10 missing from petty cash. There had only been a tenner in the box and I hadn't taken it. I'd been stitched up. But I was kinda relieved when he bellowed: "You're sacked!"

I was on a roll.

6. Eastern eye

'We used terrorism to establish our state'

An Israeli Defense Forces Major once invited me for a beer in his front garden after work. As I sat with him, he said: "You have a good attitude to life...and an Eastern eye."

Then he pointed to a huge tree in the distance and said: "I see a snake."

As the most senior military operative on 'my' kibbutz (effectively a commune in Israel), he was in charge of it in times of military conflict. During the first Gulf War, 1990 to 1991, Saddam Hussein's Iraq was lobbing Scud missiles over to Israel. The kibbutzniks were ordered to the air raid shelters on hearing the codeword "Snake" (in Hebrew). But after a while, most of them stopped going down into the shelters, instead standing on the roofs to watch the Scuds fly over, much to his frustration and annoyance.

Some time after the war ended, 'Major' was watering the plants in his front garden and was bitten by a highly-poisonous snake. He fell to the ground within moments and was lying there, prostrate, croaking: "Snake!"

His next door neighbour heard him but she got the wrong end of the stick and said: "Snake, yeah, yeah."

She did eventually realise what had happened and called for an ambulance. He nearly died during a six-month stay in hospital. No wonder he sees snakes everywhere.

Major is my favourite in an extensive collection of father figures: Funny, warm and wise. He was a "sabra", which means Israeli-born. Sabra is the name of a prickly pear fruit, which is dangerous-looking on the outside but sweet on the inside. The idea is that Israelis are much the same and I tend to agree, on the whole.

He was best described, physically, as a better-looking version of Monty Python legend Michael Palin. This military man with a heart of gold had a lot of young women swooning over him, even though he was entering the latter stages of middle age. I visited him in his open-air metal workshop once and a talk radio station was blaring out. He was shouting down the phone. Then he hung up abruptly and I realised he'd been on the air!

I found it hard to think of him as a soldier, let alone a major. He was such a softie. But there were little tell-tale signs. He told us that a fellow kibbutznik had become a famous violinist and invited him for a performance in London. He had the best seats in the house, in the royal box. During the interval, Major ordered a "black beer" and was served a Guinness. However, "black beer" is non-alcoholic in Israel. He didn't realise and, as a light drinker, he started getting sleepy during the second half. He resorted to an old army trick to stay awake — playing with an earlobe. It must have looked a bit odd, especially because he was in such a prominent position.

He once took the "volunteers [guest workers from abroad such as me]" on a trip around northern Israel. It was a great day. But I would start playing with an earlobe every time he started giving rambling history lessons. He took the hint. Major carried what must have been the world's oldest rifle on the trip. It was straight out of World War One. And I found it highly-amusing that he would phone ahead to our next port of call on the coach and speak English in a thick Israeli accent to fellow Israelis. It must have left those on the other end of the line a bit puzzled. I asked him why he did it and he smiled: "Because I am representing you and I want you to hear what I am saying."

He had such a big personality but he kept himself to himself on the kibbutz. I asked a younger guy who worked with me in the almond fields why Major was such an isolated figure. My kibbutznik colleague said: "I'll tell you a story about him [Major]. There was a group of us who spent an hour trying to open a jammed wagon holding the 'fruit'. He [Major] eventually approached us and said, 'I know how to open it.' He got a crowbar and, with one dig in a particular spot, it opened. We were like, 'Arrrrghhh, that man.'"

I once asked Major directly why he kept himself to himself and he said: "My job now is just to make my wife happy."

She was happy.

...

I was on a plane from London to Bombay when I was 19 and there was this incredible sunrise around halfway there. The colours were screaming: "Middle East."

I can still recall telling myself: "I'd like to go there one day."

I didn't have long to wait, ending up on Kibbutz Yizreel at the beginning of summer 1993 aged 20 after a Jewish friend from my Pimlico days had headed there and encouraged me to join him. For the uninitiated, a kibbutz is not some hippy campsite. Mine was quite luxurious in its own way and there was a lot of lucrative industry going on there. For instance, they had a factory dedicated to producing pool-cleaning robots, which were used at the 1992 Barcelona Olympics.

It was such a beautiful place, overlooking the stunning Yizreel Valley, with Nazareth perched on a huge hill in the distance. There was also a natural spring mentioned in the

Old Testament on the kibbutz's land. A great place to have
a cool dip under the trees which the spring fed. And we
were overlooked by Mount Gilboa, mentioned in the Bible
as being cursed by King David. A group of us climbed to
the top of it once, found a tortoise and named it "Dwain".
We took it back to our wooden shack, where it became our
pet for a few weeks before making its escape.

The kibbutz had about 600 permanent residents —
"members" — housed in comfortable homes. They all had
regular jobs within the confines of the wider commune.
Along with the small factories, there was a lot of agriculture
in the surrounding fields.

Everybody eats breakfast and lunch in the same,
huge dining room. And about half come for dinner. The
rest have it at their homes. My London friend, 'Erun',
had spent his first five or so years on the kibbutz but had
totally forgotten how to speak Hebrew on his return and
was largely regarded as a foreigner. I had little idea what
to expect and, in the days before I flew out there, I told
Erun on the phone that I was currently reading Malcolm X
and wanted to know whether that would be a problem. He
said: "Only you would ask something like that."

It wasn't a problem. It's fair to say my perceptions
of Jews were turned upside down in Israel. Erun picked
me up from Tel Aviv airport with a female kibbutznik
and, during the nighttime journey, she said all the young,
hitchhiking soldiers were "special people".

. . .

There was an episode on the kibbutz which brought out
the worst in me, I suppose. Well, make up your own
minds. The first job I had on the kibbutz was working in

the expansive dining room. It was fine. I had fun. But one of my duties did get a bit tiresome. There was this huge, electric mopping machine which was meant to be used on the whole floor every day after breakfast. The task meant shuffling around every table and every chair. Pushing that machine around was kinda akin to mowing a lawn and the whole thing took about 90 minutes. I just plugged into my Walkman and got on with it.

The thing is that job was gonna be mine until the next male (sexist, I know) volunteer turned up and then I'd be free. I did it six days a week for six weeks and then this Christian South Korean, Wun, turned up. He was in Israel because he was on the path to becoming a priest. He apparently came from an extremely wealthy family. The woman in charge of the volunteers had a high opinion of me so she sort of put Wun in my hands, which was fine. But it felt like he followed me around like a chick who thinks the first moving object it sees is its mummy. I handed the mopping machine reins over to Wun on his first day in the dining room and half an hour later he came up to me — in tears — and expressed to me he couldn't do it.

He spoke little English and he would approach me with his phrase book while I was lying in bed, crouch down, invade my space, and say: "Today, yesterday, tomorrow, yes, no."

Think about it, man.

I suppose I couldn't respect a man who was trying to teach people about religion but couldn't use a mopping machine for more than 30 minutes. What would Jesus do? He was very clumsy and got nicknamed "Wun Spencer" after accident-prone character Frank Spencer from TV sit-com Some Mothers Do 'Ave 'Em. One day, I was sitting outside my shack and I saw Wun skipping by. He proceeded to slip and have a nasty fall. He landed quite badly on his wrist and was in agony. I can't remember exactly how it came about but I became tasked with bringing him to the local hospital, again because I was a trusted figure. However, even though we got a lift into town, I felt that a Hebrew-speaking Israeli should have gone with Wun.

Things got worse. I sat Wun down and queued up in the casualty department. But Israelis can be quite brash and every time I got near to the front, Wun would run up holding his wrist and I'd lose my place in the queue. I felt like breaking his other wrist. I think he got the gist of that.

Eventually, he got seen to by a doctor for what turned out to be a minor sprain.

My problem with him was that I don't think he offered anything to the group. Not humour or strength of character or gratitude or charm or hard work. Nothing other than, admittedly, being a nice guy. I like to think I'd handle him better these days. I was only 21 at the time. A few weeks later, he left the kibbutz, citing me as the reason. He bought chocolates for every other one of the dozen or so volunteers…then he had to ask to borrow money from them to get to Jerusalem. Am I a bad guy?

That first spell on the kibbutz lasted six months and I did not want to leave. I came within a whisker of sabotaging my journey to Ben Gurion Airport in Tel Aviv for my flight home to Blighty. Anyway, towards the end of my time there, the so-called "volunteers" were due a three-day trip. We were young people, the vast majority not Jewish, who came as guests for the experience of living on a kibbutz. We would work six days a week and get paid £30 a month. That was essentially beer money. I was supplementing my income by donating sperm at the local hospital (the so-called "wank bank").

We were owed a three-day holiday in Israel but the dozen or so volunteers were offered cash, 150 shekels (around £30) each, instead of the trip. The woman in charge of the volunteers was a lovely, beautiful, Yemenite woman. But she was lazy. The cash deal suited her because it meant she wouldn't have to organise a trip. All the volunteers wanted to take the cash…apart from me. I wrestled with my conscience over this for several days and decided that £30 wasn't going to mean much to me when I was sitting alone in my Brixton flat on a grey winter's day. It was a metaphorical cloud hanging over me before having a literal cloud hanging over me.

I got on so well with the woman and she regarded me as, in her words: "Special."

So I went up to her in the dining room after she had lunch and said that, as far as I was concerned, a trip was part of the deal of being a volunteer.

I got my way and *everyone* was pissed off with me. *Everyone*. The volunteers who decided against going on the three-day trip would get nothing.

There were about seven of us who decided to go. My name was mud even among them. As we set out in a minibus, I was consigned to the back row, on my own. At that point, this adventure was disdainfully branded "Sid's Trip". But as we went through the kibbutz gates, I had this great feeling of excitement and I knew I'd done the right thing, even though I was feeling isolated and friendless. They were among three of the happiest days of my life. Everyone had such a great time, we were giddy on happiness (and booze) as we prepared to sleep on the shore of the picturesque Sea of Galilee.

That's my brand of leadership: I never seek it unless there is a vacuum.

Another time I stayed on the kibbutz, I was hanging around with a group of young, Jewish, Canadian guys who were planning to settle in Israel. They were nice but I think they felt a bit threatened by me, for one reason or another. One night, I was walking down the main interior road close to their living quarters and I overheard one of them describing me in a derogatory way as a "curry muncher". I recall it was not long after they found out that I'm Anglo-Indian, not that I was keeping it a secret. The thing is, I *love* curry. Good curry, that is. Being dubbed a "curry muncher" is much better than being called a "Paki" or a "mongrel". Then I heard a huge, young, Jewish, South African guy I'd befriended tell them: "Sid's the wrong guy to mess with."

I didn't have any problems with the Canadians after that and I didn't hold a grudge. I just think it's so sad the way that these racist sentiments are passed down the generations. You kinda get used to it over the years. Of course, I do have my boundaries but they didn't get nearly that far.

...

Bearing in mind my ineffective punches in the playground at Pimlico, I was at a point of my life that, despite a hardcore attitude which warded off a lot of aggressors, I didn't know how to *really* fight. But I thought of a novel way to tackle this. There were a lot of Russian Jews on the kibbutz and they were all into some form of martial arts or boxing. The Top Dog was a relatively small guy called Oleg, a classic boxer. There had been quite a lot of friction between him and one of the volunteers, who was a 6ft 4ins former Royal Marine. It never came to blows, though. I asked Oleg to teach me how to box. His English wasn't good so there was a lot of translation going on through his English-speaking Russian mates during negotiations. But something got lost in translation…

We set a date for me to turn up to his caravan. These were massive mobile homes, really. They had a bedroom at each end and a huge living area in between, which was cleared for lesson one. Actually, quite a good space for boxing, especially because of the flexible floor material. There must have been half a dozen Russians looking on as we eventually got going. I wasn't prepared for what happened next. I don't know how long this lasted, I honestly couldn't say whether it was five minutes or 45 minutes but he absolutely battered me, relentlessly. I mean, I didn't even get close to landing a single blow as he stung me from every angle like a swarm of a thousand angry wasps. I was regretting not bringing a towel to throw in. I was so relieved when it eventually ended.

It then emerged that Oleg had thought I was challenging him to a duel as the Marine's proxy, which wasn't the case. I was in fact myself at loggerheads with the Marine. Oleg was so apologetic when this became clear. And I certainly won his respect for taking a beating. Suddenly, we were friends, such are the dynamics of alpha males. I became his student and he did start to teach me, from the basics of how not to break your arm when you deliver a punch to angling your fists to deliver maximum damage.

I took to it, looked forward to it, not in the sense of a party or a hot date but the challenge, the physical confidence it gave me as I got better and better. I still wasn't landing punches but my defence was improving a lot and I realised that it's an "eye game". That, as a boxing fan, was a revelation to me, that our eyes were locked during virtually every moment of every round.

I had black eyes and a bruised nose for the entire time I was doing this. The hardest part was keeping my guard up, it's so tiring on the arms. The first time I let my guard down a bit, Oleg would stop and say: "Siddy, I am not a woman."

He would repeat that line the second time I let my guard down. The third time, he would punch me in the face. I remember thinking: "He is not a woman."

Hate to be sexist, just that's what popped into my head at the time.

Oleg would teach me one new thing every session and I was a good student. One time, he got me to punch solid parts of the caravan to improve my haymaker technique. Another time he showed me this trick where he would look like he was going to throw the left jab but would quickly retract it and land a haymaker using his right. But being Siddy, I tried an *experiment*: Instead of flicking out my jab and hitting with the right, I flicked out the left jab, quickly withdrew it before following through with said *left jab*. I caught him flush on the chin and he started to stagger backwards towards an open window. His mates had to run to stop him falling out.

It was the only time I ever caught him. I realised it was a cheap shot because he was teaching me a particular discipline and I subverted it. But still, it was a good feeling and he kinda rated me for it, although that was the last lesson.

Oleg, I am not a woman.

. . .

The first year I was on the kibbutz, I was very much a boozy Brit. I'd turned into a bit of a yob. One time, me and these three English lads I hung around with decided to

buy some cheap booze in the local town, Afula, rather than
going for the quality stuff on the kibbutz. It was about six
miles away and we used to hitchhike there. It was always
a little adventure. Religious Jews would often pick us up
and try to indoctrinate us. But they would quickly lose
interest when they discovered we weren't Jewish. Once,
this religious guy picked us up and when it became clear
we were gentiles, he sincerely tried to persuade us that
Jews were the master race and we were inferior. I mean,
he genuinely thought he would win us over to his point
of view.

Thanks for the lift.

It's actually quite surprising how many secular Jews
hate the religious types in Israel. Not a story you often
hear but incredibly prevalent.

We went to the supermarket and bought four crates of
"Nesher" beer, which wasn't a bad brew and very cheap.
It's fair to say that four blokes hitchhiking with four crates
of beer isn't something you would often see in England.
We made our way to the pick-up point and waited patiently.
But it seemed like, for once, no one wanted us. Not even
religious zealots. Eventually, this rusty, canvas-roofed
army 4x4 stopped for us. We piled into the back with
our booze and, just before we got going, the fat, middle-
aged soldier behind the wheel turned around and gave us
a huge, dirty, manic smile. Suddenly we were starring in
Mad Max II. Yikes.

However, all seemed fine as we set off, although he
was definitely breaking whatever the speed limit was.
Then we started to get closer to the halfway point to the
kibbutz, where there was a huge hole in the road in dire
need of repair that we were all too familiar with. The
driver turned to us and started laughing manically before

putting his foot to the floor as we approached the hole. Then we hit it and us in the back were sent flying up, all cracking our heads on solid parts of the roof as bottles started exploding, covering us with beer. The driver was still cackling away as he dropped us off. Our legs were like jelly.

Thanks for the lift.

To be fair, *most* of the beer remained intact. More intact than us.

That evening, my English mates made a beer-drinking contraption from a plastic tube and a funnel. The beer was poured into the contraption and you could work out all the fizz by alternating the high point of the tube endings. Then we'd put the tube in our mouths, raise the funnel and drink a whole bottle's worth in one gulp. It was a massive hit and we were already plastered before we got anywhere near the pub.

We brought the contraption with us and, at some point after we staggered there, I was sitting on a bench inside the pub/disco next to this sexy, busty Dutch volunteer. Somehow we ended up snogging, wildly, on the bench. But the guy sitting next to me put the funnel on one of her boobs and sucked the other end of the tube. She withdrew her tongue from my mouth, stood up and poured a full glass of beer all over me. I don't know how she expected me to suck her tit when I had my tongue down her throat.

It stands as one of the great injustices of my life.

She was quite a tough woman, though, and it was all laughed off the next day. I've got a nice picture of us sitting together outside my shack during her last day on the kibbutz.

There were tensions among the volunteers. A young, white South African guy who I *thought* I got along with was due to leave the kibbutz a few weeks after I arrived. A Dutch mate told me this guy was joining a Jewish "cult" in Jerusalem. I thought nothing of it. But two nights before the South African left, I had this incredibly vivid dream that I was hit on the back of my head while walking into the shared bedroom of my shack. In the dream, I tried to look back to see who did it but as hard as I tried, I passed out. Instinctively, I decided I didn't want to sleep in my room the next night. Good move.

It was a pub night and I ended up sleeping in a young kibbutznik's flat. It emerged the next day that the South African had pulled out a knife and told the other volunteers that he was going to stab me. This apparently led to a bizarre confrontation between him and an otherwise incredibly shy, female volunteer. He departed the next day, leaving me convinced that the dream saved my life. In the next few weeks, I started to access the thought processes which led me to have that dream. I managed to narrow it down to a casual conversation weeks before when he was telling me about this particular Ninja "sect" which had no compunction about attacking from behind. Nice.

In fact, that episode was worse than my personal experience of Armageddon...

Friday was the only pub night on my kibbutz. Sometimes we would drink in Afula or just hang around with a few cans outside the shacks. So we jumped at the chance to go to Kibbutz "Megiddo" — Hebrew for Armageddon — which is a ten-minute drive from my kibbutz, for a midweek pub night.

There were only half a dozen of us there and we sat at the bar getting progressively pissed on the most popular Israeli beer, Goldstar. We eventually got onto tequila shots and then the barman put some porn on the TV, which was a great touch and certainly grabbed our attention. But we noticed at some point that the sneaky sod had started trying to pass off cheap, nasty, Israeli vodka as tequila. We weren't best pleased.

Not the end of the world, though.

...

When I was 22, I took a break from the kibbutz to go on holiday again to a backpacker resort called Dahab in Egypt's Sinai desert, with two English mates I'd met during previous spells on the kibbutz. A surprising number of Israelis used to go on holiday there, pre-army and post-army. Youngsters, either way.

We ended up hanging out with four pre-army Israeli girls aged 17. I made a move on this interesting and sexy girl. Her English was excellent and she was smart, to what degree I had no idea of at the time. We sort of ended up getting cosy in a particular restaurant, where a whole gang of us would hang out all day, lying on the carpets and cushions, smoking shishas and eating spicy tuna pizzas. It turned into a relationship which spanned several years. Long-distance relationships are awful. But I never would have dumped her. She dumped me not long after starting her two-year stint in the Israeli Defense Force. I did love her. Maybe I should have told her that.

She held some racist views when we first met. I can be very pragmatic and I took her age into account but I think *I* would have been doing the dumping pretty early on if she hadn't quickly dismantled her prejudices. I mean, I'm half Indian. I inspired her to talk to her black cleaner at her massive and impressive house in one of the most exclusive parts of Tel Aviv. She was intrigued to find out that he was gay and quickly built a friendship with him. Then she came to visit me in Brixton and, with her friend, walked the quick way to the Tube station on Muggers' Mile, even though I had expressly told them to go the long route. And after she met Mr. T, she said: "I have to admit, he is really nice."

Rewind a couple of years and she was talking about how "black is shit" being the *"thing"* in Israel at the time. There's a knack to knowing who you can and cannot enlighten. Partly because of that relationship, I probably spent about three years in Israel during the Nineties. I was a guest at her family home for some of that but most of the time I was on the kibbutz.

My stock rose there over the years in the sense that I got to do more and more interesting and challenging jobs. The first year was mainly spent in the dining room, which was where the volunteers tended to work. But I managed to move on thanks to my determined mindset and hard work. My first job outside the dining room was in the extensive, communal gardens. I would spend many hours mowing the lawns on a mini-tractor. And I got to use loads of different contraptions.

My mum is a professional gardener, so it must be in the genes. I certainly have an aptitude for certain aspects of it. My boss used to let me decide how I was going to tackle certain projects. One day, he left me with a massive, over-grown bush to tame. He came back towards the end of the day to monitor my progress and said: "That's not how I'd have done it but it's pretty good."

However, my favourite role was out in the almond fields during the harvesting season. I got to drive tractors and work as part of a well-oiled machine. The greatest compliment was that I was more trusted than paid Israeli workers from outside the kibbutz. Some aspects of the work got me super fit and I loved being out in those fields. More happy in my work than anything else I've ever done. Journalism can be great and compelling but it's a different sort of thrill.

We came across all manner of wildlife in the almond fields, from chameleons to porcupines to rabbits. And the kibbutz's two smartest dogs used to come along for the harvest period, just for the craic. The camaraderie with the humans was brilliant as well. There was about a dozen of us using all sorts of vehicles and techniques to harvest one tree of all its fruit inside 90 seconds before moving to the next one. We were The A-Team. I was probably the bonkers one.

Using cutting edge farm equipment, we probably collected about 97 per cent of the fruit we induced to fall from the trees using a specially-adapted vehicle to shake the fruit from the trees (it's amazing to see the tree shake and shed its load for the first time). But there was still a fair amount left behind. The kibbutz employed Palestinians to pick it up off the floor. That was a shock for me because Israel is a first world country and they were so third world. I'm guessing they were from inside the nearby West Bank because Arab Israelis generally seemed far better off.

One of my Israeli colleagues pointed out how the middle-aged Arab women used a different technique to us to save their backs. We would crouch down, bending our knees but they would keep their legs straight and bend from the middle of their bodies. However, my abiding memory of the Palestinians there was of being chased after by them for water when I was in the area on one of the tractors. Of course, I obliged but it meant I had to drive all the way back to the supply point, wasting 20 minutes.

Why weren't these people being supplied with water in the first place?

My feeling at the time was that the Palestinian boss was responsible for that. That was my reading of the situation, for what it's worth. What also stuck out in my mind was that some of the teenage boys were wearing trousers and jackets in the middle of an Israeli summer. Don't know what that symbolised to me but it wasn't good. I suspected they were the only clothes they had.

In my opinion, if you don't understand what is going on in the Middle East then you don't understand what's going on in the world. It is my belief that this planet revolves around Jerusalem. Tribes have fought over the Old City for thousands of years and the Israelis are just the latest in possession of the prize.

There was a lot of optimism for peace in 1993 when I first pitched up in the region, thanks largely to the Oslo Accords agreement for an Israeli-Palestinian settlement. Negotiations had been going on behind the scenes for some time. And, that year, Israeli PM Yitzhak Rabin and PLO leader Yasser Arafat shook hands on the White House lawn under the auspices of the US President, Bill Clinton.

It seems like a lifetime ago.

Rabin was effectively in charge of the Israeli Defense Force during the 1967 Six-Day War and consequently became an iconic military hero. He was pictured as one of the first Israeli soldiers to enter the Old City after the stunning victory had been secured. But he was genuinely looking for an enduring peace at the point he was assassinated — by a by a lone wolf right-wing extremist Jewish Israeli opposed to the Oslo Accords — at a 1995 peace rally in Tel Aviv attended by 100,000 Israelis.

For many, including me, the chance of peace in my lifetime died with Rabin. He had the military credentials and had made the journey from his hawkish tendencies, which enabled the Israeli public to trust in him with their collective future.

Rabin's widow, Leah, who died in 2000, became known as "The Lioness of Israel" following the assassination, mothering a nation whose dreams of peace had been shattered. In 1997, she said: "We [the Jews] used terrorism to establish our state. Why should we expect the Palestinians to be any different?"

I took my now ex to Jerusalem in 1999 and we had a drink in the swanky King David Hotel cocktail bar. The hotel had housed the British administrative HQ in Palestine when it was bombed on Monday, July 22, 1946, by militant right-wing Zionist underground organisation the Irgun. The death toll was 91, including 28 British citizens. There were 46 non-fatal injured.

Palestine was under British mandate then but most of it was declared the Jewish state after the 1948 Arab-Israeli War. Former Irgun leader Menachem Begin went on to become Israeli Prime Minister between 1977 and 1983.

Despite my political views on the Middle East, I would say there's much to commend about Israeli society. They do tend to be hard on the outside and soft on the inside, I'm talking of the vast majority, secular society. They know how to live in the moment and can't get their heads around the idea of "entertaining" people. They are open, honest and direct. And if they offer you something — such as food, drink or shelter — they mean it.

One of the things I revelled in was that Israel has a hybrid population and I found some sort of shallow sense of belonging in that. Cars would often stop at the hitchhiking spot in Afula, look past a dozen Israelis and pick me out to ask for directions. Israeli friends told me I had a face that made people want to know who was behind it. The funny thing is that I would often be able to give them directions because I grew to know the area quite well and most of them speak English to a decent standard (thanks largely to Hollywood).

One of the themes that always popped up was that the women choose the men in that 'cool' society I was temporarily part of. Actually, at this point of my life, I think women choosing the men is more prevalent across the world than I'd grown up to believe.

Of course, there are some disturbing aspects to Israeli society. Firstly, there's a lot of friction between Israeli Jews with Arab country backgrounds, such as Moroccans and Yemenites, and those of European extraction, such as Germans and Americans. And it goes without saying that racism is rife towards Arabs. It got progressively worse even during my time from 1993 and 1999. But there was contact. Some Arab visitors used to be friendly with certain kibbutzniks and pop by for a cup of coffee on their rounds. And I recall that in my last year in the almond fields, an Arab farmer was being recruited at vast expense to run the whole operation all year round.

...

At the time of writing, I would describe myself as anti-Zionist but NOT anti-Semitic. Jews saved me. My kibbutz days were amongst the happiest of my life. I still have Israeli friends. One of them stayed with me and Brian in Brixton during the mid-Nineties. She was a lovely girl, quite sexy: Think bosomy Gwen Stefani. We thought it was hilarious when she tried to buy stamps at the Brixton branch of…NatWest. Not totally unconnected, she was quite into dope at the time, as were we. She would spend much of the time getting blasted and looking out of the window at the rough pub across the way on Railton Road, which was, with no sense of irony, called "Harmony". There used to be police and paramedics there on a regular basis.

One stoned evening she gasped and said: "Someone's just pulled a gun out!"

I went over to have a look and said: "Yeah."

Then I swiftly returned to the sofa and continued to nurse my joint. I can't say I saw guns every day in Brixton, in fact that's one of the few times but most Israelis have them, being as the country has a civilian army and they're afraid of Arabs. I suppose life on The Frontline was pretty fascinating for her, as was life in Israel for me.

Whatever my current point of view on the Middle East, the kibbutz was my equivalent of going to university. I had access to many, many incredibly intelligent people: Poets, sculptors, musicians, military heroes and so on. It put me in a different context, like they saw beyond my accent, my hard edges, even my occasional bad behaviour. That gave me a lot of confidence for when I reluctantly returned to Britain. It also gave me a much-needed break from cannabis.

Thank you, Kibbutz Yizreel.

Part II: Media

7. GOTCHA

'You're a one-man subculture'

After the press conference was over, I cornered the Times correspondent who had interrupted me when I was asking my question and snarled at him: "You're just lucky we're inside Scotland Yard [London police HQ]."

I felt like smashing his face in. Wanker. The sheep had just turned up to be spoon-fed the story, collect their press packs and satisfy their desire to be titillated by terrorism aimed at black and Asian people. This was the London nail-bombing campaign of 1999.

The first device targeted the black community in Brixton, where I was living at the time. I was out shopping for clothes on Oxford Street, central London, when it went off. I didn't know what had taken place but passengers were ordered off the train one stop short at Stockwell and I walked to Brixton from there. My mum had to make the same walk 18 years earlier after the 1981 riot, leaving us in Leicester so she could do a shift at The Ritzy.

The centre was cordoned off and, even though I still didn't know what had happened, I vividly remember seeing an abandoned, old Routemaster red bus with the film title "Blast from the Past" emblazoned on its side. I was Editor of Eastern Eye at the time, a weekly, red-top, British-Asian tabloid newspaper. After finding out what had gone on, my gut reaction was that it was a racially-motivated attack and maybe the Indian subcontinent capital of Europe, Southall, would be targeted next. The following day, I went into work and I decided to go with the front page splash headline: "BRIXTON BOMB: SOUTHALL NEXT?"

Some of my colleagues thought it was scare-mongering and in the end I decided to phone the Publisher, who backed me. A few days later, a bomb went off on Brick Lane, east London, which is the heart of Britain's Bangladeshi community and barely a mile from our offices. I decided to call up a reporter to ask her to go down to the scene with me and the police gave certain media outlets, including us, access to the crime scene, which was yards from a small police station which had been closed as it was every Saturday. But my reaction was that, if a little paper like ours feared a racist attack, it should have been open.

In fact, an Asian man who thought a sports bag, which contained the bomb, looked suspicious headed to that police station only to find it shut. So he put it in the boot of his car, where it went off, otherwise the casualty list would have been far worse. These are the circumstances that led me to attend the press conference in New Scotland Yard, where a CCTV screen grab of the suspected bomber was being circulated. My question was something along the lines of: "Why was Brick Lane Police Station closed when you were aware of the Asian community's fears after the Brixton bomb?"

The Times reporter next to me said: "We're not here for polemics."

I didn't know what "polemics" were but I got the gist and knew he was having a pop at me. The officer conducting the press conference — an assistant commissioner — looked me squarely in the eyes across the room and reassured me that everything was being done to protect London's ethnic minority communities. I found his baritone monologue quite chilling. But at least he was respectful enough to answer. I'm asking you now, was mine not a reasonable and pertinent question? I did, still do, and that's why I approached the Times reporter afterwards. He wasn't quite so confident when it was just me and him.

When I got home, I looked up "polemics" in an old dictionary and the definition was something about "challenging the Christian consensus". The interesting thing is that modern, online dictionaries make no reference to the "Christian consensus" element, it's more a "verbal attack". But I bet that reporter knew, like it was a dog whistle comment for the consumption of his exclusively white, male, mainstream peers, and policemen, in that room. And yes, if you haven't got it by now, I *am* challenging the Christian consensus.

It's a bit hazy after all these years. But two days before the Brixton bomb, we received a letter from a group calling itself "The White Wolves" — apparently a splinter group of fascist para-military group Combat 18 — ordering all non-whites and all Jews to leave before the end of 1999, or face "extermination". After the first explosion, I phoned Brixton Police Station to inform them of the letter that eventually led me to speculate "SOUTHALL NEXT?". They didn't get back to me.

I didn't think much of it at the time because we used to get quite a few racist letters. But after the Brick Lane bomb, we got another letter — supposedly again from The White Wolves — claiming responsibility. It felt like the world's media descended on our little office in Bethnal Green, east London. I prepared "packs", with copies of the letters, a press release and the previous edition of Eastern Eye, in which we had speculated that an Asian area would be targeted next.

It was a crazy time. I must have done ten TV interviews and countless on the radio. I had to draw the line when a Japanese TV station wanted to do a bit on me. But I vaguely recall doing a 6am radio interview and I have no idea what I said but do remember veteran broadcaster Anne Diamond telling me to go back to bed. One LBC radio quote of mine which kept popping up was that "the police are just glorified football stewards". Also, some big-hitting Asian journalists from here and India came to see me. Some interesting conversations. And I was invited to Private Eye's editors' lunch. Quite an honour and a measure of how Eastern Eye's profile had sky-rocketed.

In the middle of all this, I heard that a guy in marketing had said I was lapping up the attention on a "personal tip". In fairness to my boss, he told him: "When you're on that wave, you've just gotta ride it."

I felt like the bomber was following me around and I decided to go with my now ex to visit Brian in Ireland. We were there when the third bomb hit, inside gay pub The Admiral Duncan in Soho, central London. Scores of people were injured and three, including a pregnant woman, lost their lives.

Lots of crazy things happened during that time, including a bomb alert across the road from our office, which led our ex-army security team to evacuate the building. The back entrance gates were shut so dozens of us were ordered by the security guards to crouch down in the yard, head on knees and put our index fingers in our ears. The bomb disposal squad carried out a controlled explosion and there was a tiny pop. A bit of an anti-climax. Apparently, it was big news for a few hours on broadcast media. An old colleague asked me whether it was a publicity stunt in the context of how Eastern Eye had somehow found its way to the centre of the story. It wasn't.

There were lots of abandoned bags in the surrounding area, presumably left by racists wanting to scare the local, largely Bangladeshi, population. The streets were desolate, like there was a revolution going on because every 30 seconds to two minutes, you could her police sirens sounding, going in all different directions, presumably dealing with hoaxes.

Eventually, the bomber, Neo-Nazi militant David Copeland, then aged 22, was arrested. His father appeared on TV a lot at that time to distance himself from his son's views and actions. The most surreal thing is that I was in Shadwell Tube Station in east London around that time and, wearing a cap, Copeland's dad, who had quite distinctive blonde hair, was the only other person on my platform. I don't know whether he recognised me from my 15 minutes of fame but he turned on his heels when he saw me and walked back up the stairs.

It emerged in his son's trial that Southall *had* been the next target, as opposed to Brick Lane but Copeland changed his mind at the last minute.

...

I've always had a love-hate relationship with education. When I left Merton College aged 18, I sort of knew I wanted to be a journalist. I sat a test for a National Council for the Training of Journalists (NCTJ) course in (bleak) Harlow, Essex, when I finished my A-levels. But I didn't make the cut. After my first stint in Israel, when I was going nowhere fast, my mum presented me with an advert for broadcast journalism at Vauxhall College, south London. I evidently passed with flying colours and the lecturer overseeing the exam asked me on the spot whether I wanted to take their NCTJ print journalism course test for people from ethnic minorities. Again, I aced it.

Thanks, mum.

After getting into my stride on the course, I noticed a headline in The Express, which read something like: "MP in nig-nog race row."

I pointed this out to my partner in crime: A sharp, black woman called Nadia. We started to dissect why we found it so offensive. Looking back, we were quite naive, especially regarding The Express's political line. We felt the word "nig-nog" should have been partly asterisked out because it was an abusive term. In our letter to The Express, we asked if they would print the headline "MP in fucking bastards swear row"? This approach triggered a mixed reaction from our lecturers. One of them, who was a lovely guy but a bit straight, said: "You can't say that."

I thought it was spot on and showed good journalistic instincts. Much to our surprise, and I'd even say, delight, The Express wrote back and acknowledged, on a point of journalism, the word "nig-nog" should have been in quotes in the headline, at the very least. They noted that by not putting those words in quotes, a racist term had become part of the paper's own language. It felt like a small but significant achievement...and we got a taste for it.

Things went a bit pear-shaped for me by the end of the course and I'm not even sure what sort of qualification I obtained, if any. But the positive was my work experience at Eastern Eye. I can vividly remember when I first got the sense I could be a journalist. It was deadline night there and I was only getting £60 a week at the time. By the early hours, it was down to just Nad, who was Production Editor, the Editor and me to put out the paper.

I was enjoying being part of this little club and, as it approached midnight, the front page headline was the only thing left to do. It was about a Bangladeshi-British teenager who had been battered half to death by a racist, white gang. There was a picture of him in his hospital bed with wires and tubes inserted into various parts of his upper body. I think he might have been on life support.

The Editor had written "RIVERS OF BLOOD" into the headline slot but he wasn't happy with it, thought it was a bit laboured and cliched, especially considering it comes from a famous anti-immigration speech by extreme right-wing Tory politician Enoch Powell in the late Sixties.

We sat around for ages discussing it in front of the screen. I loved the banter and the way we were knocking about ideas. Then it came to me: "THE SCARS OF RACISM."

The Editor's eyes lit up, he wrote it in the slot and said: "Done."

Then he said: "Siddy's the third man."

It was an interesting time. The real highlight, though, without any shadow of a doubt, was interviewing Pakistani cricketing and shagging legend Imran Khan (who is Pakistan's PM at the time of writing). He was based in London and was all over the tabloids for his sporting and sexual prowess over a number of years. He got caught up in the whole ball-tampering scandal — even though he'd retired — and got stitched up.

This English writer was doing a biography on Imran, which he co-operated with, and there was this bit he offered up about how he *had* tampered with a ball but openly and as a prank during a *charity match*. Of course, some of the papers got hold of the story, took it out of context and put a negative spin on it, no pun intended. All of a sudden, Imran was just another foreign cheat.

Eastern Eye had a contact with a hotline to Imran, hence me and Nad ended up interviewing the star in a private room at his High Street Kensington office (for his cancer hospital charity in his homeland). Being of Pakistani origin and a cricket nut, Nad was totally in awe. He conducted the first half of the interview well. Imran probably thought I was a white photographer as I listened patiently. Then the enormity of the situation dawned on Nad and he ran out of steam. I jumped in and got things going again.

Imran was a nice guy. Not snotty but not over-friendly. Genuine. We told him how football icon and high-profile broadcaster Jimmy Greaves had been slagging him off over ball-tampering on an ITV panel show called Sport in

Question (it was the sporting equivalent of BBC politics panel show Question Time). Without saying anything, Imran stood up and walked out of the room. We were stunned and didn't know what to do. Had we offended him? Should we leave? Was he an arrogant narcissist after all? But five minutes later, Imran came back into the room and said: "I'm on the show on Thursday."

That's juice.

He asked if we wanted to come along. Regrettably, we had to decline because it fell on a deadline day at Eastern Eye. But it was great tuning in while we were at work in the evening and saying: "Wow! We got him on that."

The show went well and there was total respect from Greavsie to Imran after he had told his side of the story.

Aside from sport, Nad's main job at Eastern Eye was as Production Editor. He was a brilliant headline writer. When then England cricket captain Mike Atherton was caught ball-tampering, Nad put the screen grab on the front page and the headline was "GOTCHA". It was a reference to The Sun front page headline for the scandalous sinking by the Royal Navy of Argentine warship The Belgrano during the 1982 Falklands War. The 44-year-old vessel was outside the security zone and moving away as fast as it could.

The banter with Nad was first class. He once wore a pair of blue velvet trousers to work and I mullered him over it. The next day, I came in a bit early, made an authentic-looking, Highway Code-style "No blue velvet trousers" sign, using my layout skills, and pinned it up on the wall. Another time, he dug out some publicity shots of himself from when his career first started. I made a point of getting everyone who came into the office have a look at them. It was excruciating for him. He took his revenge by somewhat undercutting me. Whenever a woman came in, he would ask them: "Do you think Siddy's a ladies' man?"

He added: "Because he was just telling me that he's a bit of a ladies' man."

If. Fucking. Only.

The worst was when they would genuinely reflect on the question. That was excruciating for me and a ceasefire was promptly agreed.

· · ·

I got fired in my first spell at Eastern Eye for being too disruptive, like I was back at school, and even though I was only on £60 per week. So I was going nowhere fast in my early 20s. At one point, I was unemployed and down to my last £100.

Some English friends I met on the kibbutz said I would find agency work in Reading, just outside London, and could stay with one of them while I sublet my flat in Brixton. In a matter of months, I went from interviewing Imran Khan to doing night shifts loading lorries at a Waitrose chilled warehouse somewhere in Berkshire. We worked in pairs and, because I was "just" an agency worker, I ended up working alongside a moody staffer, Steve, who was not popular (he was going through a bitter divorce).

One night, he was driving this mini-forklift loaded with hundreds of bottles of milk and managed to tip it over. The bottles all burst and milk went everywhere. Fucking everywhere. It was a lake of milk. Steve somehow found a dry spot, threw his hat down on the floor and started jumping up and down on it while screaming. Everyone gathered around in silence for this Basil Fawlty-style meltdown. And then, totally deadpan, I said: "Steve, there's no point crying over spilt milk."

Everyone cracked up. A few days later, the alarm sounded for our break and I made my way up to the canteen. When I went back down 20 minutes later, Steve came right up into my face and screamed: "Don't you ever fucking well leave me on the ramp alone again."

His poor wife.

He carried on ranting and raving at me, I couldn't even make sense of what he was saying. Bearing in mind that I'm not usually a violent man, he was firing flecks of spit at my face and, as an instinctive reaction, I tipped my head forward. Unfortunately, I caught him flush on the nose with my forehead. I suppose it could have been described as a head-butt. The stupid thing in this farcical situation was that he started stumbling backwards and I moved towards him to try and stop him falling. But he thought I was going in for the kill. He smashed into a trolley/basket and I was sacked on the spot.

I came very close to going back to the kibbutz after that. My mum was so concerned about her son seemingly just drifting through life. But a few days before me and Brian headed there, Nad phoned to ask if I was interested in becoming his production assistant. I was! It was so exciting, I was on top of the world. His rationale was that I'd behave myself if I was on a proper wage, £8k. He had struggled to push this through with the Editor, who said of recruiting me: "It's like Miss World is in the next room and she wants you to fuck her…but you know she's got AIDS."

Charming.

I did get the job, though. Nad confessed years later that the real reason he took me on was because I was "fun". But after a while, he said to himself: "Oh, this guy can do newspapers."

Nad was a great teacher when it came to the technical side of page-designing software. He started by drawing, on screen, a "shadow box" (they used to feature in tabloids but not anymore). The point was that a shadow box covers all the general elements and principles of layout software. I didn't look back.

During that time, our Imran contact delivered us a googly. There were rumours the star was about to get engaged to white, English heiress Jemima Goldsmith. But our contact assured us it was just idle gossip. We published a story on the front page with the headline: "Imran will never marry a white woman."

We all saw the funny side of it when the engagement was announced a few days later.

. . .

Deadline night was always an event at Eastern Eye, it was tough. These affairs could go on to 6am and there would be a cabbie from the printers waiting for us to finish for many hours on end so he could take the disks. But at around 11pm one night, two of my colleagues came in and said one of their cars had a smashed window. We all piled out and there was this tall, black guy smashing in another car window. He scarpered and one of my workmates gave chase, caught him up and smashed down the bottom of his right, upper arm on the suspect's shoulder. He fell to the ground and we caught up.

I ended up subduing him on the floor. Unfortunately, one of my Asian colleagues was a racist, particularly towards black people (but also towards me for being mixed race). He started kicking the guy as I held him down. I told him to stop. The thief started pleading his innocence at this point and I told him: "Shut the fuck up, I'm your fucking saviour!"

I told the racist colleague that I'd let the guy go if he didn't stop kicking. He stopped but started screaming racist abuse. Then the police turned up and they told my colleague he'd be arrested if he didn't button it. Quite a dramatic night. I think the black guy was a junkie. He was big but he wasn't strong and I have no idea what he was hoping to find in the cars. We went back to finishing off the paper. Epilogue is that the thief was prosecuted and, I recall, jailed.

Deadline night certainly wasn't without its charms. The Editor's brother used to pick up smoked salmon and cream cheese bagels from a legendary Jewish outlet on Brick Lane. We would take little breaks to have arm-wrestling contests and general banter. I loved it. Loved getting home to a joint even more, though.

The Editor could be a bit of a monster and, even though we worked so late, he would insist that we came in the next day. Me and Nad never made any agreement about what time we would pitch up, even though he usually gave me a lift home after we'd put the paper to bed. But we always surfaced at the offices around the same time. I mean, we'd both turn up nearly together, whether it be 1pm or 2.30pm. It was uncanny and everyone noticed. I guess we tuned into each other in the fog of war.

Despite not being Muslim, one of the things I loved about those days was Ramadan. The observants weren't allowed to eat or drink during daylight hours but they would feast when the sun went down and we'd all be invited to tuck in after those fasting had first dibs in the conference room, which sounds grander than it was.

People would bring top-notch Indian subcontinent food, takeaways and home-cooked grub. It was great bonding. I did fast one day and I did okay. I found the hardest thing was not the hunger but cleaning up my thoughts. It was great when I finally did get to eat. A lot of observants actually put on weight during Ramadan.

I left Eastern Eye to work for black newspaper The Voice in the mid-Nineties, enticed by bigger money. It was probably good for me to get out of my comfort zone but it was a bit frustrating at times, especially because I wasn't getting to write headlines. I could have done that job in my sleep…and virtually did at times. They were based in Brixton and I used to go home for lunch and get stoned. It wasn't usually a problem but it was a bit challenging when the Editor tried to engage me in conversation about a page when I was shit-faced.

The highlight of my time there was posing, pre-Ali G, as a "wigger [a white man who acts black]" for a photoshoot. It was hilarious being told by two black men how to be black. We were in bits. I've still got some of the photos.

I left The Voice because of a cantankerous white woman. She was confrontational over the pettiest thing. I lasted two years there. My line manager said some in my role only lasted two hours because of that woman.

I went back to Eastern Eye on what was meant to be a temporary basis. The Editor was concerned about my friendship with Nad because he'd left to work for a rival, East, which had been launched by colourful, left-wing politician George Galloway. I used to meet up with Nad once a week at the Burger King on Tottenham Court Road. We never shared anything that could damage either publication and, eventually, I was confirmed as Production Editor of Eastern Eye.

The Editor had been quite preoccupied with launching an Asian fashion magazine at the time and took me aside after a while. As someone never far from trouble, I was worried. But he told me that I'd been holding the paper together for months and that he was extremely grateful (although there was no extra money). It was a proud moment. I hadn't assumed control but as Production Editor, I had to monitor the workflow and the Editor's absence gave me a bit of licence to set the editorial line.

I later brokered Nad's return to be Editor as the sitting Editor became Publisher. I started to get atheist Brummie

Nad into gangsta rap, particularly Ice-T. And, aware of my Anglo-Indian background, my mixed class background and my upbringing in a black area, he declared that I was a "one-man subculture". It stuck (and was the original title for this book).

They were happy days. One of the funniest things was when a talented, gay feature writer had done a piece about himself and his hobby of appearing on TV gameshows. He wasn't a very assertive guy and if he wanted to say something he would be "umming" and "ahhing" for ages before spitting it out. He was making corrections during lunch to the gameshow feature (because he didn't trust me) and he noticed there was a picture file in the page folder I'd called something like: "Uhhhhhummmmmmmaaaahoooohhmmm."

He double clicked on it and a huge photo of *him* popped up! Apparently, he was totally incensed and wanted me sacked on my return from lunch. But the Publisher thought it was the best thing since sliced bread. He was a terrible boss, a megalomaniac but he did have a brilliant, dark sense of humour. Still does.

His brother had a column in the paper and I wanted to update his picture when I became Editor. There was a small studio and I went there with the columnist and the photographer. I don't know why I joined them but the session got underway and the gormless snapper just pointed the camera at his subject. *That* is why I joined them. Running out of patience, I started calling the columnist a "wanker", doing the hand gestures and everything. It's fair to say that it did the trick and he had a huge smile across his face. Good pics.

Eat your heart out, David Bailey.

...

Sri Lanka won the 1996 Cricket World Cup and weeks later the team held a press conference at an Asian restaurant in west London, which me and Nad went along to. I'm not a big cricket fan but I had a soft spot for Sri Lanka, having covered the team's comical antics leading up to securing the sport's ultimate prize. At some juncture in the preceding years, most of the team were dropped for being what the selectors described as "overweight and oversexed".

The restaurant was packed with stereotypical white, English, public school cricket correspondent types. But they could not find it in them to ask a single question of the world champions. It was an awkward moment and I felt embarrassed for the players. So I asked their cool dude captain, Arjuna Ranatunga: "Do you have a message for the selectors who dropped you for being 'overweight and oversexed'?"

He turned to some officials behind him and they had a whispered chat. He turned back and, with great understatement, said to me: "I think they've learned their lesson."

The ice was broken and the questions started to flow. We had some awards with us for their star players and chatted to them afterwards. As we sat in Nad's car before the journey home, we saw Sanath Jayasuriya and Muttiah Muralitharan walk past, clutching the awards we'd just given them, and it struck us how down to earth they were. The most humble people you could ever wish to meet. I find it tragic that there are such awful sectarian divisions in Sri Lanka. I've always had a positive view of those on both sides of the conflict.

...

Looking back, my Eastern Eye experience played a huge part in shaping me as a person, in a different way to the kibbutz. It was a natural development and helped me to access my Asian side. The earliest memory of my Indian dad was when I was five. I just didn't see him as my father when he visited us in our Brixton squat. I was a ward of court because he had threatened to kidnap me in previous years. Then there was the three weeks with him in India when I was 11. After that, I did get some sense of my Indian family when he visited during the dinner parties with London-based relatives. But to be honest, when my Eastern Eye placement from Vauxhall College was arranged, I kinda thought: "That'll be good, Asians are nice."

That was a naive reading of the situation. I did feel like an outsider at first and I wasn't confident. In reference to their parents, a few second generation British-Asians, including Nad, told me: "You have to be Asian to understand."

But after a while, I started to find my place there. It was quite a chaotic environment which would leave most white, English people tearing their hair out. We had 1,500 viruses on our computer network, for instance. And it was a challenge to get through the day without tripping over loose wires. I dubbed it "The Krypton Factor", after the TV gameshow that ran from the mid-Seventies to the mid-Nineties, in which physical stamina and mental capabilities were put to the test. It toughened me up and made me more adaptable. I could have done without *all* the extra obstacles, though.

I've always been respectful of other cultures, a good quality to have in that environment. I used to look, listen and learn a lot of the time as I strove to find my place in the jamboree. In the early days, I was changing trousers in the office and someone, outraged, piped up: "You're such a white man!"

The point being that I was doing this in front of the Editor's wife. I didn't see the problem because I was wearing boxer shorts. But I took my cue from the prevailing culture in that office. Another time, one of my colleagues told me: "You drink white man's tea."

He had his with milk but it was very dark and very strong, just like him (he was the one who caught the junkie window-smasher). I didn't copy the way he did it but I formulated my own take on teabag tea that I still abide by.

Nad was the key, though. We made each other laugh and he took me under his wing. It was a good place to be, everyone loves Nad because he is a super-smart and genuine guy. He is not the biggest but is definitely an alpha male, in his own way. His lethal weapon is his mind. I don't know where I'd be without him.

...

I reprised my role in the ethnic minority media for six months, starting in 2001, for the launch of a newspaper called Asian Xpress. It was a rollercoaster ride from start to finish. The key players were ex-Eastern Eye and I had some experience on the national papers to draw on. But Asian Xpress was basically me and Nad. We worked 36 hours straight on a few occasions, which was a measure of our commitment to that labour of love.

We garnered loads of mainstream attention. Nad was initially the Editor and he did the morning paper review on Sky News. I followed in his path after I became Editor. Weird being driven to a TV studio in the back of a limo.

Our designs and headlines were getting ripped off left, right and centre by national newspapers. But we took it as a massive compliment because it was clear that major players in the mainstream media were taking notice of what we were doing and saying. We did loads of great stuff, including an exclusive interview with News of the World investigative, "fake sheikh" reporter Mazher Mahmood in the week he exposed Sophie, Countess of Wessex. I wrote all the questions and the Publisher did the actual interview. It was dynamite.

I also managed to get News of the World showbiz columnist Rav Singh to do an interview because I'd recently been editing his page. He supplied us with pictures of him meeting dozens of the world's most famous people. I conducted that interview myself but didn't take a byline.

We were rivals to Eastern Eye and I recall that, as its Editor back in the middle of the nail-bombing campaign, I had offered £10,000 to anyone for information which led to the nail bomber's conviction. We thought it was funny when the reward was claimed but it would have been a bit awkward if I'd still been at Eastern Eye.

The end of the line at Asian Xpress came not long after I sacked a black designer on being told we needed to shed a member of staff. I hated doing the deed, he is one of the nicest people I've ever known and was training to be a preacher. When I escorted him next door to do the paperwork, I told him how gutted I was for him. He said: "Don't worry, I've got God on my side."

I didn't sleep for three nights. Even copious amounts of cannabis wouldn't knock me out. I felt so guilty. I should have told the bosses to do their own dirty work and sack him themselves. The next week, we were "given" a female, Asian designer. It dawned on me that my colleague had been pushed out by the racist wanker who'd kicked the black car thief.

What a piece of shit that man is. I resigned a few days later.

8. It was like Beirut

'I have the power to kill you'

Speeding through a checkpoint manned by armed soldiers in Beirut is definitely the most adrenaline-inducing moment of my life. But I don't recommend it.

The Publisher of Lebanese Gazette had this cool mate when I was Editor. Mo was a scuba-diving, pothead dude with dreadlocks. One evening he was giving me a lift home from the paper's office in a swish part of town. We chatted away as he drove his old, white Merc but he suddenly hit the brakes. About 50 yards up the road was an armed checkpoint.

Mo said: "Shit!"

He started moving slowly towards it but then, as we got close, he put his foot to the floor and we sped through. I heard a slight commotion behind us. I was expecting them to open fire and Mo was far from calm as we continued to accelerate. I barely had time to react, just clutching the side of my seat and ducking by leaning my upper body down into my lap.

The backstory is that they were Lebanese soldiers and they had to ask the Syrians if they could wipe their own arses back then. But I didn't know that until after the incident. The Syrians were virtually an occupying force. If they had manned the checkpoint we'd have been shot dead there and then. Why did Mo do it? He'd "lost" the documentation for "his" car. From The Frontline in Brixton to the Green Line in Beirut.

Adrenaline-inducing but not as scary as being strangled half to death by Morgan.

I had somehow managed to pick up a job for an English-language broadsheet paper — The Daily Star (not to be confused with the British version) — in Lebanon during the mid-Nineties between spells in the ethnic minority media and on the kibbutz. I took a cab from the airport to downtown Beirut and my studio apartment (which was just a nice hotel room with a kitchenette 3ft from my bed).

I woke up the next day to the sounds of birds, hustle and bustle. I was dying to get out and explore. I started going for a walk and it occurred to me that it was like a cross between Haifa, Israel, and Bombay. This was the Arab world.

I felt right at home but after three hours, it occurred to me that, not only was I lost, I didn't know what part of town my hotel was in, so I couldn't even ask for directions. It took me another three hours to find my way "home". What a relief. Looking back, I suppose I could have found my newspaper if push came to shove.

It was sunny but the heat wasn't oppressive and I didn't feel bad vibes. I mean, this was *Beirut*. We used to joke how adding "…in Beirut" would enliven the end of any sentence.

"We played pool…in Beirut."

"We went for a walk…in Beirut."

"We bought a pint of milk…in Beirut."

Of course, for many years, saying "it was like Beirut" was a way of saying somewhere was war-torn, lawless and chaotic. There was a bit of that. But it was a rare period of peace when I turned up. I wasn't into the thrill of being a war correspondent. I was trying to angle my life away from conflict. My hotel was in Hamra, which is technically on the Muslim side of town, west Beirut. But it was actually quite cosmopolitan. Yes, you would see women in burkas on Hamra Street but equally, you would see others in mini-skirts. There were loads of great, little takeaway spots, which would be open until the early hours. And there was a fantastic shop full of magazines and newspapers from around the world. Hamra was *the* place to be in Beirut. Pool halls, amusement arcades, cinemas, restaurants and so on.

I didn't watch much of US drama series Homeland but one episode I did see was called "Back to Beirut". Hamra Street was depicted in 2012 as being ruled by militia men. It destroyed any credibility the show had in my eyes. Lebanese Tourism Minister Faddy Abboud said filming "did not depict reality". He added: "We want to take action, we want to write to the filmmakers and producers and demand an apology. And we are planning to raise a lawsuit against the director and the producer."

Twentieth Century Fox, which produced the Emmy-winning series, declined to comment. *My* abiding memory of Hamra Street was take-away eatery King of Chips, not militia men. Great falafel at 2am.

On that first day, I ended up in The Daily Star newsroom on the opposite side of town, in the Christian quarter. I was so excited. They were new offices and I instantly took to the elfin-figure Editor, Peter Grimsditch (I read that he had "a penchant for black, silk shirts"), who, coincidently, was the launch Editor of The Daily Star back in Britain in the late Seventies and is still known by most as "PG". I'd read a few funny stories about him online and it's fair to say that he wasn't a disappointment. The paper was done by about 1am. The Pope had arrived in Lebanon on the same day as me and the front page splash headline was: "Welcome to Lebanon."

PG said the headline was dedicated to me (I later learned that the saying has a double meaning). Then all the Western sub-editors piled into his Jeep and he drove us back to Hamra and a little pub called The Evergreen. We were the only ones there and about half a dozen of us, mainly English, journalists stayed on for an 11-hour bender until 12 noon. PG picked up the tab.

I had arrived.

Apparently, I got dubbed "Peter's Angel of Death" at The Star because of my boisterous personality and compulsion to say it the way I see it. A camp Brit with Pakistani roots once asked me: "Do you *feel* anything, Siddy?"

I found it a bit bizarre. I mean, of course I feel things. If anything, I wear my heart on my sleeve. I'm sure he was alluding to my rough edges. But I'm genuinely interested in the truth and am more than capable of empathy and compassion. I'm sure there were lots of people who could see that I felt things, especially the women.

I was once having a lunch date with a Lebanese girl sitting outside a restaurant when an old but powerful-looking BMW did the maddest-ever 360-degree handbrake turn on the crossroads junction we were overlooking. The driver stuck his head out of the window and yelled as he punched the sky before speeding off, burning rubber. I thought it was fucking awesome but I was expecting my date to say something like: "What a wanker."

Actually, she was quite impressed, as was I by motorcyclists doing outrageous wheelies on the closest thing Lebanon gets to having a motorway. That's a typically Lebanese attitude. The handbrake turn incident gave me a sense of how crazy life must have been during the civil war, which ran from 1975 to 1990 and claimed 120,000 lives. Some said they were happier during that time because it made them treasure life, not take it for granted.

A cool, Lebanese graphic artist on The Daily Star grew up in Beirut during the civil war. He recalled how he used to sleep while firefights were breaking out in the surrounding streets. As an insight into the principles of Arab hospitality, the fighters used to go and drink tea with their enemies during lunchtime ceasefires. Then they would return to their positions and start shooting at each other again. There would be shame in breaking the Arab cultural code of how you host your guests. It's a principle I try to abide by. It's all too alien in the West.

The cab drivers in Beirut were generally friendly, open guys, so I used to ask them what they did during the civil war. Most of them were in one militia or another. And, such is Arab hospitality, they would often offer you a cigarette. If you told them you didn't smoke, they'd say, in all seriousness: "Have one anyway."

There was a young, Lebanese-Dutch girl who did work experience at The Daily Star who, incidentally, was quite appalled by my chaotic working practices. She was highly-educated and well off. She used to ferry around me and my foreigner mates as we explored Lebanon. We were blown away when she took us to her family home, a mansion up in the hills. I could not get my head around why they didn't leave during the troubles being as they were so rich, her father specialising in high-end smoked meat and fish.

She explained that the civil war wasn't continuous for the 16 or so years. There were months when it went quiet and they stayed because they thought the fighting was finally over. Like a metaphor for my marriage.

One late night I was reading a brilliant book, Pity the Nation, about the civil war, written by legendary, Beirut-based English journalist Robert Fisk. I was sat up in bed and suddenly a bolt of lightning hit pretty close to my flat in Hamra. I nearly jumped out of my skin and for a few, terrible moments thought it was an Israeli airstrike, such was the power of that book, how engrossed I was in it.

One night in the office, we heard an explosion. For about ten minutes, we were all wondering whether war had broken out again. I was considering my position. I didn't get out of Brixton to be placed in an actual, recognised war zone. It was stupid the way certain journalists revelled in conflict. I'm not saying all war correspondents are like that, in it for the titillation but some of them are and I find it pathetic. It turned out that the explosion was down to a film being made about the civil war. I was so glad. I didn't want to leave.

The mainly English production journalists largely kept themselves to themselves but there was some interaction with foreign aid workers. I struck up a friendship with a lovely French girl, Carole. She took me for a long weekend in the a demilitarised zone in southern Lebanon, policed by United Nations Interim Force In Lebanon (UNIFIL). The soldiers at the time were Fijians and they were lovely. We got stopped once at a checkpoint and a huge Fijian soldier gave me what seemed like a five-minute handshake, with a huge smile on his face. A gentle giant.

It was a quiet area because of the regular engagements between IDF and Hizbullah fighters. We found somewhere for lunch, this incredible outdoor restaurant, which was delightfully shaded by grapevines. We splashed about in a paddling pool before we ate a delicious meal and enjoyed first class hospitality for the price of two McDonald's meals in London. I suppose we could have been a nice couple but we had such a strong friendship, to the degree that she set me up with a beautiful, incredibly well-endowed, blonde, Greek aid worker. Those few days in southern Lebanon were amazing because it was like a paradise war zone.

But Carole also took me to a Palestinian refugee camp, which wasn't quite what I expected. There were no tents.

It was just a dirt poor area of shoddy, concrete buildings. A ghetto. A hellhole. The camps were largely established in 1948 as Palestinians fled what soon became Israel. There are dozens and dozens of jobs which Palestinians are not allowed to do in Lebanon, as part of the conditions for what was meant to be a temporary solution.

Another trip with Carole was also memorable. She was going out with this handsome English guy. I think he was a teacher. But he was such a bimbo, it was unbelievable. It drove her mad, which is why I got invited along for a day trip to Byblos, thought to be one of the oldest cities in the world, with an incredibly scenic coastline.

At one point when Carole was trying to park, she got in a jam with two Arab men inside their car. Carole — who's tiny — gave them the finger and they both got out of their car instantaneously and were hotfooting it towards her. I was sitting in the front (because she could not bear to try and make conversation with her gorgeous boyfriend) and immediately got out and tried to calm the situation, while lover boy sat still in the back. I explained to the Arabs that she is French and such a gesture is no big deal in Paris. It worked but fuck, this is Lebanon we are talking about. I told a Lebanese colleague about the incident at work the next day and he said that, in their culture, if women use abusive words or gestures in anger with men, the gloves are off.

...

Winter in Beirut wasn't too bad. There was always at least three hours of sunshine each and every day. It never got cold. But when it rained…

It fucking *poured*.

At times, it was so torrential that umbrellas wouldn't have helped. If I was walking the streets on my way home then I would just give in and get soaked to the skin. I loved it. The rain wasn't cold and I knew it would make the hot shower even better when I got in. I found a wonderful sense of freedom in those moments.

Like in Israel, I fitted in physically to my surroundings. I looked Lebanese. Both Israel and Lebanon have largely hybrid populations. It's interesting from an anthropological examination to assess how I'm perceived in different places and how that impacts on my treatment. I do think my mind is in the Middle East. There was a downside, though.

When we went on road trips around Lebanon, we'd get stopped at checkpoints and soldiers would take particular interest in me and shine their torches in my face. It turned out they were looking for draft-dodgers. I heard horror stories about young men with Lebanese roots from the Americas being snared, even when they were just over for a few weeks to catch up with distant relatives. One kid lived near a Jewish area in Brazil and he ended up right on the frontline with the Israelis' buffer zone because they thought he was a spy.

...

Everyone remembers where they were when they heard that Princess Diana had died. Me and my posh flatmate (I eventually moved out of the hotel) were taking a break for a few days with a Lebanese friend in the fertile Beqaa Valley, which is infamous for its cannabis production. When we got home to Hamra, my flatmate put the BBC World Service on his fancy radio. I used to hate this, thinking: "'Tim', we're in fucking Lebanon having a great time, forget about fucking Blighty."

It was like he was updating his British mind software.

And the content of the broadcast seemed, at first, to be tedious beyond belief: What would happen to the young princes, William and Harry? On first take, I thought they were talking hypothetically, hence my growing frustration with Tim. But then we suddenly got it: Diana was dead. The next shift at The Daily Star was a bit surreal. The Arab staff offered their condolences to us which, frankly, we thought was hilarious. And they were feeling, as Arabs, bad about Dodi, which we weren't prepared for, either.

We generally used to hang out at a classy cafe in Hamra and a load of us watched Diana's funeral over coffee and scrambled egg on toast. It was a small place but a party of around ten, loud Americans managed to squeeze in. I'm not exactly sure why I found it so funny but one of them blurted out: "What do you mean, The Queen Mother's still alive?!"

...

I spent much of my teens to early 20s getting stoned rather than drunk. I was a bad drunk. Pubs and clubs were not my scene at all, apart from on the kibbutz (which was more like a disco and there were loads of beautiful girls). But I loved Beirut nightlife. Classy. It wasn't cheap but not unreasonable, either. About US$100 for a good night out. The music wasn't deafeningly loud. I mean, The Evergreen was something else, I'm talking about where the trendy Beiruties went and we followed on our days off.

It was so civilised, the only drunken yobbery came from me. They used to pass around free shots in the nice places, which usually did great party food as well. Lebanon historically used to be the Saudis' playground but has now been superseded by Dubai. It's not a strict or uptight country. They even brew their own beer, Almaza, which is part-owned by Dutch giant Amstel. And it's good. Better than Amstel.

Drunken yobbery is not something taken into account by the Lebanese, so imagine my horror when I got up one morning and found a "tank trap" in my living room. They are kind of like four 4ft-long steel girders being arranged to stand up and had painted red and white stripes. The idea is that they get caught up in the tanks' undercarriages, halting their progress. It turned out that Tim and another English toff had taken it from outside a government ministry. The problem is that if a tank trap is removed in Beirut, people tend to assume that the next thing that's going to happen is a tank zooming in.

I was pissed off — just on the level of what our landlord would say — and I let Tim know it. That thing was so fucking heavy, I have no idea how they managed to get it there. My conclusion: Booze. Would they need to get drunk to take it back? I don't know what they did but it was gone the next day.

...

PG gave an American journalist friend a job in Beirut. British hacks do, in my experience, look down their noses at their US counterparts. Most newsrooms are vicious places, to one degree or another. And Mike cut a lonely figure, trying too hard to fit in rather than getting his head down and waiting for us to warm to him. It was like he was speaking but there was no eye contact or warmth, he seemed totally two-dimensional.

Towards the end of his first week and shift, he made a little boat out of a newspaper, put it on a small filing cabinet and filled it with boiled sweets. No one had touched them by the time he'd left. But as soon as he was gone, we all piled in. The next day we came into work to be told that he had committed suicide by jumping off a cliff near Beirut's iconic Pigeon Rocks.

The hat was still sitting there with a few sweets left.

It was a weird, emotional day. PG wasn't there to start with. The story was that Mike was staying with him and turned out to be a raging alcoholic. This guy's behaviour became more and more erratic. He had drunk almost everything alcoholic in the flat while PG was at work and then started on a bottle of vinegar.

I apologise to PG if I'm getting any of this wrong but the story went that he reached the end of his tether and asked his friend to leave. Next thing PG knew, Mike had jumped or fallen to his death. PG spent the day being grilled by the relevant authorities but he came by in the evening to rally the troops.

We headed to The Evergreen after work, this time without PG. It was a tiny, windowless place that would stay open as long as people were drinking. The proprietor — known to us simply as "Amigo" — would serve spaghetti bolognese at three in the morning. It was yum. But there were no takers that night. We all felt guilty, especially about the sweets hat. When it came to ordering drinks, I was asked by my colleague what I wanted and, under my breath, I mumbled: "I suppose it should be Scotch on the rocks."

That is my English, gallows humour.

My colleague told everybody and they thought it was hilarious but I wasn't expecting the quip to be shared. As I said, I'm not a cold person but I have a dark sense of humour and it just sort of fell out of my mouth. It was a tragedy and we were all there thinking he might still be alive if just one of us had reached out to him, even in the smallest of ways. Like that might have made the difference.

Those sweets. Tragic.

The Arabic newspapers weren't afraid to show pictures of dead bodies and they printed a small shot of Mike on the slab. The talk of the town was that "the Israelis did it". Everything always came back to "the Israelis". But the reality is that there were two words that you couldn't say in Beirut back then, "Syria" and "Assad". The Syrians didn't have an embassy there because they regarded it as their territory.

...

My dad — best known as "Peso" — must be one of the few people to have been taken hostage in Beirut *before* the Lebanese civil war even began. He was a drug-smuggler, mainly cannabis, and he and an English friend decided that a big hit in Amsterdam would be Lebanese Red, regarded by some as the best hashish in the world.

The problem was that they didn't have enough cash to finance the operation when they got to Beirut so Peso had to become a hostage with the supplier until his friend did the deed and paid for his freedom with the proceeds of the smuggling. But his friend somehow got ripped off and Peso got stuck.

I only know this story because my mum was approached to stump up the cash to free Peso by a British military man's English wife. She was having an affair with Peso's partner in crime. But we were broke squatters at the time. I don't think my mum would have paid even if she could, anyway. How that story ended is a mystery to me but my guess is that — not for the first or last time — Peso's parents bailed him out.

My time in Lebanon was mostly brilliant: Educational, fun and exciting. I upped my game as a journalist out there and it gave me a lot of confidence. I picked up a few other freelance jobs and in the end I decided to leave the broadsheet to become Editor of a new paper aimed mainly at students, Lebanese Gazette. But at Christmas I was in this phase where I was serving out my notice at The Daily Star, editing LG and subbing a magazine, called Society. I actually did a 100-hour week. After I went awol for a week from the mag, I sort of snuck in and got to work. After about five minutes, the owner walked in, scowled at me and said: "I have the power to kill you."

He meant it.

My greatest achievement in journalism relates to my brief spell as Editor of LG. There was this story for the health section about a girl aged five who had a heart condition but her parents were too poor to pay for surgery. I decided to put it on the front page with a picture of the girl, Mariam, and her crying mum. Headline: "Don't let my little girl die."

There was a great quote in the story when Mariam's younger sister said: "Don't let her die — or I'll break the fridge!"

We started an appeal and there was this whole buzz about it. I don't know whether we raised quite enough, US$10,000 I recall but it ended up with two of Lebanon's leading heart surgeons battling it out to operate for free. The snag was that they disagreed about what course of action should be taken. The reporter who brought in the story, who had mixed feelings about me, asked which surgeon the family should go with. I was like: "How the fuck should I know?"

The reporter told me she grew to hate the story. I had to sit her down and tell her the facts of journalism life.

I don't know what happened to Mariam. But we gave her a chance.

Out of loyalty to PG, my Editor at The Daily Star, I worked through Christmas because most of the others went home to England. It was tough but I got through it. Things calmed down a bit but I decided to leave Lebanon altogether after losing patience with my childish, bullshitting LG Publisher (a pattern is developing here), whose uncle, incidentally, is the leader of Hizbullah, Sheikh Nasrullah.

Actually, I liked that Publisher in some ways. He reminded me of Nice Guy Eddie from Tarantino flick Reservoir Dogs. But he was an awful publisher, a spoilt prat. The thing is that I was owed holiday money by The Daily Star and felt my Christmas efforts for them meant they should pay me what I was entitled to in my contract, even in the Wild East. I went to the offices a few days before flying home and tried to see the Publisher/owner — a rich, nasty man. His PA tried to stop me going in to his private office but to no avail. I entered, waving my contract. I was determined. He called me a "pesky individual" (it was straight out of Scooby Doo) and I called him an "inadequate conman".

If I'd have sworn at him then I wouldn't be alive to tell the tale. Then I stormed out and he came after me. At that point I realised he had five security guards on duty rather than the usual two. They grabbed and held me. It was surreal because the Publisher was the aggressor and I was the passive one. He gave me the hardest slap across the face he could muster and I got bundled into the lifts. Fortunately, the security guards were fine with me once the boss was out the way. I had feared a beating.

These guys were ex-militia men. Killers.

I was walking down the street with my heart pumping and could still feel his handprint on my face. I left a few days later. One of my nicknames in Israel and Lebanon was "CD", as in "Compact Disk". Apparently, one of the Publisher's thug personal security guards, a giant of a man and one of the arse-kissers, said: "CD is now cassette tape."

I also later heard that if ever the Publisher had a disagreement with someone, particularly foreigners, they were always "drunk". Lebanese society is feudal and I was at the sharp end of that a few times. In some ways, I feel I could have settled there. But ultimately, that feudal aspect is something I couldn't stomach.

I was ready to leave. I'd had enough. My naivety had got the better of me again. I made my way by cab to Beirut's airport, which I now know was and is run by Hizbullah. Initially, everything was fine. Then, as I checked in my luggage, I was led away by army security guards to this little, empty room which only had a small, wooden bench. I sat down and wondered what the fuck was going on... for at least an hour. Then the door opened and the security men said: "Come with us."

I was bricking it. Who was behind this? I had got a new passport with no Israeli stamps (years later, I learned that it is actually against Lebanese law to have been to Israel). Then the security guards took me along a narrow corridor and opened up a door which led outside onto the runway. There was a car there and they told me to get in. Then it sped off to my plane. The built-in steps were down at the back and they told me to get out and hurry up. I needed no encouragement. I found my seat and within one minute the plane was moving.

I have to admit that, as the jet engines kicked in and we started to accelerate down the runway, the thought in my head was: "Back to civilisation."

9. Slaughter of the innocents

'A few Arabs die, there's no harm in that'

I sat with ghosts on a warm winter's evening in a desolate south Lebanon village square.

The ghosts of children.

They were among the victims of an IDF atrocity that ended 106 civilian lives, destroyed many more and changed mine. Half of those killed were kids. Sitting among the dozens of tiny graves, the eerie silence was deafening. Where was everybody? Then, with hardly any prior knowledge of the facts, I had an epiphany: "This slaughter was no accident."

The Qana massacre — during the IDF's "Grapes of Wrath" operation — happened on April 18, 1996, a year before I arrived in Lebanon. It was a war crime I can throw fresh light on. It's a revelation that haunts me.

The victims were among 800 locals taking cover in a known UN compound in the village as the Israelis and Hizbullah engaged. It was Carole and another female aid worker who took me to Qana. They knew I had Israeli sympathies and I guess they wanted to "flip" me. They did. But they did it in a way to let me come to my own conclusions, which I tend to respond to. I have no doubt in my mind that Carole wanted me to "feel" something, as opposed to just read, write and think about it, as most journalists do. I had figured the Israelis were just a bit misunderstood. Until then.

Qana was a vitally-important strategic location from a military point of view because it has a five-road junction under Hizbullah control, just outside the then IDF "buffer zone" in southern Lebanon. The slaughter happened during 17 minutes of shelling. I can barely imagine that one shell that doesn't kill or maim you would be pretty fucking scary but 13 in 17 minutes. It must have seemed an eternity. For those who survived.

Legendary English journalist Robert Fisk described the scene that met him when he arrived during the aftermath of the shelling, writing: "When I reached the UN gates, blood was pouring through them in torrents. I could smell it. It washed over our shoes and stuck to them like glue. There were legs and arms, babies without heads, old men's heads without bodies. A man's body was hanging in two pieces in a burning tree. What was left of him was on fire.

"On the steps of the barracks, a girl sat holding a man with grey hair, her arm round his shoulder, rocking the corpse back and forth in her arms. His eyes were staring at her. She was kneeling, weeping, crying and, in Arabic, over and over, saying, 'My father, my father.'"

It turned out, in the years that followed, I was spot on to think the massacre was deliberate. Testimony to that effect comes straight from IDF soldiers who were there and deserve credit for bravely speaking out to an Israeli publication, albeit anonymously. During the onslaught, one senior officer, in Hebrew, told them: "Look at how many Arabs there are and how many Jews."

He said they're "just a bunch of Arabs", adding: "A few Arabs die, there's no harm in that."

In the days after the atrocity, Nobel Peace Prize winner and then Israeli PM Shimon Peres claimed the shelling was a "mistake". Writing in The Independent, Fisk continued: "Peres announced that 'we did not know that several hundred people were concentrated in that camp. It came to us as a bitter surprise'.

"It was a lie. The Israelis had occupied Qana for years after their 1982 invasion, they had video film of the camp, they were even flying a drone over the camp during the massacre — a fact they denied until a UN soldier gave me his video of the drone."

Fisk added: "The UN had repeatedly told Israel the camp was packed with refugees."

Years later, it was rumoured that the Israelis were trying out new artillery hardware in the operation. The Lebanese were collectively so angry about Qana, especially the slaughter of children, that there, of all places, sectarian differences were put aside to condemn the slaughter. The *lifestyle* magazine I worked for, Society, dedicated its front cover and much of an issue to the atrocity. Like with the picture of US journalist colleague Mike on the slab, Lebanese publications did not shy away from printing graphic images. Maybe they are right to, so we can get a sense of what war is really like. This is war.

A UN enquiry concluded that the massacre was deliberate and was thus accused of being anti-Semitic by Israel. There had been a pattern of systematic bullying of United Nations Interim Force in Lebanon (UNIFIL) soldiers during the whole time the IDF were an occupying force in southern Lebanon. On my last full day in the country, I somehow ended up sitting in a pub's private room with an English colleague and two Fijian UNIFIL soldiers who were in the Qana compound just before the shelling started.

For all the millions spent on reports, enquiries and everything done to establish whether the IDF knew what they were doing when they targeted the compound, one of the Fijians told me: "They phoned us before the strike and told us to save ourselves."

They phoned.

That call gave the Fijians just about enough time to get out, although four were injured. I asked one of them what he thought about this and he said: "This is war."

Am I betraying the Fijians by revealing this? I don't think so. He knew I was a journalist on my way home to Britain the next day. He wanted me to know, even if it means the IDF don't phone up the next time they decide to murder children. I don't even know how I ended up in that room with those Fijians.

UNIFIL soldiers had the option of going to Israel or unoccupied Lebanon during their time off. One of those Fijians from my last day in Lebanon turned up at at my kibbutz to watch rugby training the following summer. He was a bit shaken when he recognised me. Shocked to see *me* on the other side of the border. Did he think I was a spy and, if so, who was I spying for? I'm not a spy, I'm a journalist.

Hizbullah were accused by the Israelis of using the compound as a human shield for their activities on the afternoon of the slaughter. It was reported that they were firing 200 yards from the compound at the IDF. That seems quite far. It was also reported that two or three Hizbullah fighters entered the compound, where their families were holed up. It is not clear whether they entered before or after the IDF shelling.

Hizbullah have quite a one-dimensional image outside of the Middle East: Terrorists. But many would say that they fought a just cause against the Israeli occupation of southern Lebanon, which ended in 2000. Despite only having around 5,000 military combatants, largely made up of local farmers and shopkeepers, they are said to be highly respected by the IDF for their military capabilities and commitment. And Hizbullah's powerful and popular political wing is often cited by many to be the least corrupt of Lebanon's major institutions. They provide education and vital services for the country's Shia community.

It's probably true to say that they are led by Islamic fundamentalists and I didn't like it that children wore fake suicide vests on "Jerusalem Day" in Lebanon. But I equally respect that they have the courage of their convictions. I can still see in my mind's eye a picture of their charismatic leader, Sheikh Nasrullah, beaming with delight the day after his son died fighting the Israelis and thus becoming a martyr.

...

I dearly wished there wasn't an epilogue to the Qana massacre but there was. During the 2006 Israel-Hizbullah War, the village was targeted again, this time with an air-strike on a three-storey residential home housing two families, claiming 28 civilian lives, including 16 children, with 13 people missing. The building had no military significance. Then UN leader Kofi Annan urged the UN Security Council to condemn Israel for the massacre. It didn't.

Washington Post reporter Anthony Shadid described the scene that day: "Most of the dead had choked on flying dirt and other debris. Their bodies, intact, preserved their final gestures: A raised arm called for help."

He added: "Twelve-year-old Hussein Hashem lay curled in the foetal position, his mouth seeming to have vomited earth. Mohammed Chalhoub sat on the ground, his right hand broken. Khadja, his wife and Hasna, his mother, were dead, as were his daughters, Hawra and Zahra, aged 12 and two. As were his sons, Ali, ten, Yahya, nine, and Assem, seven."

Israel had directed civilians to flee the conflict but they were bombarding the escape roads. One of eight survivors of the blast said those attacks discouraged the families from leaving Qana. Throughout that war, Israel pursued a strategy of not differentiating between civilians and combatants in order to minimise Israeli casualties. That was not a suspicion, an IDF general admitted it freely.

In response to global criticism, Israel agreed to suspend air strikes in the area for up to 48 hours, which allowed for more civilians to flee, as well as an investigation of the incident. In return, Hizbullah halted rocket fire into Israel for that period.

Just a few years ago, a colleague and friend told me about visiting the Nazi Auschwitz concentration camp in Poland and said: "It's true, the birds don't sing."

It was the same when I was in Qana, although it didn't occur to me exactly like that at the time. But that place was dead. Where was everybody? I couldn't feel the wind yet somehow I could hear it.

I hate to think what's it's like after the second atrocity.

The 1996 Grapes of Wrath operation was designed to boost Peres's military credentials and popularity ahead of a general election, which his Labor Party lost. This was a man who, as then Foreign Minister, won the Nobel Peace Prize in 1994, along with Israeli PM Yitzhak Rabin and PLO leader Yasser Arafat. It was for the Oslo Accords agreement, designed to create a lasting settlement between the Israelis and Palestinians.

But in 2002, members of the Norwegian committee that decides who gets the award stated that they wished they could have recalled Peres's because he had not acted to prevent Israel's re-occupation of Palestinian territory, had not lived up to the ideals he expressed when he accepted the prize and was involved in human rights abuses. Despite this, Peres went on to become Israel's President (a ceremonial role) in 2007 and remained in the post until 2014. He died in 2016, aged 93, not as a peacemaker but as a mass murderer.

10a. No

'I've shat better headlines out me arse'

My desk was three feet away from Sun Editor Rebekah Brooks's on the newsroom floor. Our chairs were back to back. She didn't spend much time there apart from when Rupert Murdoch was in town, mostly preferring to take command from her executive office. One evening, I arrived to do my shift as Late Chief Sub, a grand title but which essentially meant I was doing the middle-management "graveyard shift" until 2am. Brooks (then "Wade") and Murdoch were assembled around her desk with his small entourage.

I was running a bit late, around 5pm, carrying a huge gym bag for my break, wearing a bulky jacket and holding the teas for my comrades. I managed to cause a bit of a kerfuffle as I tried to manoeuvre myself into position, narrowly managing to avoid whacking the VIPs in the head with my gym bag. Right in the middle of causing this blatant, cringeworthy irritation, my mobile phone rang. I felt like Mr Bean. It was Nad calling from next door at the News of the World, wanting to know if I was up for a fag.

Without deliberately earwigging, in the middle of this scene I was at the centre of, I overheard Murdoch, in a thick Aussie accent, say, "Blaaaiiiirrrrr [Blair]", "xenaphobeeeaaa [xenophobia]" and "the Beee Beee Seee [the BBC]". It was like he was being a parody of himself and everything he stands for...and against.

The epilogue was that the then Chief Sub pulled me into a vacant executive office the next day. I had no idea what the issue was. After we sat down, he said: "Now, I don't like talking to people about the clothes they wear.

But someone *very, very* high up has complained about the [check] shirt you wore yesterday."

In fairness, he saw the funny side. But I didn't wear that shirt again until the last day of my first spell at The Sun in 2007. Did Murdoch complain about my shirt? I still wear it from time to time when I'm feeling rebellious.

. . .

Before I got onto national newspapers in 1999, I was Editor of red-top British-Asian paper Eastern Eye but I fell out with the Publisher and resigned. I put together packs containing copies of a particularly good issue I'd edited, with my CV and sent them out to the editors of every national newspaper. I did shifts or was offered them by almost all of them. The Guardian Editor was the only one who didn't reply.

I don't know what it says or said about me but something clicked from day one at the News of the World, known in the industry as "The Screws", as in "the Screws of the World". And when it comes to "sub-editing" or "subbing", I feel increasingly honoured to have turned up there at that time.

The Screws was like a resting home for Fleet Street legends back then. I could write a book about them. They were a hilarious bunch — I cheekily dubbed them "Dad's Army". But they knew what they were doing. It's sad to hear every now and then that one of them has passed away. I got invited to the pub by for the first time by Derek Prigent, a true gent and a total sweetheart. Very chirpy, and young at heart.

Some of them were a bit bigoted to start with but ultimately, decent. I was able to get through to them and I gave them an experience as well as them giving me an experience. By the time I left a few years later, I think they actually rated me more *because* I am not white. Many had never interacted with black or Asian people before. So it was an eye opener for them. They used to ask for my views on all sorts of race and culture-related stories. I believe I made a huge impact from that point of view at The Screws and at The Sun. And being half white helped me find ways to relate to them.

Veteran sub Al Barter immediately caught my eye when I entered The Screws newsroom for the first time. The Tommy Cooper of journalism, he simply had funny bones. Al was a six-footer in his late fifties/early sixties with a grey, pudding bowl haircut, a massive, reddish, pin cushion of a nose, jam jar spectacles, a substantial pot belly and a grubby, egg-stained, blue jumper. He was like a stereotypical old hack who wouldn't have been out of place on Eighties satirical TV puppet show Spitting Image.

I did hear him talking about "Pakis" in my early days there but he was quickly told to "shoosh" by a younger, female sub. After I'd been there for a while, he was chatting to another old hack, 'Big Man', who was there as a casual but was quite senior next door at The Sun. There was a lot of coverage of India's Kumbh Mela (millions of wild and wacky pilgrims gathering for a religious festival) at the time and I overheard Al saying something to Big Man like: "We need to civilise them."

I marched over to him and said: "Come on, Al, no one's trying to stop you doing *your* mad thing over there in the corner."

That was an affectionate way of making my point. I did like him and, incidentally, I thought he was just trying to impress Big Man, who had quite an intimidating presence.

It was quite sweet, actually. These two old men probably had the same dynamic going for most of their working lives. I could almost envisage the scene being played out between them as boys in the school yard.

I'm calling him "Al" but he was "Al Barter" to everyone, like his first name and surname were married. And he had his own dialect. He called the (female) Chief Sub "Miss". He would identify a story which had the required elements as "got the gear". If you were a young man then you were a "lovely boy" and everyone was "Herberts". He would go on endlessly about a magazine he once owned and ran. The stories were gripping...the first time. He had evidently ended up in court several times because his mag's lonely hearts column had played a part in several murders.

He kindly used to give me a lift in his white, Leyland minibus to cut half an hour off my journey time and we had some interesting chats. Al was extremely curious about my background. But during one lift, he mumbled something about me never asking him about *his* background. Then he mumbled something about "Aldershot". Another time he put it to me that the immigrants who'd made their way over here from the Indian subcontinent were "the creme de la creme". I told him that, in fact, most of those coming over are from poorer backgrounds, looking for a better life. I also explained that there are millions and millions of rich Indians who wouldn't dream of abandoning their opulent lifestyles over there. India has more US Dollar millionaires than any other country in the world.

I paved the way for Nad to join The Screws and Al took it upon himself to mentor my Pakistani, Muslim friend. What a turnaround. Nad used to call him "Al Qaeda", which he hated. But he who lives by the nickname...

Al had no less than ten kids (hence the minibus) by two different women, called his wife "John" and apparently gave outrageous nicknames to all his bosses in his heyday at The Sun, using them to their faces. Al was famous for leaving his coat on the back of his chair so the executives thought he was returning after his pub break. He'd actually fucked off home early and drunk during a shift. He nearly got sacked over something else but was described as a "necessary evil" by the Editor, who saved him from the chop.

Sadly, Al died aged 70. He'd had serious health problems for some time but worked up to a year before he passed away, to support his family for as long as possible. My heart would always smile whenever I saw him around after I'd migrated to The Sun. And I can vividly remember the last time I ran into him, in Fortress Wapping, although I didn't know then that it would be the last time.

Al was walking out of the building with a few work chums and I was on my way back in after a pub break with my work chums. We both had a little chuckle as we approached each other but didn't saying anything. Then I grabbed hold of his substantial stomach and we had a belly laugh, before moving on.

. . .

Despite my experience and development on The Screws, I got a massive culture shock next door after being taken on by The Sun for the first time in 2002. There was this clutch of middle-aged guys, a gang, and some of them could be pretty nasty. I went drinking with them on my break but my dislike of several of them led me to just try and wind them up. I'd done the business next door so I didn't feel like I should have to prove myself again. One colleague — who I'll call 'Arrogant Twat' — actually told me to "shoosh" when another "sub" had asked for help with captions and I chipped in. Like I didn't have the right to make a suggestion, irrespective of how good it was.

I'd been pretty much exclusively writing the most read column in the English-speaking world a few months earlier at The Screws, the "Rav" showbiz page. That paper was shifting four million copies every Sunday at the time. I got on with Rav. While he was phenomenal at bringing in a succession of top-notch exclusives, he wasn't a great writer, though he gave me plenty to work with. I fully appreciate that it's easier to find a good sub than someone who has the social skills to get celebrities to spill their secrets at 3am in Stringfellows. He was incredibly hard-working and a reasonable guy. But it *was* a pain when he filed his column directly to me over the phone from an F1 race somewhere in Europe.

...

Sometimes people ask me what "subs" actually do. If it seems a bit banal at first, bear with me. There are essentially two types of journalists on papers, editorial and production. In many ways, being a reporter on editorial — which includes interviewing stars, foreign travel, press conferences, attending crime scenes, sitting in courtrooms and building up contacts — is the more exciting side of the industry. But it's not for everyone. I am a production journalist, a sub-editor, or "sub".

The reporters and correspondents collect the raw material and we edit the stories and write the headlines. Subs are hired for writing ability and might, for instance, be given 2,000 words to crunch down into 200. We might be processing one big story on a shift or up to 15 small ones, and everything in between. The production department is the engine room in most tabloids. As Nad said: "The reporters provide the ingredients but the subs are the chefs."

I was once given a picture story of supermodel Kate Moss crossing the road wearing a black and white striped coat. I said to my boss: "Woman crosses road, that's interesting."

He gave me an icy stare and snapped: "It will be when you're finished with it."

Compared to the story originally filed by the reporter, I had to pretty much start from scratch on that one, apart from the facts. My intro went something like: "Many say supermodel Kate Moss is just a clothes horse but she looks more like a zebra crossing yesterday."

Sometimes it's about making something out of nothing, "a bit of poetry", as it is known on papers. Other key responsibilities include querying "holes" in stories. Or subs may request additional information or quotes to enhance a story. Working with lawyers is also part of the job and most subs tend to develop a feel for libel.

Referring to subs, Murdoch himself once said something like: "The News of the World journalists can do what The Sunday Times journalists can do but The Sunday Times journalists can't do what the News of the World journalists do."

The Sunday Times subs were a bit put out by that. And yes, that was in the days before the phone-hacking scandal.

A former colleague uses one of my headlines to illustrate to his chums outside of the industry what subs do. The story was a short one about how a school teacher in America got sacked for featuring in a porn movie. My workmate asked me for a headline and I came up with

"JOB BLOW". It was borderline even for The Sun but it's a perfect example of how a simple, good headline (just switching two words around) can bring a story to life. And to give an idea of what goes into producing a well-written tabloid paper, I once spent eight hours subbing the News of the World spread...and I'm quick. Sadly, subbing is a dying art because the internet is taking over and there's now a relentless demand for instant news.

National newspaper production departments have a strict hierarchy. The "backbench" subs are the most senior. They have an overview, "draw" the pages, write the lead story headlines, select which stories are going where and basically make the decisions after being briefed by the Editor earlier in the day. The "middlebench" subs are handed the pages, give out the stories to the "downtable" subs and revise those stories before the pages are sent. During a period as a downtable sub, I was once given a story about the world's biggest penis weighing 2lbs. My headline: "Wahey-ing in at 2lbs."

The middlebencher, 'Roy', changed the headline to: "19-inch willy just 2Ibs."

"Just"!

I emailed him to say that "my daughter weighed less than that when she was born", which is true, and that I reckon 2lbs seems quite a lot for a willy. I added in the email: "Unless you've got something to tell us..."

He changed it. But I nicknamed him "Big Roy" after that.

One of the funniest moments came during my first incarnation at The Sun when I was sitting at my desk and the colleague next to me had his head buried in The Times. The Editor, David Yelland, was walking by and suddenly did a double take. He turned on his heels, peered over my colleague's shoulder, pointed to The Times front page and said: "That's a strange headline."

Without looking up, my relatively young colleague quipped: "Yeah, I've shat better headlines out me arse."

Yelland's whole body jolted to attention. He spluttered "quite" before turning on his heels again and marching off in his original direction. I asked my workmate years later whether he'd known it was Yelland. Sadly, he confessed that he hadn't and only realised when the boss was walking off.

Most people presume The Sun newsroom is a raucous place, full of "monsterings", gesticulation and rows. It simply wasn't like that. Sorry to disappoint you. There was banter but it's a very involving process producing a daily paper in this day and age of endless redundancies and shrinking sales. Of planned decline. And if you stop and listen in the last few hours before the deadlines start kicking in, all you can hear is the furious tapping and clunking of keyboards. There's a lot of edgy emails floating around as the pressure builds and a few, pertinent words whispered in certain ears. All very passive-aggressive stuff. But also a generally high level of professionalism.

There were exceptions.

Even during my time on the nationals between 1999 and 2016, the culture changed. Especially the drinking culture, as in there was less of it. I thought it was a shame. But some things changed for the better. A particular incident, which would probably involve severe disciplinary action these days, springs to mind. During my first spell on The Sun, Arrogant Twat and one of the executives wrestled a younger colleague to face flat on a desk and pretended to take turns to arse fuck him, in front of the whole office. It was shocking, and I'm not easily shocked. What compounded the horror was that the "victim" was more pissed off that they'd destroyed six months of physiotherapy work on his back inside 60 seconds. The humiliation wasn't even the worst part for him, he was in agony.

I could sense the guilty pair getting nervous. Arrogant Twat headed home soon after but phoned up the office ten minutes later, begging for forgiveness from the victim, which was denied. The other offender was an untouchable executive.

Arrogant Twat reenforced his standing as an arsehole soon after when there was a late night raffle for one of the five or so subs to get to go home before the end of the shift, which we called an "early cut". Arrogant Twat was slightly older than most of us and he had a tantrum because, as a "senior" sub (which is how he described himself, although there was no such title), he wasn't automatically afforded the privilege. I genuinely thought he was joking to start with. Arrogant Twat got his way. What a man of the people, which is also genuinely how he saw himself.

. . .

I was on the middlebench during the mid-Noughties and I was generally Late Chief Sub (LCS), which I quite liked, despite the hours. It was usually quiet but the odd time a major story would drop. I enjoyed that challenge, especially as it was only every now and then.

Then I started doing the Late Night Editor (LNE) shift. A misleading title for that position. Basically, I was proof-reading every version of every page and being the last line of defence. It was pressure but okay to start with, maybe doing it once or twice a week. Then the Chief Sub pulled me to one side to say I was brilliant at it (which played into my complex about needing approval from experienced hands).

The bit he said he liked the most, aside from the obvious task of spotting mistakes, was how I would go above and beyond to identify potential problems up the road while pages were still being put together. I used to come up behind the middlebenchers *and* backbenchers and deliver my observations, like I was the Editor! Whatever I could say about some of their characters and however they felt about me, they were all professional and savvy enough to lap it up.

Then it came to my appraisal with my boss. It was great. But at the end, I brought up the subject of the LNE shift. I said I was prepared to "do my fair share but I'm doing way more than my fair share". He seemed to be understanding about this. Then the next rota was published and I was down for even *more* LNE shifts. I was grinning and bearing it for a few weeks but one evening I cheerfully came in for an LCS shift and, before I had even take my coat off, let alone sat down, my line manager asked if I could be LNE a few days later.

I said: "No."

He said: "You don't even know why."

I said: "I don't care."

Then the whole office, of about 200 people, went silent and he didn't know what to say, so I said: "You can sack me if you like but I'm not doing it."

A stunned but tickled backbencher stood up and piped up: "Talk about throwing down the gauntlet!"

You could almost hear jaws dropping as my line manager told me to go and sit "downtable". I said I'd go, "happily". Admittedly, looking back, I was manic.

Not everyone was impressed with my line manager's management style but he had a few supporters. One of them was the late Vic Mayhew. He was a character. Old school. I heard he was very senior back in the day and, incidentally, used to be a policeman.

I ended up sitting next to Vic after being effectively demoted on the spot and, every time I walked behind him, he would propel backwards on his office chair so I had to avoid him smashing into me. He was obviously doing this deliberately, trying to push me over the edge. But I just got my head down and got on with my work. Then, at some point, Vic tried to distract me and worked "soixante-neuf" into the a conversation he was trying to have with me. I didn't know what it meant ("69" in French) and he blurted out the fact I didn't know to the whole office: "Hey, Elaine, Siddy doesn't even know what soixante-neuf means!"

I told him: "I've had enough of your shit."

Then I *really* lost my temper, telling him to "go find someone to fuck", in *Hebrew*, to make my point about language knowledge, swiftly followed by "your mum's cunt", in *Arabic*. The newsroom fell silent again and I added: "I've had enough of your shit…you racist. You're not Father Christmas [he used to grow a grey beard in the winter for his grandkids], you're a sad, old git."

One of the top subs said he'd only seen a scene like that once before in his career and it also involved Vic. You know, the stupid thing is that I didn't hate Vic. I just think he was corrupt. Corrupted by having too much power too early in his career. You knew that if you messed with him, you were messing with the whole organisation. He might have been a genuinely nice guy if he'd never been corrupted in that way.

Obviously, what happened in those few hours was a turning point for me at The Sun. I was pulled into a private office the next day by my line manager to be presented with a written warning for "insubordination". I thought it was funny, like it was the army. Insubordination! Yes, I was in an episode (thanks to a little help) but how did it deteriorate in weeks from me being given a glowing appraisal to being given a written warning? I'm willing to take my share of the blame but ultimately, it was a failure of management.

. . .

Big Man (the hack Al Barter was trying to impress) was on the backbench at The Sun my first time there, as well as doing casual shifts as a downtable sub at The Screws. I first caught his attention when he was subbing The Screws front page lead story in 2000. It was around the time of the truckers dispute and, as Blair's Government floundered, Labour rapidly lost popularity and went behind in the opinion polls for the first time in many years. The Screws headline was: "TORIES AHEAD."

It was based on an opinion poll that gave them the lead after being way behind just six months before. But I somehow managed to pull it from the air that the Tories were way behind in a poll just *two weeks* previously. I told Big Man and he put a query into the newsdesk. It turned out I was right and that fact obviously added great weight to the story, which was otherwise pretty lame by their standards.

The following week, Big Man came into The Screws, marched up to me, shook my hand and said: "That was a great front page last week and it's all down to you."

He was another who was more than smart enough to identify that I had a hunger for validation from father figures. Experienced hands telling me I'm talented: I am a needy person in many ways. But Big Man needed his own sort of validation. He was a workaholic, hence doing Screws shifts when he didn't need the money. Several years later, I ended up working with him closely on page two of The Sun, which exclusively features politics.

This West Country character was a talented journalist and massive physically and mentally. He was one of the few people on the floor who Murdoch would talk to when he visited and once asked Big Man: "How are you?"

Big Man replied: "Apart from working in the only sixth-floor basement in London?"

It was a reference to the newsroom floor being surrounded by executive offices, which meant we got little natural light. That miraculously improved over the following few years. He was very protective of subs below him.

He rated me highly and used to pass on my opinions (such as having "freedom" to wear veils and hijabs) up The Sun hierarchy. I was told by a colleague that I "handle him really well". The thing that made me chuckle the most about Big Man was when we were doing a story about Snoop Dogg and, in his thick, West Country accent, he enquired: "Isn't his full name 'Snoop Doggy Dogg'?"

Snoop *had* shortened his name over the years but I thought it was remarkable and hilarious that Big Man of all people had absorbed this detail. I didn't have him down as a gangsta rap aficionado.

I used to be quite open with my views, even when I was "middlebenching" page two. It was my baby for a year and I was never put out by the finished product. Never offended. That's thanks to Big Man. Someone once asked me how I reconciled being a "politically black"

Brixton boy with working for Murdoch. I would say that I maintained my integrity and used whatever autonomy I had to make a contribution because a newspaper is, at its core, a collection of hearts and minds. I was part of that. And, for instance, while I think The Guardian and the BBC are great institutions in their own way, they don't want the likes of me. Maybe you the reader can work out, in the context of this whole book, why that is. I'd like to know. I'm sure most people outside the industry would be surprised at how much movement there is of journalists between papers with diametrically opposed editorial lines. Essentially, for most, it's about earning a crust. I'd say you only realise why "cynical hacks" become cynical hacks when you've become one.

And many of you may be surprised to know that morale was at rock bottom at The Sun the afternoon after the EU referendum vote came in, despite the paper's pro-Brexit stance. I'd say at least 90 per cent of those who were in any way vocal on the newsroom floor about the result were Remainers, of which I am one. I asked a white, male colleague why he was against Brexit and he simply said: "They've been sold a pup."

The Sun actually ran a page lead that day on all the ways that leaving the EU was going to hit Brits in the pocket, especially in the light of Sterling plunging on the currency markets. The newsdesk was bombarded with calls from angry readers for days. You have to remember, there's only one opinion that counts in the Murdoch Empire: Murdoch's. Once you've realised this, then you have to decide what, if anything, you're gonna do about it.

...

I didn't work for two and a half years because of my mental health problems from 2008 but was thankfully taken on for my second spell at The Screws in late 2010. The subs department was a great place to work, like family. A lot of the same people were there from the first time. Part of the reason it had a different atmosphere to The Sun was because it was a Sunday paper. The week would start gently on a Wednesday and build up to long shifts on Fridays and Saturdays, when it would get pretty intense. The early part of the week allowed for a lot of bonding and banter. I loved it. I was back home, although I should probably point out that the subs desk was a bit like a small, paradise island surrounded by sharks. Unfussy eaters at that.

I was totally gutted when The Screws folded in 2011. Tears. It was strange to be part of that experience, being at the centre of an international news story on the last day. But as media people, we took it in our stride. We knew that the news agenda moves on relentlessly and we'd be left feeling quite hollow about the gravity of the story inside a week. The lasting impact would be missing our comrades, tea parties in the office, Christmas drinks.

I put a lot of the special atmosphere down to the subs' boss, Fran Goodman. A lioness. She was there the first time and gave me my big break. She was in a tricky position, straddling between being management and looking after her staff. I've never worked with anyone who did it better. Incidentally, I got a nice headline into that last ever edition of The Screws, a bit of history. It was a (boring) story about how prospective house buyers are put off by bad mobile phone reception. Headline: "HOME HANG-UPS."

There is a tradition in newspapers called "banging out". If someone is leaving the paper then everybody in the newsroom bangs on their desk until the departing colleague leaves the office. I got a bit of a shock the first time I experienced this. I had no idea it was going to happen and thought the revolution was on! It's a hangover from when the printers did it with bits of hot metal when one of their co-workers was leaving in the olden days (Vic told me that). But the last night at The Screws was particularly unusual because *everybody* was leaving. So what happened was that the Editor and Fran banged everybody else out, hitting the desks with rulers. There were two policemen waiting at the office door, preparing to seal the newsroom off as a crime scene.

When we came down into the atrium and congregated before facing the world's media, there were a few tears (not mine at the time). But what sticks in my mind was that the journalists from The Sunday Times crowded around a few floors up and banged us out by hitting the windows. Then we made our way outside to be met by the cameras, while I peeled away for a fag. The company put on a free bar at the nearest pub and we were respectfully left alone by the media to have our farewell party. It was actually a good night. At one point, editions of the last-ever Screws turned up. Then we made our excuses and left.

End of the World.

...

I returned to The Sun in 2011 and things had deteriorated. Sometimes people didn't see the humour in the funniest of things in what was an even more toxic atmosphere than before. I had totally lost my ambition, my mental health issues being a major factor. I didn't see happiness when I looked up so I didn't fancy the stress of trying to climb the slippery pole.

There is a saying in national newspapers: "Going over to the Dark Side."

It's usually a gradual process but I've never known anyone to come back, not gradually or otherwise. About four or five years ago, I was subbing a page lead on Real Madrid footballer Gareth Bale buying a company for his parents in his native Wales. I finished the story and sent it for revision. It went through 100 per cent how I'd written it. Job done. A few hours later, though, my boss came up behind where I was sitting and asked if I'd subbed the Bale story. He knew I had. Boss man told me to pull up the page, which I did. I was suddenly worried that I'd dropped a huge clanger. He told me to zoom in on the byline. It read: "By GARETH BALE."

I burst out laughing and said: "You'd think he earned enough playing for Real Madrid without having to moonlight for The Sun!"

I turned around to my boss, honestly expecting him to be chuckling away but he was just glaring at me. Obviously, it would have been embarrassing if that mistake had been printed but we were supposed to have checks and balances to prevent that sort of thing. It's not like it got printed, just a wanker wanting to give out to someone, which he thought better of in the end. I've caught hundreds of potentially far more catastrophic mistakes over the years which nearly did get printed, processing thousands of words on every shift. But I make one silly error and I get clobbered. That's the reality of newspapers at times. If, as a journalist, you can't have a laugh at my Bale byline then part of you is dying or dead.

. . .

Because local papers are dying out, the last 20 years has seen graduate schemes provide national newspapers with new generations of journalists. It's creating a huge culture shift on newsroom floors. I don't like it. I'm glad I built up my life and newspaper experience before getting on the nationals. When The Sun's first graduate trainee scheme got underway in the mid-Noughties, the staffers wouldn't talk to them. The consensus among my colleagues was: "They're training them to take our jobs on a fraction of the money."

They were right but I could not sit back and watch a basically decent bunch of young people flounder. So I was the first staffer to talk to them.

The shit thing was that I did my best to mentor a black graduate towards the end of my second period at The Sun. He was a nice guy and smart. But I found him to be the sort of person who thinks that if you do everything asked of you, play it by the book, you'll be fine. I tried to get it across to him that it doesn't always work that way.

He always dressed immaculately, in a suit and tie. Always clean shaven. And he was polite and friendly. I tried to explain to him that racism is still alive and kicking in newsrooms but it's been driven underground. A decade earlier, an Irish guy doing shifts on The Screws was the one who said: "The Sun is full of unscrupulous barrow boys."

That's true to an extent but it's not all bad. They respect you if you stand up for yourself rather than be: "Yes, Sir. No, Sir."

I tried to give some tough love to that lad but just ended up alienating him. He wasn't taken on, even though most of the other trainees were. Let's just say that I don't think he was operating in a meritocracy. I did more harm than good and it's not a nice feeling.

I honestly don't think that *my* genetic make-up stopped my career from progressing. It was more about not being prepared to stay "on message" in the Murdoch Machine. My feet wouldn't have touched the ground if I wasn't any good. But a theoretical Establishment would prefer me to be on the inside pissing out than the reverse. My mixed race, "politically black" views were the problem, not my blood. The author of bestseller Why I'm No Longer Talking to White People About Race, Reni Eddo-Lodge, sums it up well:

"It's truly a lifetime of self-censorship that people of colour have to live. The options are: Speak your truth and face the reprisals, or bite your tongue and get ahead in life."

I blazed a trail from the ethnic minority media into the mainstream and that's something I'm proud of. I changed a lot of racial attitudes on both Murdoch red-tops. And I can imagine there was a lot less casual racism when I was around. I once overheard a backbencher talk about "spear chuckers". He looked up, saw I was there and immediately retracted the remark. The thing was that he grew on me. He respected me and my ability. This guy was one of the rising stars of the company. But he treated me as an equal even when he was Night Editor.

Many years later, when he was more senior again, we had a fag together out the front and he was genuinely grateful for my observations on his section. He got shafted by the company in the end after a row with the bigwigs over yet another cull of subs. He was a good guy for standing up for them.

I can be very patient and try and see the best in people. I'm also quite adaptable, not ramming home my point until I've build up a bit of stock. I had the ear of some pretty powerful people at times. But I'm a known quantity.

. . .

Paul Davidson was one of my colleagues and friends in my first period at The Screws, from 1999 to 2001. He was a bit younger than the hardcore of the Fleet Street legends club and much of his career was spent as a reporter, as opposed to a sub. But he was more than competent and always had a string of fascinating exclusives for our ears only, from well-informed contacts he'd made during his spells as a crime correspondent.

He was doing shifts on The Sun to top up his pension pot after The Screws folded in 2011. He finished at 11pm one night and ended up getting on a train home with another Essex-based workmate. Paul got off to change. He had a heart attack on his second train and, despite the best efforts of off-duty medics, he died. It was a shattering revelation the next day. I was determined to go to his funeral, in Essex. It was an amazing turnout and there were plenty of laughs during the speeches. His best friend, who was the top sub on The Screws, told me afterwards: "Paul admired your talent."

I was incredibly touched. Paul was always a nice guy and I felt he warmed to me and what I represented, which took him away from where he was when we first made friends. And vice-versa. Such a terrible shame he wasn't able to enjoy the comfortable retirement he'd worked so hard for. It's not an uncommon scenario. Life expectancy isn't great for subs on the nationals. I've lost track of all the heart attacks, strokes and stress-related illnesses over the years. I myself, obviously, got pushed to the brink mentally, to the extent where I could have lost my own life.

Paul once told me a remarkable story, the darkest of humour. As a reporter in his younger days, he drove out to interview an elderly couple whose two, adult children had tragically died at separate times and in different circumstances. Paul had a good manner and I can just see him sitting with the couple, listening to them pour their hearts out. Losing a child has to be one of the most devastating blows life has to offer. To lose your only two is beyond comprehension.

It was emotional even for Paul as he started to wrap up the interview. The couple then described how cathartic it was to open up about their feelings. Paul was parked on their driveway and before getting into his car there were hugs as they prepared to wave him off.

He eventually got in, fired up the engine and reversed over their cat.

10b. GOOD SH★T!

'That kinda pisses on my idea'

Some of my choice headlines and captions during my time on British national newspapers, followed by a few which didn't make it…

Story: Artist paints Cheryl [then] Cole with antlers.
Headline:
**Cheryl's
doe oil
painting**
- *The Sun*

Story: Elastics firm goes out of business.
Headline: **Elastics firm was overstretched**
- *Sunday Mirror*

Story: Irish farmers' daughters beauty pageant finalists chosen.
Headline:
**Farm girls
dung good**
- *NoW*

Story: Punch-up at a psychiatrists' conference.
Headline: **Freudian slap**
- *NoW*

Picture story: Identical quadruplet blonde babes flown over from the US to promote "four chances to win" the Lotto, when its slogan was: "It could be you."
Headline:
**It could be you or
you or you or you**
Camelot dropped the slogan the next day.
- *The Sun*

Picture story: North Korean despot Kim Jong-un is mobbed by adoring female soldiers.

Headline: **GIRLS JUST WANT TO HAVE UN**

- *The Sun*

Story: Teacher in US sacked for appearing in porn film.

Headline: **JOB BLOW**

- *The Sun*

Story: Peruvian cannibal who used to eat priests goes vegetarian while in jail.

Headline:

**Cannibal gives up
priests for lentils**

(My absolute favourite)

- *NoW*

Story: Threesome caught having sex in the ruins of Pompeii.

Headline:

**Rumpy
Pompeii**

- *The Sun*

Story: Scientists alter a gene in mice that they have in common with humans and it makes them more intelligent.

Headline:

**Of mice
& Mensa**

- *The Sun*

Story: Teacher in India sacked for getting naked to teach his pupils about human anatomy.

Headline: **SCHLONG DIVISION**

- *The Sun*

Story: Baby Spice Emma Bunton is dropped by Virgin Records in Christmas week.

Headline:

Virgin drops Baby

- *NoW*

Picture story: Queen Mum meets Santa.

Headline:

'Hello, and
what do
you do..?'

Private Eye nicked the principal idea behind it for their cover later that month.

- *NoW*

Story: Seaside town maze is closed because students are having naked parties there at night.

Headline: **AMAZEBALLS**

- *The Sun*

Story: Two members of Eighties punk band The Damned are reunited after 30 years, both recovering on the same cancer ward.

Headline: **I'LL BE DAMNED**

- *The Sun*

Story: Survey finds people in northern town Carlisle are the happiest in Britain.

Headline: **GRIN UP NORTH**

Evening Standard ripped it off for the BBC's Salford TV launch a few weeks later.

- *The Sun*

Story: EU president Herman Van Rompuy lays into then PM David Cameron.

Headline: **PM IS HERMAN MONSTERED**

Night Editor said: "The headline was more than the story deserved."

- *The Sun.*

Story: Burglars steal 30 turkeys from a butcher during Christmas week.

Headline:

It's turkey

swizzlers

- *NoW*

Story: Town residents are left puzzled because they keep digging up biscuits in their gardens.

Headline: **CRUMBSTRUCK**

- *NoW*

Story: Prisoner in the US escapes jail but is caught hours later getting drunk in a nearby bar.

Headline: **ON THE RUM**

- *The Sun*

Story: Outstanding charges against Saddam Hussein formally dropped six months after he is executed by hanging for gassing the Kurds.

Headline:

Saddam

off hook

Middlebench took it out but backbench restored it.

- *The Sun*

Story: Madonna announces world tour dates from a toilet.

Crazy For Loo

("Pooper Don't Preach" didn't fit)

- *The Sun*

Story: Hollywood star Colin Farrell tipped to star in East End gangster flick.

Headline:

Lock, stock
and Farrell

- *NoW*

Story: Gamer dies after getting DVT in front of the screen.

Headline: **CONSOLENCES** (it was tasteless)

- *The Sun*

Story: Bandits in South America make a priest swear on the Bible to get him to reveal where the church safe is.

Headline: **BLASPHEMONEY**

- *The Sun*

Story: Star Trek legend William Shatner infuriates locals in an English village when he says it's "laced with prostitution" while he is guest host of BBC satirical TV show Have I Got News For You?

Headline:

Shat app
you face

(I think it was quite an achievement to get the word "Shat" into a Sun headline)

- *The Sun*

Story: Council officials put up signs warning people they will be fined if they poo in a park.
Headline: **JOBBIESWORTHS**
- *The Sun*

Story: Lag spends day in a pub after being mistakenly let out, before eventually handing himself in.
Headline: **ANY CHANCE OF A LOCK-IN, LANDLORD?**
- *The Sun*

Picture story: Strictly presenter Tess Daley in sexy photoshoot.
Headline: **HOST TESS WITH THE MOSTESS**
- *The Sun*

Story: TV presenter Michaela Strachan gets ill on location.
Headline: **MICHAELA STRICKEN**
- *The Sun*

Picture story: Demi Moore looking washed out after husband leaves her.
Headline: **SEEN A GHOST, DEMI?**
- *The Sun*

Front page lead story: Andy Murray becomes the first British man in 77 years to win Wimbledon.
Headline: **AND OF HOPE AND GLORY**
- *The Sun*

Picture story: Prince Andrew talking to a woman in the sea.
Headline: **THE PLAYBUOY PRINCE**
Making something out of nothing.
- *The Sun*

Story: Maradona banned from playing football again after cocaine is found in his system.

Headline: **END OF THE LINE FOR MARADONA**

- (Beirut) Daily Star

Picture story: A bush is delivered to Kate Winslet's house.

Headline: **KATE BUSH**

- The Sun

Story: Kebab shop which featured in a Beatles Magical Mystery Tour film gets a plaque to mark its history.

Headline:

Magical

my shish

story tour

CPR on a tedious page three story.

- The Sun

Story: Diplomatic row between UK and China over Hong Kong.

Headline: **HONG KONG DING DONG**

- The Sun

Story: Live link between then President Obama and US astronauts on space station.

Headline: **All the President's spacemen**

The Night Editor, who became Editor and then COO of Murdoch's UK operations, wrote another headline and I suggested mine. He said: "But that kinda pisses on my idea."

I said: "Yeah but mine's better!"

He changed it.

- The Sun

Story: Recently retired tennis legend breaks down in tears as he receives career achievement award.

**Sampras at
break point**

- *The Sun*

Story: Cape Town is voted the best city break destination.
Headline: **GREAT ES-CAPE**

- *The Sun*

Story: Scientists have found that adults carry around 3kg of bacteria in their guts.
Headline: **A LOT TO DIGEST**

- *The Sun*

Story: Range of knickers to indicate the wearer is on her period, with slogans such as "riding the crimson wave", is launched.
Headline: **PANTY ONE-LINERS**

- *The Sun*

. . .

Picture: Then UKIP leader Nigel Farage as fictional character Andy Capp in story about which comic icon politicians would be.
Caption kicker: **If the cap fits...**
An achievement getting a Bob Marley reference about racists into a Murdoch paper.

- *The Sun*

. . .

Headlines that didn't make it (for various reasons):

Story: Lags are banned from having pictures of topless women in their cells.
Headline: **Behind bras**
- *NoW*

Picture story: A serial rapist being whipped in Iran before being publicly hanged (somewhat over-egging the pudding).
Headline:
Any lashed
requests?
- *The Sun*

Story: Rock star Meatloaf feared he was going to die after collapsing on stage.
Headline:
MEATLOAF: I THOUGHT
I WAS BROWN BREAD
- *The Sun*

Story: Rapper Kanye West is paid millions to do a private gig for the son of an Asian dictator. Can't remember the country, in the Kazakhstan region.
Headline: **WEST-ERN HIP-HOP-CRISY**
I wonder why that headline didn't make it in a paper with The Sun's political leanings? Changed to: KANYE'S HIP-HOP-CRISY
- *The Sun*

Story: Dope being grown in a Portaloo in the US.
Headline: **GOOD SH*T!**
- *The Sun*

Picture story: Paris Hilton posing in revealing string outfit.
Headline:
Paris in
the string
- *The Sun*

Page one lead story: Angry Arsenal players chuck pizza at then Man United manager Fergie after hot-tempered match at Old Trafford.
Headline:
'You wanna
pizza me?'
Night Editor had it on his screen but eventually went with WAR AND PIZZA.
- *The Sun*

Part III: Influences

11. Small axe

'He kissed the noose so that we may be free'

On the morning of April 13, 1919, Nad's paternal grandad resolved to attend a protest against oppressive British laws in the Indian province of Punjab. But his bicycle had a puncture, which meant he couldn't go to the event in what was his home city, Amritsar. It turned out that Nad might not have existed if his grandad had gone. If it hadn't been for that puncture. And something happened at the demonstration which triggered a chain of events which brought me into existence…

The draconian laws in place limited civil and political liberties for Indians. Then Lieutenant Governor of the Punjab Sir Michael O'Dwyer was one of those laws' most powerful proponents. Following the deaths of five British civilians days earlier during rioting in Amritsar, in which many Indians lost their lives, a curfew was introduced and all political rallies were banned.

The admittedly illegal protest was intended to be peaceful in Amritsar's huge, walled garden, Jallianwala Bagh. Estimates of the numbers attending ranged from 5,000 to 20,000 and it was made up of exclusively unarmed men and women — many elderly — and kids. Despite the nature of the gathering, many of those came from surrounding, peasant villages and did not even realise the strict restrictions were in place. The law included indefinitely extended detention, incarceration without trial or judicial review and a ban on public gatherings. And even though the event was also celebrating the Sikh festival of Vaisakhi, half of the crowd were Muslims.

Between 50 and 90 "native Indian" British Army troops were dispatched to the scene by O'Dwyer. Two

armoured cars with mounted machine guns were also sent
but were unable to squeeze through the main entrance
into the garden. The soldiers were under the command of
Punjab-born Brigadier-General Reginald Dyer. Within 30
seconds of entering, he had lined up his men and ordered
them to fire at the crowd, without warning. Some soldiers
initially shot into the air with their rifles. Dyer was said to
have reacted by barking: "Fire low. What have you been
brought here for?"

It was reported that he also directed his men to shoot
where the crowd was at its thickest. I'm not sure how
those troops could possibly obey such an order, especially
against their own, innocent people, and I wonder how the
part they played in the atrocity impacted on them during
the rest of their lives.

The only viable exit was sealed off by soldiers and
many tried to escape by climbing the walls. Others got
trampled to death in the stampede. Even those who lay flat
on the ground were fired at. Many jumped into a massive
well out of sheer desperation. The shooting lasted between
ten and 15 minutes. Some 1,650 rounds were spent. There
was no provision for the injured and the curfew Dyer
had imposed on the city prevented aid being given those
lying on the dusty floor until the next day. According to
British Government figures, 379 people were killed. But
other estimates put the death toll as high as 1,800, with
thousands more injured.

One of the survivors was a 19 year old Punjabi Sikh
called Udham Singh. He was born a poverty-stricken
villager in 1899 and taken in by an orphanage at an early
age after his dad, a railway crossing watchman, died. It is
unclear what happened to his mum. He left the Amritsar
orphanage in 1919, the year of the massacre, and had been

serving water to the crowd. Understandably, the slaughter had a profound effect on him.

The seed had been sown.

The next day, Dyer issued a press release in Urdu. Chillingly, the last line warned that, if he was not "obeyed", "revenge will be taken upon you and upon your children". Dyer also asserted in his own testimony that he would have used his machine guns if the armoured vehicles had been able to enter the garden. The atrocity sparked widespread outrage across the world. Most of the Punjab was kept under strict martial law for months. Restrictive policies included Dyer's infamous "crawling order", which forced people to crawl on the ground belly-down instead of walking.

He was labelled "The Butcher of Amritsar", although many historians contend that O'Dwyer premeditated the massacre. It seems to me that they were equally culpable but we will probably never fully know. One thing is for sure, O'Dwyer described the massacre as a "correct action" and, initially, publicly, gave Dyer his unwavering support. The Governor was relieved of his post later that year.

Dyer was, by all accounts, an inflexible military man who described himself as "a soldier". A man who followed orders. If O'Dwyer ordered the massacre then Dyer probably wouldn't have given him up. O'Dwyer had contended — without evidence — that Dyer's actions were justified because the gathering was part of a rebellion conspiracy. It was supposedly timed to coincide with a rumoured Afghan invasion.

O'Dwyer created the conditions and context for the massacre.

In the fallout, Dyer's testimony revealed he was not remorseful. When defending his actions, he kept changing his justification for the slaughter from sending out a wider warning to feeling physically threatened by the size of the gathering. He was removed from the Army in 1920 but without further punishment. Anecdotal evidence suggests he had become unhinged in the years leading up to the massacre, fearing a full-scale insurrection in India when it was probably not on the cards at the time. There had been much direct action against British rule in the Punjab, including riots but the disturbances were probably not anywhere near as co-ordinated as the British seemed to fear.

Dyer became a hero among those in favour of the Raj. There was praise and condemnation for him during debates in the UK Parliament. And he was described as "the man who saved India" by English writer Rudyard Kipling, who was based there. But even Winston Churchill distanced himself from the affair, while serving as War Secretary at the time, later saying it was a "monstrous event, an event which stands in singular and sinister isolation [during colonial rule]".

On his exile to Britain, Dyer was presented with £26,000, well over £1million in today's money, from a fund set up for him by The Morning Post, a newspaper which later merged with The Daily Telegraph.

Dyer wrote: "It is only to an enlightened people that free speech and a free press can be extended. The Indian people want no such enlightenment."

He did, however, according to some sources, privately admit that his part in the massacre tortured him. He died in 1927, aged 62, after a series of strokes and other debilitating conditions. Some said God dealt with him.

Back in the immediate aftermath of the massacre, Udham Singh resolved to become active in the revolutionary political movement and was eventually jailed in India for possessing unlicensed arms. He was released in 1931 after five years behind bars. Udham was put under constant police surveillance but managed to give the British the slip and eventually made it to London in 1934, where he found work as an engineer.

But gainful employment was not the limit of his ambition.

On March 13, 1940, O'Dwyer was scheduled to give a speech at Caxton Hall, Westminster, London. Udham entered and found a seat. When then 75-year-old O'Dwyer started to speak, the Indian revolutionary stood up, walked towards the speaking stage and, with a revolver he'd been concealing, shot O'Dwyer twice. Once through the heart and once through his right lung. He died instantly. Udham also shot three other British officials who were on the stage but they survived.

The assassin made no attempt to escape and was swiftly apprehended. There's an iconic picture of him being led away in handcuffs with a big smile on his face.

Reaction to the assassination varied. Mahatma Gandhi referred to it as "an act of insanity", stating: "I hope this will not be allowed to affect political judgement."

Indian National Congress leader Jawaharal Nehru, who went on to become India's first Prime Minister, said the action was senseless. But somewhat surprisingly, The Times of London dubbed Udham a "fighter for freedom", the shooting "an expression of the pent-up fury of the downtrodden Indian people".

In Udham's diaries from 1939 and 1940, he occasionally misspells O'Dwyer's surname as "O'Dyer". Some historians have speculated that he may have confused O'Dwyer and Dyer. But it seems to me that he knew exactly who to shoot in Caxton Hall. Udham was remanded in custody at Brixton Prison, which I get a kick out of because it's so close to my current home. I think about him being there when I go past. Maybe the powers that be will one day put a blue plaque up on its walls in honour of him.

He went on a 42-day hunger strike there and was eventually force-fed. Asked to explain his actions during police interrogation, Udham, who spoke poor English, said: "I did it because I had a grudge against him [O'Dwyer]. He deserved it. He was the real culprit. He wanted to crush the spirit of my people, so I have crushed him.

"For full 21 years, I have been trying to wreak vengeance. I am happy that I have done the job. I am not scared of death. I am dying for my country. I have seen my people starving in India under the British rule. I have protested against this, it was my duty. What greater honour could be bestowed on me than death for the sake of my motherland?"

His trial began at the Old Bailey on June 4, 1940. Udham was found guilty of murder and sentenced to death a few days later. He made a speech which the judge, Mr Justice Atkinson, ordered not be published by the press. In it, Udham said: "I have more English friends in England than [Indian ones] I do in India. I have nothing against the public.

"I have great sympathy with the workers of England but I am against the dirty British Government. You people are suffering the same as I am suffering through those dirty dogs and mad beasts. India is only slavery. Killing, mutilating and destroying. We know what is going on in India, people do not read about it in the press. Hundreds of thousands of people being killed by your dirty dogs."

Mr Justice Atkinson mentioned the Amritsar massacre. Mentioned.

Udham refused to plead insanity, which would have saved him from the death penalty, and was hanged at

Pentonville Prison on July 31, 1940. His remains were initially buried in the grounds of the north London jail but were exhumed and repatriated to India in 1974. Some of his ashes are retained inside a sealed urn at Jallianwala Bagh and he is now generally referred to in the Indian subcontinent as "'Shaheed [martyr]' Udham Singh".

Nehru reversed his stance on the revolutionary in 1962, proclaiming: "He kissed the noose so that we may be free."

I was totally blown away when I first read his story during my early days at Eastern Eye in the mid-Nineties. Despite being someone almost unknown outside the Indian subcontinent, to many, he was more crucial in the fight for India's independence than Gandhi. However, Udham is still regarded as a terrorist by some, particularly in Britain.

In my mind, there is a simplicity, purity, integrity, bravery and symmetry to his story. He is my ultimate hero, not because he was an Indian who killed a Brit but because he meted out natural justice and was prepared to make the ultimate sacrifice for the sake of others. This dynamic could be transferred to many different struggles against oppression, such as Apartheid South Africa or the Palestinians' ongoing struggle. Despite being a Muslim, Nad's late father also regarded Udham as his ultimate hero.

Most of the leaders who decide to take their country to war never have to face the consequences of their murderous decisions. Tony Blair springs to mind. I'm not advocating the former British PM's assassination but I think he should be spending the rest of his life in jail for launching the illegal Iraq War, which has claimed hundreds of thousands of civilian lives.

Have things changed as much as we'd like to think?

It's my guess that the assassination of O'Dwyer sent shockwaves through the British Establishment.

The idea of being slain for outrages committed decades earlier must have sent a chill down their collective spine. Accountability. Never knowing when they might face the consequences of their misdeeds. It was justice that it was bullets which tore through O'Dwyer. And it was fitting that Udham, who had no escape plan, "kissed the noose".

So, it occurs to me that I wouldn't exist if it wasn't for Udham. He changed the course of human history. Of global geopolitics. A lowly, humble, orphan villager from the Punjab. Obviously, Gandhi played his part but I believe his MO fed nicely into the British colonial agenda of peddling the myth that peaceful demonstration was the key to freedom from slavery and oppression: The victims of the Amritsar Massacre were peaceful demonstrators...

One of my favourite Bob Marley tracks is Small Axe. The key lyrics are:

If you are the big tree,
Let me tell you that: We are the small axe
Sharpened ready ready to cut you down (well sharp)
To cut you down

Udham Singh was the small axe.

My personal philosophy is more along the lines of another Bob Marley line: "He who fights and runs away, lives to fight another day."

Punjabis have made a huge impact on my life. They certainly punch above their weight regarding impact on the wider world. My Punjabi Sikh now ex's dad was a carpenter. I was working with him once, trying to chop down a little tree with *my* small axe. But the head kept flying off the handle. Becoming increasingly frustrated as I smashed the head further and further down the handle,

I took it to him. He put the head in place and, with the whole thing upright, rather than using brute force, he started gently tapping the bottom of the handle with a hammer. *Very gently*. The point was that the head made small, angular gains down the shaft of the handle, gripping it tighter and tighter. It worked!

My now ex's dad said: "It's an *Indian* idea."

Udham had an *Indian* idea. It worked!

The amazing thing for me personally is my links to India via my English side. My maternal, white grandfather was actually born in India and went on to become a navigator in the British Royal Navy after coming to England when he was young. He also had bipolar. His father was an India-based colonel in the British Army at the time of the massacre. He commanded a Muslim regiment and then a Sikh regiment, both in the Punjab.

My mum became concerned in recent years about whether her grandfather was linked to the Amritsar massacre. She managed to determine that he wasn't and said she didn't think a local regiment could have carried it out.

The rules of combat and geopolitics have changed so much since then. Maybe it's because powerful people are better protected these days but most terror atrocities strengthen the political leaders' hands because they mean increasingly draconian laws can be imposed on us, like in 1919 Punjab. Udham's actions are in such stark contrast to much of what goes on today, which largely targets innocent civilians or military pawns.

If Sir Michael O'Dwyer was a knight, Fusilier Lee Rigby was a pawn...

He was the 25 year old British Army soldier slain near the Royal Artillery Barracks in Woolwich, south east

London on May 22, 2013. The killers were British citizens of Nigerian descent in their 20s. I am totally against what they did, it was barbaric and inhumane. It's therefore hard to make my point on the subject. But I will try.

Father of one Rigby was wearing a hoodie promoting British armed forces charity Help for Heroes when he was run down by the killers' car. They then used knives and a meat clever to attack him, trying to cut his head off at one point.

Absolutely sickening.

One of them encouraged passersby to film them on mobile phones at the scene of the crime, while his blood-soaked hands held the meat cleaver and knife. I find it noteworthy that he didn't reference 72 virgins in heaven or anything particularly religiously extremist (although his actions were obviously pretty extreme). He was saying that his motivation and willingness to die for his cause was British foreign policy.

I was one of the millions who congregated in Hyde Park on February 15, 2003, to oppose the impending Iraq War. It was the biggest protest in British history. But to no avail. So, in an uncomfortable way, politically, those who opposed the war and British foreign policy are singing from the same hymn sheet as Rigby's murderers. That does not mean we agree on how to oppose policies we disagree with. But frankly, at no point during that rally, when the police helicopters were circling above us, drowning out the speeches, did I think it would make a blind bit of difference. Blair was hellbent on war and nothing was going to stop him. It's made the world a much more dangerous place for us all.

I got extremely wound up at The Sun as I saw the propaganda machine wind up before my eyes in the lead up to the Iraq War. I was naive to think I could persuade my colleagues that, as Arab League chief Amp Moussa warned: "The gates of hell will open

Eventually, one of my senior colleagues sat me down and, pointing to a computer screen, said: "Let me show you something."

He pulled up a website called "onwar.com" and I punned: "Warons."

Then he showed me the history of British wars: No less than 86 since 1610. This is a warring nation. In the lead up to the Iraq War, later deposed and executed leader Saddam Hussein was mocked when he said it would be "the mother of all battles". Actually, I happen to think he was deliberately misunderstood by the Western media, which portrayed the quote as something along the lines "the motherfucker of all battles". He was simply saying that the "mother of battles" would *give birth* to all other "*battles*".

I was at The Sun on the day of the Rigby slaying and at one point I went outside to have a cigarette with a few colleagues. One of them said "bloody Muslims" before bursting out laughing. I, darkly, told him: "Don't lose your head over it, 'Les'."

My crack was in bad taste but I felt it was a justified way of countering Islamophobia, in that context. Frankly, I just wanted to shut him up.

I feel sorry for Rigby's family. It was a horrible way to die and he was a tiny pawn in an almost unprecedented geopolitical phenomenon plaguing the planet for the last few decades. Are we living in what historians will look back on as World War Three?

As a journalist for many years now, I feel qualified to say that I believe the media as a whole is insane. Think about how much coverage Rigby's murder garnered compared to those of British squaddies sent halfway round the world to die fighting in an illegal war. In some ways, Rigby's death was just an aberration of geography as far as the British state is concerned. And, aside from the disturbingly barbaric nature of the killing, the Rigby slaying shook this country as much as it did because it happened on the streets of London rather than, for instance, Baghdad. As one of Rigby's killers said: "When you drop a bomb, do you think it hits one person? Or rather your bomb wipes out a whole family?"

Rigby, from Middleton, Greater Manchester, was in many ways just a "worker". And Udham himself said in court: "I have great sympathy with the workers of England but I am against the dirty British Government."

I feel that history is repeating itself and that the vast majority of people fail to see the current parallels with centuries of colonial rule.

...

One of the most horrific terrorist atrocities committed on British soil occurred at Manchester Arena on May 22, 2017, as members of the public were leaving after a concert by US singer Ariana Grande. Including the terrorist, the suicide bombing killed 23 people, more than half children. The youngest was an eight year old girl.

The next day, I posted this on FaceBook: "I want to start off by saying that I totally condemn the Manchester atrocity. The callous murder of innocent children, in particular, is utterly despicable.

"As the father of a young daughter who dreams of the day when I take her to see Lionel Richie in concert,

I cannot begin to imagine what the victims' relatives are going through. This should all go without saying.

"But for me, there is a but...

"My timing might be spot on or it might seem totally inappropriate to many of you. But let's get a bit of perspective: Western-led wars caused the death of four million Muslims since 1990, according to a 2015 study by the Washington DC-based Physicians for Social Responsibility. I don't believe in subscribing to the numbers game but imagine if the boot was on the other foot.

"I am not alone in thinking this but most people who hold such views feel nervous about expressing them openly. In my opinion, Western foreign policy is the root cause of this war, a war which seems to have been designed to never end. I put this to a white, presumably Christian, nurse in her mid-20s who attended the scene of the Westminster atrocity in March. She agreed but said anyone expressing such opinions at her hospital would be swiftly ostracised.

"Of course suggestible, disenfranchised young people are going to be brainwashed into committing terrible atrocities when the West's continuing, murderous, colonial adventures give them an otherwise absent sense of purpose.

"To the credit of the British people, Tony Blair is a pariah in the UK for his shameful role in launching the Iraq War...just imagine how they feel about him and the West in the Muslim world.

"Don't get me wrong, I don't want to live under Sharia law and I enjoy the relative freedoms and prosperity that the Western world provides me. But when so many of us are no longer able to openly express our views, it no longer feels like a society I'd be prepared to lay down my own life for."

As American-Jewish philosopher Noam Chomsky put it: "It's only terrorism if they do it to us. When we do much worse to them, it's not terrorism."

12. Drive-by of thoughts

'I ain't dying over no fuckin' record'

I walked into the venue on Brick Lane, east London, and Ice-T was standing there, on his own, leaning against a wall beside a toilet door with his hands behind his back. He was a little shorter than I'd expected (about 5ft 10ins), even though I'd seen him in concert a few times before.

I bowled straight up to him and said: "Thanks for bringing me up."

He stuck out his right hand like a flick-knife and we shook on it. His eyes were clear, actually beautiful, not full of anger and hatred as I'd half expected. I wanted to tell him about Udham Singh, the ultimate cop killer. My Indian now ex wrote the name down on a piece of paper. So I told Ice-T about this guy and asked whether he'd be able to find out about him. I said the story would "change your life". He said: "I've got people who can track that shit down for me."

I pronounced: "Indian gangstas."

I was a little "high" at the time, in a bipolar sense rather than a recreational drug sense. But you have to bear in mind that I'd been seriously into Ice-T since I was 15 and I thought he was the coolest man alive, still do. To hear those words burst out of him in person decades later was electric.

It's weird, I'd been spending all my quiet time at The Sun chatting on his website forum during the preceding two weeks. Then he came on and said that he reads every single entry and he'll be making a personal appearance, not doing a gig, a few days later on Brick Lane, which is in an Asian (especially Bangladeshi) area. It's about a mile from Murdoch's "Fortress Wapping", where I was working. Bearing in mind that he is based in LA, it seemed like it was meant to be. And even my ever-skeptical now ex said: "You magicked him up."

I consider Ice-T to be the Malcolm X of his generation. And before you sneer…

Yes, it would have probably helped his credibility if he'd been assassinated in a killing forever shrouded in conspiracy theory intrigue. But as he says at the end of each album: "Told ya, ya shoulda killed me last year."

Ice-T is the living embodiment of Malcolm X's mantra: "By any means necessary."

I understand the point of that saying as: If you are being enslaved, oppressed or facing a genocide, you have the right to do whatever it takes to gain your freedom. Anything. The responsibility for acting with *integrity* lies with the oppressor, not the oppressed.

To Ice-T, "by any means necessary" has meant getting his message out via hip-hop and heavy metal. It's a question of evolving tactics in these days when news outlets are run by fewer and fewer corporations, which are getting bigger and bigger, totally focused on the bottom line, at best.

Political hip-hop is guerrilla tactics. As he raps the year after "The Controversy" in Message To The Soldier (1994):

They never meant us to speak
They had planned to keep the black man weak
But rap hit the streets
Black rage amplified over dope beats

The Cop Killer affair is the biggest controversy in the history of the music business. In 1992, the US Government was threatening to charge Ice-T with "sedition", which equates to treason and, ultimately, carries the death penalty. His record company, Time Warner, refused to pull the track. Ice-T said this was not because they agreed with its content but because they didn't want politicians dictating what they could and couldn't sell in the future. In the end, Ice-T pulled it himself, saying: "I ain't dying over no fuckin' record."

Though the track became associated with the 1992 LA riots, it was actually written in 1990 and Ice-T had been performing it in 1991, the same year black motorist Rodney King was stopped by four, white LAPD officers for a traffic violation before being repeatedly kicked, and beaten more than 50 times with batons. The recorded version of the track, which references the King case, was released in March 1992, just as the cops charged with King's assault were acquitted – that outrageous injustice was the *real* catalyst for the riots.

Obviously.

What was so controversial about Cop Killer? It was about fighting back against police brutality. He says the inspiration came from friends who were telling him the police were out of control in black areas of LA. One told Ice-T: "We need a cop killer."

So he wrote about it. Ice-T said it "targeted police who feel it's not their job to solve problems but to perpetuate them". And here's the thing, it was not a *rap* track. It was a heavy metal track with his then newish band Body Count. But during The Controversy, he was universally described in the media as "the *rapper* Ice-T". To me, that is a manifestation of the unconscious AND conscious racism towards the rap genre. Like these people have nothing to say. Actually, they are literally *saying* things — "rap" essentially means "talk".

Ice-T also said the problem the powers that be had with the record was not its content but that it was the

"Bugs Bunny" company giving him a platform. He also maintained he was not interested in the "freedom of speech" First Amendment argument because, as he states on Message To The Soldier, the Constitution was written at a time when black people were "considered nothing but property". He added: "The expectation of having black people speaking on records never came to mind."

The irony is that Message To The Soldier is actually a far more incendiary track than Cop Killer on a political level. He was unbowed. Ice-T says he knew he was in deep shit when he saw then (Republican) Vice President Dan Quayle slamming him on TV. Right-wing film legend Charlton Heston — who became National Rifle Association President in 1998 — also came out to pour scorn on Ice-T at Time Warner's shareholders' meeting. Heston was at the time campaigning to prevent a ban on an armour-piercing bullet dubbed "the cop killer". As Ice-T said: "He's got his shit twisted."

It's ironic that staunch Republican Heston starred in one of the most subversive Hollywood films ever, neo-Marxist 1973 blockbuster Soylent Green.

Ice-T's 1989 track Freedom Of Speech was a prophecy of The Controversy. He raps:

Freedom of Speech, that's some motherfuckin' bullshit
You say the wrong thing, they'll lock your ass up quick

In reference to founder of the Parents Music Resource Center (PMRC) and Second Lady wed to former Vice President Al Gore, Tipper Gore, Ice-T continues:

Think I give a fuck about some silly bitch named Gore?
Yo PMRC, here we go, raw
Yo Tip, what's the matter? You ain't gettin' no dick?

You're bitchin' about rock 'n' roll, that's censorship, dumb bitch
The Constitution says we all got a right to speak
Say what we want Tip, your argument is weak
Censor records, TV, school books too
And who decides what's right to hear? You?

And he picks it up:

And say America's some motherfuckin' apple pie
Yo, you gotta be high to believe that
You're gonna change the world by a sticker on a record sleeve
Cos once you take away my right to speak
Everybody in the world's up shit creek

Ice-T was not, as was assumed, dropped by Time Warner after the affair but it became clear when they refused to sanction artwork for the cover of his next album that his creative freedom would be restricted in a way it hadn't been before. He decided it would be best to move on and start his own record company. The first album, Home Invasion, featured some seminal tracks, including Message To The Soldier.

. . .

Slavery isn't something talked about that much in black popular culture. In many ways, it's a private pain. But Ice-T wrote in 1994: "Fifty million blacks were killed during our Holocaust, and we ain't got a fuckin' dime."

He also states: "Whites don't want to let go of the advantage they've built up over hundreds of years."

Despite this, Ice-T has a lot of white fans. In 1993 track Race War, he raps:

Fuck John Wayne
I don't hate whites
I just got a death wish for muthafuckas that ain't right

I reckon a big part of how he attracts so many white fans is because of being what he describes as a "linear" rapper. His lyrics are clear and easy to understand — totally direct, not "coded". I find myself *absorbing* coded rap lyrics and that keeps the music fresh for me. And Ice-T himself says that, for instance: "Busta Rhymes is rapping on a whole different level."

But Ice-T was the original "gangsta" rapper and he says his message, initially, was: "I was like, 'If you do this and that, you're going to jail.' Then NWA (Niggaz Wit Attitudes) arrived on the scene and were like, 'Fuck it, we're going to jail.'"

Despite my Brixton background, I first came at his music in my early teens as, essentially, a "white" fan who appreciated the way he told it straight. He is, without doubt, the biggest influence on my writing style — direct. A TV interview with him brought my now ex out in hives because of the way he was shooting from the hip. In his 1994 book, The Ice Opinion, he said: "A reporter might mumble before an interview, 'I'm on your side, and I know what you're saying. My editor isn't but fuck him.'"

I'm always curious about his opinion on things, whether it be in his music or an article or a TV interview. I thought his take on OJ Simpson's 1995 murder trial acquittal was particularly thought-provoking considering that he thought the former American football superstar was guilty. He said: "It's good [that he got off] because it shows that money is more important than race in America now."

Well, he is the Original Gangsta.

If you want another point blank opinion, white House of Pain rapper Everlast told Ice-T that he doesn't think black people hate white people, it's just that they don't trust them. And he doesn't think white people hate black people, it's just that they're afraid of them.

Regarding Donald Trump's presidential election victory, Ice-T said: "He's pretty much scared the shit out of everyone in the world and we could be on the precipice of a World War Three. I've never watched so much news in my fucking life. It's getting serious."

That scares me coming from him. He has previously stated that WW3 "will largely be fought out in people's minds". The likes of Ice-T are speaking the uncomfortable truth and rap culture in the last 30 years is totally underrated. I believe some of these artists have vastly more to say about how the human race should be progressing than they are given credit for. The word "black" was reclaimed in the Sixties, largely by James Brown, and it's been rappers who have reclaimed "nigger"/"nigga". And it's a word that only they can use. I only feature it in quote marks, not my own language. A boundary has been set, a red line. That's power. Snoop Dogg, meanwhile, has rapped about how he "brought the Afro back".

This is the cutting edge of a gradual power shift which would have Enoch Powell turning in his grave. Good. I'm also intrigued by the discussions that take place between the black audience and black artists. On Nigga 4 Life, in what was surely a reference to the likes of Michael Jackson, Snoop Dogg raps:

You can paint your face and change your nose and buy new clothes

But you know what…?
You can't change who the fuck you are
You's a motherfucking nigga for life

However, I believe some things are going backwards. With the benefit of hindsight, I realise that when I was growing up, black people didn't have to assert their "blackness" in Brixton because, crudely speaking, it was their "territory". But I was playing football a few years ago at a five-a-side complex in Elmers End, south east London, which is a predominately white area, and I noticed how racially-defined the teams were. It seemed those racially-defined teams were competing to be the loudest in the dressing room. To be dominant.

Growing up, this ultra-confident and loud talk was known as "fronting". It means, effectively, putting on a show, *acting*. I felt particularly sorry for the young, black guys, like they've bought an image sold to them about how black people should be. Sold a pup. It gave me a headache. A few miles south of Brixton and where I live now, West Norwood, has some young, black guys who seem to be under the impression they are living in South Central Los Angeles. Ice-T was all about *getting out* of the ghetto. In 1991 track Escape From The Killing Fields, he raps:

No one wants to
Live in an urban war
You live there cause
Your parents were poor

He picks it up:

Ya gotta get out! Why?

Cause the fields
Are where you die

Rap has been a big part of my life since me and two white friends started getting into Ice-T when we were 15. We would sit there in a bedroom somewhere or other, get stoned (incidentally, Ice-T doesn't do drink or drugs) and listen to his albums. It seemed like the best thing in the world at the time. I, for one, wasn't doing it to be 'cool'.

I was immersed in black music — soul and reggae as well — from an early age. Jamaicans can be noisy people, in my experience. I mean, especially the ones who use industrial-sized speakers inside or outside their little shops in Brixton. But I loved that atmosphere, it was such a colourful place. Culturally rich. That was normality to me and it marks me out from my immediate, white family. I can't say what's going in their minds but for whatever reason, I think differently from them. It's a big part of why I'm writing this book. To try and help them understand.

Ice-T served in the US Army when he was young and went on to be heavily involved in criminal activity as a civilian. I was reading an interview with him recently in which he revealed that when he walks into a commercial building, he automatically takes note of the location of the alarms and the exit points. It's just become part of him. I laughed when I read that. Ice-T is rich now, he doesn't have to raid jewellery stores anymore and I'm not on the breadline now so I don't have to rely on the newspaper stand lady giving me too much change.

I'm not trying to *push* my views, I'm just saying that the way each of us sees the world is through the prism of our own experiences. My mum grew up in one of the poshest boarding schools in the country. Some of her dorm mates had titles, such as "Lady". Obviously, she's going to see the world in a different way to me. For her, Brixton life was just a phase but I spent my formative years there. What I object to is being told that, for whatever reason, my viewpoints aren't a valid contribution to the discourse. Despite being confident in my own abilities from a young age, there's always been a part of *me* that feels my viewpoints aren't valid because they deviate so much from this society's collective consensus.

My time at Eastern Eye had a huge impact on me. It made me realise that I was not alone. I can still remember hearing Nad say: "We're all politically black."

That was the first time I realised I was politically black. That I am not part of the 'club'. That actually Ice-T was speaking the truth, cutting through the crap. That's why much of rap excites me like no other type of music. If I want to soothe my soul, I listen to Roberta Flack. If I want to bond with my daughter, I listen to The Four Tops. If I want to feel my strength, I listen to rap.

It is not in the slightest bit contrived but notice how they are all black voices.

...

My old, Irish flatmate Brian once showed interest in a Dr. Dre baseline so I played him Redman and Method Man track Tear It Off, which has a banging baseline. His reaction: "That's not music."

And he told me I'm "not black". I've never acted black or thought of myself as black (except when I was posing as a "wigger" at The Voice). Actually, that's not totally true about the 'acting'. I was at West Norwood's B&Q in in the mid-Noughties trying to buy two deckchairs. The mixed race (half black) staff member working the floor was particularly unhelpful and told me that they had to be sold as a four, which I knew was bullshit. Then he turned his back on me and started serving a white woman. He was all over her. I was so wound up and went searching the store for another staff member to help me, which she did. I got my two deckchairs. As I made my way to the checkout, I held them up with each arm and muttered to the unhelpful prick: "See? Two."

Next thing I knew, he had collared some black co-workers to follow me to the counter and accused me of being racist! He told them that I was doing an impression of a monkey when I was holding the chairs up and down. He genuinely believed it. I turned around to him and and his pals and bellowed: "I was just telling you, 'TWO!'"

Then I had a schooldays flashback and, in a Jamaican accent, bellowed: "You bloodclaat!"

A lot of black customers burst out laughing. I totally humiliated that prick and he deserved it. I guess that was a rare example of me *acting* black. But all I was trying to do was deploy an effective way of defending myself against the accusation of racism. It was a pretty decent strategy as it turned out, not that I had exactly planned it.

I digress.

. . .

Rap music peaked in the Nineties for me and I hated the whole "bling" culture that followed. In a nutshell, it got commercialised. But there's still an undercurrent of meaningful music in the genre. The existential elements of some material is seriously disrespected. If you look back to aspects of Nineties gangsta rap, there is a theme of sex and dope. There were rappers out there saying that was enough to keep them contented.

Without going into the language of that whole *subculture*, because it is consistently taken out of context, a lot of what Dr. Dre and Snoop were doing was encouraging the people they were representing to get stoned and fuck rather than getting jailed and/or shot. Indeed, Dr. Dre's 1992 debut solo album was called The Chronic, a reference to a high-grade type of cannabis.

In the post-LA Riots era, the LP marked the invention of G-funk. "G" as in "gangsta". It was a natural evolution from the funk era pioneered by the likes of James Brown in the late Sixties. When I was 21, the idea of lots of sex and dope seemed pretty fucking attractive. But I'm relieved my life has taken me in many other directions. I still shudder to think what would have happened to me if I hadn't been fired from The Ritzy.

I might still be there.

Rappers aren't taken seriously in mainstream culture, even by many black people and I find it troubling that certain artists are looked down on because of their medium of communication. Most of the ones who actually have something to say are from poor backgrounds, so it's a class as well as race thing. The irony is that the mainstream entertainment sector has an insatiable appetite for black culture, which is constantly evolving in the West, as it is consumed by the dominant, white culture.

On Rap Games Hijacked, Ice-T raps: "Just being black is hijacked."

And presumably referencing the West's Jekyll and Hyde approach to black culture, Missy Elliot rapped on Lick Shots: "For those of you who hated, you only made us more creative."

She could have been referring generally to black people in Western societies.

. . .

I had an interesting insight in my early days at The Sun in 2002. The London edition was printed beneath us at Wapping, east London, so we used to get a first edition copy before we went home. I was leafing through the paper one night and noticed that in a story about Dr. Dre they had mistakenly used a picture of fellow rapper Tone Loc. I went over to the features department and pointed it out. I expected them to just fix it but a disinterested, irritated executive insisted on sitting me down and sighing: "So, what do you want to do here?"

Like *I* was being awkward!

That stupid Stepford Husband had such a bad attitude. I was left with the feeling the Dr. Dre 'mistake' was deliberate, in the "all black people look the same" vein. I have ultimate respect for Dr. Dre, he is one of the most influential people in the music industry. He grew up in Compton, which is a particularly tough part of LA. But he is now said to have a personal fortune of around £550million, making him the third richest rapper on the planet. You have to have something pretty fucking special about you to make that sort of leap from poverty to wealth.

I like the way Ice-T puts it in his 1994 track Straight Up Nigga:

Those who hate me, I got sumthin for ya
A nigga with cash, a nigga with a lawyer

I was doing a story during my second period at The Sun about R&B singer Chris Brown, famous for assaulting ex-girlfriend Rihanna. The beginning of the intro of my story was changed to "Bad boy rapper". I was at pains to point out that he isn't a "rapper". It turned out to be a bit of a struggle to get the executive to change it. I got there in the end but it didn't do me any favours. That's the tip of the iceberg. No pun intended.

...

You may be surprised to know that, musically, Ice-T isn't my favourite rapper, not even close. Dr. Dre's beats are better and Snoop's rapping voice is like honey. He's even invented a new language. Dr. Dre's The Chronic is my favourite rap album. Brilliant on every level. The best track is Stranded On Death Row. The last passage:

Cause only the weak, will try to speak
Those who are quiet, will always cause riots
There's three types of people in the world
Those who don't know what happened
Those who wonder what happened
And people like us from the streets that *make* things happen

13. Soul power

'Boom bloody boom'

There's a line in Tarantino flick Kill Bill where the Uma Thurman lead character says men who grew up without a father collect father figures. Guilty as charged. Four Tops lead singer Levi Stubbs was one of mine, especially because he really did Reach Out to me.

I got into them in my early teens and I eagerly anticipated seeing them live at Camden Palace on a date with a beautiful, blonde, French, country girl when we were 16.

Though Motown legends, they were out of vogue at the time. There were probably only 500 people in the auditorium, so we went right up to the stage, to the left hand side. Despite the poor turnout, the Four Tops were putting on a great show. I suppose they'd been in the business so long that they were hardened to going in and out of fashion. You could tell that they just loved to sing. I think there's a lesson in life in there.

I thought it was a bit unfair that Levi was the tallest, most handsome and most talented of the quartet. He had a way about him that seemed to be everything I wanted and didn't have in a dad. A loving soul poured out of him via his vocal chords. And something unforgettable happened when they sang what was then my favourite, and the most emblematic, of their tracks — Reach Out, I'll Be There.

As I gazed up adoringly at Levi, he caught my eye, made his way in my direction, about 20ft across the stage, crouched down in front of me and put the microphone up to my mouth for me to sing the chorus. I sang with the muthafucking Four Tops, people!

The French babe was impressed.

I can't believe a movie hasn't been made about them. They were remarkable in so many ways. They all lived within a few blocks of each other in Detroit for virtually their whole lives (only one still alive at the time of writing and he's still performing with replacement Tops), despite Motown relocating to LA. Levi could have gone solo and made bundles more dosh. But he said all the money in the world would be worthless without his buddies. He even refused to have separate billing. I believe he would have been regarded in the same light as the likes of Marvin Gaye and Al Green if he had gone solo.

He was diagnosed with cancer in 1995 and, after suffering a stroke in 2000, he was no longer able to go on tour. I recently stumbled on a YouTube video of his last proper performance, in the mid-Noughties. It came during an Aretha Franklin concert in Detroit. They had been close friends for much of their careers and collaborated on several occasions, flirting outrageously on camera at times.

Levi was confined to a wheelchair as the surviving Tops brought him out on stage to rapturous applause. Aretha urged: "It would be nice if you remained standing."

She really didn't need to ask.

Her favourite Four Tops track was I Believe In You And Me (which is my daughter's favourite song full stop), so they chose that and Levi's talented 'replacement', Theo Peoples, got things going before handing over to Aretha. Not knowing that she was the Queen of Soul, my then six year old daughter took an interest and said: "Wow! That woman can really sing."

(I'm teaching her well).

Then Levi cut in — and the voice was still there.

"A miracle!" Aretha exclaimed. One of the Tops had to whisper the lines into his ear as the others mopped his brow and wiped away his tears. *That* is why he never went solo — as I explained to my daughter — love. Levi died in 2008 at 72, the same age as my dad.

The vital similarities ended there.

· · ·

Soul music was my first love. Culturally, I've never followed the trends. Not a deliberate thing to try and be different but I'm like that to this day. As a journalist, I'm all too aware of spin and image management. I try not to do either because I've seen from a relatively young age how dangerous that can be in politics and the media.

I got into "The Godfather of Soul", James Brown, in my teens. I was totally obsessed. I was first drawn to him when he featured in a video on BBC show Top of the Tops with 1988 track I'm Real, recorded with a group called Full Force. I bought the album the next day. I was hooked. JB funk gave birth to the rap era. He is the most sampled artist of all time and despite having his first hit in 1956 — Please, Please, Please — he enjoyed a popular rebirth from the mid-Eighties to the early Nineties. But my stepdad, Rob, who happened to have played the bass guitar briefly in an indy band, was quite disparaging about JB. He used to say: "Boom bloody boom."

I couldn't understand that reaction. I've always liked bassy music, maybe thanks to my Brixton roots. I'm not much of a dancer but I *feel* that bass. JB was never a political thing for me and he did some pretty awful things during his life but he also co-wrote and sang Say It Loud – I'm Black And I'm Proud, in 1968. It became an anthem in the fight for racial equality during that era and reclaimed the word "black".

I do believe "natural sense of rhythm" is something that can be said about black people as a huge, over-arching generalisation. It would almost be more remarkable if there wasn't a genetic link. Many years ago, over lunch with a white, middle class, Jewish colleague, he was telling me that the whole "natural sense of rhythm" thing is a "myth" and we're all born the same. I told him I disagreed (although, I'm sure there's plenty of black people who, like me, have no natural sense of rhythm).

The funny thing was that he was studying dance at the time. After I left that paper, Nad told me this guy performed in the office and everyone was on the floor, dying of laughter at his David Brent-like display. So I guess his proof wasn't in his pudding.

. . .

As mentioned in the previous chapter, it's interesting how little a part the legacy of slavery plays in popular black culture. So I was quite struck by some of the lyrics when I first heard this passage by the unique, late, great "gangsta soul" singer Nate Dogg's track Music And Me:

Oh my goodness, what my ancestors gave
I don't want you to think I don't know
They taught me how to reach deep down and touch
the soul

Nate Dogg had an amazing voice, up there with the greats. But his career took an unusual trajectory as a member of the G-funk scene. He carved out a little niche for himself. Much of his music featured his dysfunctional relationships with women, with breathtaking honesty and attitude. And he collaborated with an array of high-profile rappers, including the likes of Dr Dre, Snoop Dogg, Ludacris and Eminem. He died in 2011 aged 41 after suffering multiple strokes.

I find the creativity of black people as a whole is remarkable considering what they've been up against for hundreds of years. A phenomenon. And I believe I get the point about "keeping it real". To me, it's just about getting up in the morning not knowing what's gonna go down and how I'll deal with it. I cry hard and I laugh harder. There's a subtle difference between being weak and being vulnerable. I consider myself to be vulnerable because, whatever life throws at me, I keep an open heart. I wear it on my sleeve and I'm not afraid to speak my truth. I have mellowed a bit over the years but when push comes to shove...

I have a sense of my own soul and I feel a connection with certain soul singers. Sometimes it can vary from track to track with the same artist but I recall Lionel Richie saying soul music is about "revealing the soul".

Most of the white people in my life, which is about half, feel nervous when I speak my mind. It doesn't fit into normal English culture at the lower middle class level. Specifically Jamaicans, take it up a notch. I remember being on a football playing trip up to Lancashire and Mr. T played some Ice-T on some little speakers on the train. I felt uncomfortable about it at the time. All our teammates were white and his work colleagues were mainly senior to him. I guess he did it to just let them know what he thought. A power grab.

My British-Pakistani friend Nad put it to me like this: "When you are mixed culturally, there is conflict and from conflict comes creativity."

Much as I am in awe of the seemingly endless line of black music artists with amazing talent (said by some to be the result of an "oral tradition"). Don't get me wrong, I'm not against white music. My favourite song lyrics are found in Pink Floyd's Wish You Were Here. I listen to that track every now and then to work out where I am in my life. Cat Stevens is an incredibly soulful singer, I feel his soul bursting out of his music. Rod Stewart's got a great voice and I quite like Spandau Ballet. Dolly Parton is not an obvious choice but I reckon she's a seriously underrated singer-songwriter and has a distinctive way to capture and deliver lyrics. The Bee Gees were great in their own way and fantastic songwriters, up there with the very best. Love love love The Rolling Stones. And, of course, Michael Jackson.

But whether it's about boxing or music, there is a phrase which bothers me: "The Great White Hope."

Why does there have to be one? Has there ever been a call for "The Great Black Hope"? In my opinion, Percy Sledge does a better version of Love Me Tender than Elvis. The King grew up in a black area and became the white man with a black voice. I wrote that in an essay when I was 17 at Merton College and my English teacher noted on it, without an ounce of sarcasm: "I didn't know that."

Being white and handsome, Elvis was suddenly someone with a massive *constituency*. He was good but not that good. I remember when Rick Astley burst onto the scene in the Eighties, no one realised he was white until he turned up on Top of the Pops with Never Gonna Give You Up. He was good but were black artists getting a raw deal because of the commercial drive behind promoting white artists with black voices? There's a whole history of it going back to the likes of Cilla Black covering Dionne Warwick hit Walk On By. I saw the latter live in London in the mid-Noughties and she said on stage that if she'd coughed in the middle of the track, Cilla would have coughed in her version as well.

Mr. T said that when he heard Adele for the first time, he thought she was black. I didn't but the aspiration is to be culturally black in so many creative fields. I know this is not the US, yet the following point applies in the UK as well…

The Hunger Games actress Amandla Stenberg asked: "What would America be like if we loved black people as much as we love black culture?"

14. Getting physical

'We know you're a convicted rapist'

The Sun's front page splash headline on Tuesday, September 3, 2003, was: "BONKERS BRUNO LOCKED UP."

As I mentioned in the opening chapter, the former heavyweight champion of the world was admitted to Goodmayes (psychiatric) Hospital, east London, where I was locked up in the summer of 2008. There was a huge backlash to the Bruno headline.

Editor of the paper at the time, Rebekah Brooks (then "Wade"), told the 2014 Screws hacking trial at the Old Bailey that she only realised her "blind spot" when she returned home with a copy and was alerted by her then husband, EastEnders actor Ross Kemp. As the first editions of The Sun turned up at the newsstands, enraged listeners contacted BBC Radio 5 Live, calling for a boycott of the tabloid. Brooks confessed she had approved the front page. She went on: "I got home, put the proof down and Ross said, 'What's that? What are you doing?'

"Looking again, it was a complete blind spot. Ross had seen the front page and questioned how brutal it was. It was a terrible mistake I made."

The headline was changed to "SAD BRUNO IN MENTAL HOME" in later editions and the incendiary word "nut" was removed from the story. But the storm of protest from readers and charities included SANE slamming the tabloid's initial stance as a betrayal of those with mental health problems. Chief executive Marjorie Wallace said: "Such ignorant reporting does both the media and the public a huge disservice."

The furore didn't register particularly strongly on my radar, even though I was working for The Sun at the

time. I just thought it was par for that paper's course.
I wouldn't be sectioned and incarcerated for another
five years so I wasn't particularly preoccupied with
mental illness issues. I used to think my mood changes,
aggression and depression etc., were because I wasn't as
strong as most other people.

. . .

When I sat down to watch Bruno fight Mike Tyson live
on TV in the early hours of February 25, 1989, I had
no idea that the three of us have something in common:
Bipolar. Or bipolar affective disorder, to give it its full
title. England football legend Paul Gascoigne has it as well
and I wonder, with the benefit of hindsight, whether his
extraordinary presence on the pitch was linked, in some
way, to his affliction. The first England manager to give
him a cap was Sir Bobby Robson, who famously branded
Gazza "daft as a brush".

Bruno said boxing saved him from a life of crime but
I always had concerns about the portrayal of him as an
"Uncle Tom". I thought he was a genuinely decent, honest
man. I was definitely supporting him. As well as being
British, he was a massive underdog. And he was brave:
I recently watched a documentary where a second cousin
of Muhammad Ali said his relative "transcended sport" but
that Tyson, in his prime, was "the greatest" boxer of all time.

Tyson wasn't a hero of mine then, I just loved to watch
him fight. Raw energy. Raw power. Raw talent. Raw. And
despite his image, a genuine student of the sport.

Several thousand, mainly white, British Bruno fans
flew to Las Vegas to see the fight. Even they weren't
optimistic, though, with many betting against him.

I bought a DVD of that fight to research this piece and it wasn't quite how I remembered (it was over 30 years ago). Bruno actually did quite well. He gave it a shot and fought dirty, which went against his gentle giant reputation. But when you're in there with *Tyson*…

Bruno's main tactic to stifle his opponent was to hold the back of his neck. He lost a point over it but I'm sure both fighters knew it was never going to go the distance. It was gonna be a flurry of shots combo as part of a destruction by prolific knockout artist Tyson or, less likely, the slower and more cumbersome Bruno hitting the jackpot with a haymaker. The pattern of the fight sort of turned out to be a mixture of the two.

Bruno was knocked to the floor in the opening exchanges but got up on the count of four. Both continued to show aggression and with a left hook-right hand combination, Bruno rocked Tyson towards the end of that first round. It is generally acknowledged to be the first time the young champion had been hurt during his professional career. I recall legendary BBC boxing commentator Harry Carpenter vigorously urging Bruno on but the Brit was unable to capitalise on his fleeting advantage.

Eventually, Tyson's pedigree won the day and he scored a TKO (technical knockout) in round five. In the ring, he told the interviewer: "I refuse to go down."

Bruno eventually went on to achieve his dream of becoming world heavyweight champion when he beat Oliver McCall for the WBC version at Wembley Stadium in 1995. He was very emotional after that fight and addressed those who had branded him an Uncle Tom. In tears, he simply said: "I love my people."

And in a TV interview a few years ago, Bruno discussed the issue of marrying a white woman and having three mixed race kids with her. He told Piers Morgan: "No one's telling me who I'm allowed to fancy."

Again, I wouldn't exactly describe myself as a "fan" of Tyson when me, Mr. T, his brother, "Evil Stanley" and Brian would huddle together in my tiny Railton Road flat in the late evening getting "strunk" (stoned and drunk) in anticipation of his fights following his release from jail in 1995 after doing three years' jail for rape. Tyson produced the ultimate form of entertainment and I say that as a football man.

The fights in the US were generally due to start at around 4am UK time. Such a lot of anticipation. You always knew *something* would happen in his fights. Anything. Always. A savage destruction. A shock defeat. A humiliation. A bitten ear. It was savagery in the early days. He was fucking electric.

Despite the anticipation, it was a struggle to stay awake, especially under the influence, and not everyone made it to 4am (Brian). But I always did, just about, and when I saw him emerge in his emblematic black trunks, I'd get a rush of adrenalin. He had my full, undivided attention and I was totally awake. I used to imagine what it must have been like seeing him in the opposite corner before the bell went. That thought still sends a chill down my spine.

Tyson had the lot: The speed of a middleweight, relentless combinations, punching power, durability and excellent movement, with a relatively low centre of gravity, always ducking and diving. Most of all, he had killer instinct. He was similar to Joe Frazier, the opponent who gave Ali most problems when they were at their peak. But Tyson was better than both of them, in my opinion. It was like a powerful soul flowing through a powerful body.

He was The Baddest Man on the Planet, whether he liked it or not.

I believe there is reasonable doubt that Tyson was guilty of rape.

How his 1992 trial went down has been done a thousand times. Seriously, there's a book in it (there have probably been many). But to give you an idea, three of the (exclusively white) Midwest jurors have since voiced their concerns after becoming aware of evidence excluded by the judge simply because it was submitted late on. Firstly, three eye witnesses said they saw the "victim", Desiree Washington, snogging him in his limo before they entered his Indianapolis hotel room. That contradicted her testimony, although snogging is obviously not the same as consent.

Secondly, and more damningly, she told her strict, Christian father that her (white) ex-boyfriend raped her after he found out they had fornicated, some months before she met Tyson. She told her ex that she had to "cover herself", otherwise her father "would kill me" for having sex outside of marriage.

Tyson's defence team was put together by larger than life boxing promoter Don King. They were hopeless. A key piece of evidence they failed to seize on which was heard in court is that she went into the hotel room's lockable bathroom — which had a phone — to remove her panty liner because she was expecting her period. She didn't have a replacement.

I am no rape apologist, if I thought he was guilty then I wouldn't be a "fan". And I'm aware — as is he — that he's done many terrible things in his life. It's just that he doesn't want to be remembered for something bad he didn't do. Yes, he was a violent person, boxing is a violent sport. And yes, he's done some pretty bad things to women over the years, by his own admission.

But Tyson could have got out of jail a year earlier if he'd 'fessed up'. Eight years later, he gave a TV interview, saying of his so-called victim: "I just hate her guts."

He added: "Now I really do want to rape her…and her fuckin' momma!"

I have to admit that I burst out laughing when he said that, there's a sort of perverse logic to it. Somehow, not the sort of thing a guilty man would come out with, I personally sense. The female interviewer was not impressed. But how the fuck would she feel if she was incarcerated for a crime she hadn't committed and had to spend the rest of her life registering as a sex offender, with the stigma of "convicted rapist" forever hanging large over her head?

I don't know how I'd process that, do you?

He declared bankruptcy in 2003 and his boxing career ended in humiliation two years later. He was treated as a freak show for many more years, still is to this day. I didn't know Tyson had bipolar until recently. But he speaks the truth the way he sees it and I identify strongly with that. In 2013, he did a one-man theatre show called Mike Tyson: Undisputed Truth, which toured the US and beyond. In a TV interview to promote the show, he was asked: "Are you a thespian?"

Tyson said: "I don't know about that."

Interviewer: "I'm not talking about your sexuality or anything, I'm talking about a thespian being an actor."

Tyson: "Thespian is named after an actor who won the acting award named Thespis in ancient times."

Interviewer: "That's the verbal equivalent of hitting me right on the jaw and flattening me."

I saw the one-man show on TV and loved it. He's a really interesting guy. His life has been beset by tragedy but he has this indomitable spirit. He also has a long history of blowing up and becoming verbally abusive during TV interviews and I have to admit I find it funny. A guilty pleasure. The producers are parasites. They *want* him to blow up so their show goes viral.

A TV appearance promoting his stage show in 2013 almost ended in him temporarily coming out of retirement. The black, Canadian interviewer opened up by referring to Tyson meeting Toronto's mayor, who was running for reelection, asking: "We know you're a convicted rapist, this could hurt his campaign. How do you respond to that?"

It was an ambush.

Tyson: "Hey, I don't know who said that, you're the only one I heard who said that."

His white promoter cut in and tried to defuse the situation but Tyson cut back in and said: "It's so interesting that you come across as a nice guy but you're actually a piece of shit."

Interviewer: "Hey, we're doing live TV."

Tyson: "I don't care, what you gonna do about it?"

Things deteriorated further before the interviewer rapidly tried to wrap things up.

He told Tyson: "Thank you for coming."

Off camera, Tyson says: "Fuck you!"

I found it hilarious but I wouldn't have blamed him if he'd swung for the interviewer. I'd like to have seen him tell Tyson he was a "convicted rapist" on the street. There's no way Tyson would have agreed to make that appearance if he'd known the dubious conviction was going to be brought up. It was like poking a bear with a stick through the cage bars. That the interviewer was black made it all the more shameful: Racism played a massive part in what I believe was his wrongful conviction. And yes, the interview clip did go viral.

Tyson's always been surrounded by parasites treating him as a commodity. Parasite-in-chief was King. He played a shameful part in putting his client behind bars. I don't know who said it but there's a great quote about King: "He acts black, lives white and thinks green [the colour of US dollar bills]."

Tyson admits he has difficulties in his relationships with women. His mother was a prostitute and the man "said to be" his father was a pimp. Tyson grew up seeing women being abused and that was the norm for him. Legendary (white) boxing coach Cus D'Amato took the then juvenile delinquent under his wing when he was around 12 and ended up adopting him. He predicted from the beginning that Tyson would be the youngest ever world heavyweight champ and, aged 20, it happened in 1986, a year after D'Amato died, aged 77. The fighter still says that he regards the trainer as his real father. And it's interesting to speculate on how differently his life would have worked out if D'Amato had stuck around a little longer. Tyson's training as a boxer was outstanding but he was not prepared for everything that comes with being an international megastar.

He is not generally treated as a "convicted rapist" these days (think cameos in Hollywood blockbuster The Hangover and its sequel, commercials and endless network TV interviews, for instance). I don't think he did it but I guess there are only two people who know what happened in that hotel room. One thing I have to say in Washington's defence, assuming she lied, is that she was only 18 at the time. She was a kid. And one thing that has to be said about Tyson is that sexual misconduct allegations had followed him around for much of his adult life. My contention is, ultimately and simply, that the conviction was unsafe.

These days, Tyson knows he'll never be wealthy again but says: "I'm in a good place."

He added: "My past doesn't control my life and the way I live today. I just don't know why people continue to take to me and make me relevant in life. I don't feel as relevant as people make me."

...

One of the things I found interesting when I was growing up in Brixton is that I'd often be privy to black people's conversations that others wouldn't. Most of the bouncers at The Ritzy were Nation of Islam dudes and I got on well with all of them. They never pushed any of their views on me and they weren't particularly aggressive or strong, silent types. But they were all physically confident. And you gotta know that if you're messing with one of them, you're messing with all of them.

Mr. T isn't NOI but his older, half-brother is and was a bouncer. Before England played a football match one evening in the early Nineties, he mumbled a comment about one of the black players who was getting a lot of stick at the time, Carlton Palmer.

The late Graham Taylor was not universally welcomed as England boss when he took over in 1990 and his most controversial selection during an unsuccessful tenure was the Sheffield Wednesday midfielder. Palmer got vilified in the media for his gangly style and lack of panache. It all seemed such a long way from the semi-final glory of Italia 90. Gazza and all that.

Mr. T's brother expressed his anger at the way Palmer was being castigated. It hadn't occurred to me that the criticism was racially-charged, until then. I was quite colour-blind when it came to football. I totally judged players on their merits and still do.

Palmer got 18 caps for his country. He was not a creative player but in many ways, he was ahead of his time. He was perceived as being ineffective by fans and football writers. But there's one thing I'm sure about, he *was* effective. He did the tackling and he did the running. Back then, there weren't many midfield "destroyers" in the English game. Mr. T told me recently how he initially almost bought into the media narrative on Palmer and then he read something and thought: "Hang on a minute, there's 11 players out there."

Palmer was not world class but as an Arsenal fan, there have been plenty of times I've thought we could have done with a player with his fighting spirit and work rate in recent years. Anyway, I concluded there were racist undertones to the whole affair. This was at a time when England's following was still full of NF and BNP sympathisers. They refused to celebrate when a black player scored for England. The funny thing about that is, by their reckoning, the Three Lions would have actually lost 1-0 to San Marino in 1993. Fortunately, Ian Wright (black) scored four, Paul Ince (black) scored two and Les Ferdinand (black) scored one to make it 7-1.

Despite the scoreline, other results meant it marked the failure of England to reach the 1994 World Cup finals in the US and was Taylor's and Palmer's last match at international level. Funny that I probably wouldn't have had an insight into the perception of Palmer had it not been for Mr. T's brother. And I was living in Brixton.

I should have known better.

I'm all too aware that I probably don't get the full picture, all the genuine opinions, from all sides when it comes to race. But I get more than most from all sides and I treat it as a privilege and an honour, whether it's coming from Asian people or black people...or white people.

...

As far as being colour-blind when it comes to football, white Dutchman Dennis Bergkamp is the greatest player I've seen in an Arsenal shirt, not black Frenchman Thierry Henry. But my worlds did start to collide a bit when a clutch of black south Londoners started to make it into Arsenal's first team during the mid-Eighties. I identified with the likes of Paul Davis, David Rocastle, Michael Thomas, Kevin Campbell and, later, Ian Wright. There was something familiar about them, I can't quite put my finger on it. But they were all approachable in the days when the fans were much closer to the players. And they had no airs or graces. All genuinely nice guys. Even after getting in the first team, Thomas used to volunteer at the Brixton sports shop where he'd worked on Saturdays before he became a pro. He went on to score the last-minute goal that snatched the title away from Liverpool in 1989.

I recently became aware of an amazing story about Thomas and that victory in the documentary film 89, which was released in 2018. The players came back from Liverpool on the team bus that night, which was the plan all along. They had phoned ahead to find a pub that would stay open late because this was in the days of restricted drinking hours. They headed straight there and ended up spending hours celebrating with the fans, even playing pool with them and giving away their club ties. But the extraordinary thing was that one (white) fan said he left the pub at 6am with Thomas and they walked down the street and saw a bundle of the morning's newspapers outside a newsagent's door. They opened it up, sat on the ground and started reading about the historic win together.

Somehow, I can't see Thierry Henry doing that.

As well as being good men, all these south Londoners were intelligent players in their own ways and I found that inspirational. Like I could relate to that because so many people seem to think I am stupid because of *my* south London accent.

Striker Campbell didn't live up to his potential at Arsenal but he went on to have a reasonably successful career elsewhere. He was good but not quite international class and Arsenal is a big, big club. Funny thing is that he actually lived on the next street from me in Brixton at one point and is only a few years older than me. We even played in the same Brockwell Park Saturday morning league over the fence. But he was presumably banned from it by Arsenal when they signed him as a schoolboy, so I never shared a pitch with him.

Anyway, one lovely summer's day, when I was about 18, I was wearing an Arsenal shirt walking around that area. This big, blue convertible BMW with the roof down pulled up to the lights and I noticed the young black guy behind the wheel was staring across at me. With my ghetto head on, I scowled at him, thinking: "What the fuck you looking at?"

The lights went green and he pulled away. Then it hit me: It was Kevin Campbell.

Part IV: Identity

15. Brown pride

'He lived life on his own terms'

My dad —"Peso" — shagged Debbie Harry. Or so he said. She may beg to differ. He was extremely drunk when he told me the story, which was short and sweet. I've retold it a thousand times and can now do it in under a minute. It was in the late Seventies and the Blondie pop superstar was sitting on her own at the bar of a five-star hotel (he didn't say which country, let alone city) when he approached her. They got chatting and she invited him up to her room.

They did the business and fell asleep. At 6am, he heard her say on the phone: "Get this joker out of here."

Next thing he knew, a huge minder burst in, dragged his naked, brown ass out of bed and propelled him into the hallway, throwing his clothes out after him. That's all I know and the rest died with Peso in 2016, a befitting year for one of the world's lesser-known superstars to pass away.

He had a framed picture of her on his bedroom wall, among his other trophies. Don't feel sorry for him. Peso wasn't particularly proud of the story because he would have liked to have said she fell madly in love with him and they toured the world together for six months before he decided she was too clingy. Then he would have tried to snare an even sexier and more famous celebrity. Whatever life gave him, he wanted more.

He was an impossibly difficult person to be around. A tragedy on so many levels. It's hard to deal with because I am like him in some ways. Much more decent, though, which, admittedly, is not particularly hard.

Part of the problem was that Peso was a superstar in his own mind. Feeding into that were real situations such as he and my mum being friends with Indian cinema legend

Shashi Kapoor at the height of his fame. He also mixed it up with the likes of TV's Kojak actor Telly Savalas. Apparently, they sat down and put the world to rights in a hotel bar late one evening well into the early hours over a bottle of whisky. And he ended up chatting at length with one of my great comedy heroes, Dudley Moore, in an executive airport lounge bar.

There's a recurring theme here: Bars.

...

My Indian family originate from Sindh, which is a region of what is now Pakistan. Sindhis are renowned for textile trading and smuggling. My great uncle had a sari shop in London's Chinatown, where I worked for a while, and Peso...

Hindu Sindhis had to up sticks and leave what is now Pakistan because of Partition, in 1947. My family were wealthy before that, old money. But they lost almost everything. It is a huge deal to those who had to make the journey. A source of great pain and resentment.

Peso was brought up as a little prince before being torn from his home aged four. I think it defined his life and his hatred of Muslims. After being uprooted and landing in Bombay, he went to the most exclusive school in India. His parents could just about afford it. Just about. And it happened to be in the same city. But most of his friends growing up were truly wealthy and he was extraordinarily jealous of that. Thus began a pattern of acting out, which typified him to pretty much the last weeks and days of his life.

But I was always proud of my Indian side and my low opinion of Peso was never something that I equated to him being Indian. I have had and continue to have close relationships with his sister and her two, Indian-German daughters. But 99 per cent of my "Indianness" is defined through Peso and what we had/have in common.

He was a terrible father but I learned a lot from him. Mainly what not to do. He wasn't happy. Peso was a career criminal, mainly smuggling cannabis. An alcoholic. A cokehead. A drug dealer. A compulsive gambler. A womaniser. A tyrant. He could be funny and charming, although less and less so over the years. And he could be mean and abusive, more and more so over the years.

My earliest memory of him is when I was five and, presumably travelling on a dodgy passport, he came to visit me at my Brixton squat home. He wore a white suit and a dark blue shirt, with the top three buttons undone. With his hairy chest, tash and gold medallion, he kinda looked like a Mexican pimp stereotype. I hope that's not a racist thing to say, he was my dad so I feel like I can get away with it.

I don't know the mechanics of all this but he had previously threatened to kidnap me if he found my mum in London and I was a ward of court for most of my childhood. But as I grew up, my desire to get to know him became stronger and stronger. That culminated with me visiting him in India when I was 11. The plan was for my mum and stepdad, Rob, to take me there and then Peso and me would go off and we'd have parallel holidays to my family unit. My younger, half brother came with them but my half sister was only one at the time so she stayed back with Rob's parents in Leicester and, incidentally, walked for the first time.

The culture shock was incredible but I felt protected *by* him from what India had to throw at me. Yet I didn't feel protected *from* him. However, that trip opened my eyes to loads of things and I'd say, on balance, it was a wonderful experience.

The first thing that hit me when we exited the aeroplane in Bombay was the heat. The second was the overwhelming stench of fish. It turns out it was "Bombay duck" being dried out on washing lines. Warning: If you're looking for a cheap duck there, be aware that Bombay duck is actually just a certain type of dried fish.

India is a crazy country and I have a love-hate relationship with it. I'd describe it as a world within a world. *Everything* you might look for in the world is in India. From the ancient to the ultra-modern. From the absolute best to the absolute worst. If it gives you any idea of the insanity, there are prisons in India that some are breaking *into* — for a better quality of life.

A white colleague told me he went to a cinema in Bombay just for the experience. Most moviegoers in India are pretty poor and are there because they can't afford a TV set. Anyway, halfway through the film, an entire row of seats collapsed. The funny thing is that the people in that row just got up and found other seats in the auditorium.

That is India.

My Indian family home is on Marine Drive, otherwise known as "The Necklace of Bombay" because of the way street lights illuminate the arching promenade for several miles at night. I always thought it was a special place but to my surprise and delight, it was chosen as a UNESCO World Heritage Site in 2018, so I wasn't alone in thinking it is special. In my mind, I can put myself in that flat at any given moment.

Peso gave me a tour of northern India when I was 11 but the memory that sticks out on that visit is one of the few times I was around my Indian grandad. Bearing in mind he hadn't seen me since I was a baby, the day after I arrived, he quietly took me into the kitchen, sat down on a little chair, held me by the arms as I stood before him and just looked into my eyes for a few minutes. It felt natural. *Indian*. He wanted to get a sense of who I was. I will always treasure that moment.

After that holiday, Peso would visit me in London virtually every year. His trips usually revolved around the flat track horse racing season, The Oaks and The Derby in particular. He would take me for pizza and curry in Bayswater, central London. It was nice, mostly. I also did quite a bit of underage drinking, which was fun.

My mum would get tetchy whenever I got close to him.

I had well-off Indian relatives in a leafy, posh part of north London and we used to have dinner with them at their luxury, St John's Wood apartments about once every time Peso visited London. I didn't enjoy it. They would usually talk endlessly about the price of Black Label whisky and relatives' wills. I would always do or say something wrong, such as, aged 15, telling them I'd smoked cannabis. Peso would give me such a hard time over whatever I had done "wrong" afterwards. Every single time.

Back when I was a teenager, he had no understanding or interest in how I had been brought up in a white family. And he was the drug smuggler who'd been jailed at least twice. It all seemed so phoney.

Peso did his best to conform to his relatives' desire for him to be civilised but no one was fooled. The irony is that after being part of my ex's Sikh, Punjabi family for 14 years, I ended up knowing more about down to earth Indians than he did. He used to make so many faux pas with my in-laws. Different types of Indian families.

Peso was like a one-man travelling circus. It wasn't something he could turn off and on. When I still lived on The Frontline, I came with him to buy booze in Herne Hill, which is the other end of Railton Road and is actually quite well to do. We were in an off-licence and it was funny because everybody was getting a buzz off larger than life Peso. Just Peso being Peso. There was an American guy who seemed most amused...until Peso started slagging off Californian wine. This bloke took umbrage and I wanted to tell him: "You don't know what you're getting into here, buddy."

It did turn nasty but thankfully, not violent. Close, though. He always had an edge.

One of his little scams was printing travel agents' business cards to get discounts when he was abroad. I remember telling Mr. T this story on a train up North and this older, middle class, white woman couldn't help but earwig the conversation and bleated: "But that's fraud!"

Although he was obsessed with money, a lot of what he got up to was just to amuse himself — and he could afford to be much wilder in India than in Europe.

I have so many great stories about Peso, positive and negative. My favourite is when, aged 19, I was in Goa with him, my Indian grandmother and the older of my Indian-German cousins in my patchwork family. Peso was incredibly intelligent in his own way. Devious.

We turned up in Goa during the height of the season there, around Christmas time. We headed straight to the famous Taj Village hotel in the most upmarket tourist area. We went to the reception desk to secure one of the small villas, which were expensive even back then, around 1991. But they were fully booked. Peso would not accept this and demanded to see the manager. I can't remember the exact spelling but it always stuck out in my head that he was called "Mr Maskyouranus". He told Peso that he would let him know immediately when he had a vacancy (there were no rooms, just small villas dotted around a large, paradise garden). The manager gave Peso his card and told him we could use any of the facilities until a spot became available on the complex.

Within about 20 minutes of leaving the Taj, we had found a traditional Goan villa a ten-minute walk away. It worked out at something like £4 per night for two double rooms...and it was nice. So that was Peso's plan all along: Use of an exclusive, five-star hotel's facilities and two bedrooms in a villa for £4 a night. Frightfully unBritish. When a space at The Taj finally became available towards the end of our stay in Goa, we made ourselves scarce.

That's not the story.

One morning, he went off on his own, probably to score some coke, and I spent the day with my cousin and grandmother on a beach within walking distance of our villa. He wasn't there when we got back and, initially, we thought nothing of it. Then, after it got dark (I vaguely recall the sun rapidly sinking into the sea at around 6pm each evening), he turned up with two, small, Indian men in an auto-rickshaw. Peso approached me and, in hushed tones, immediately ordered me to fetch him two open bottles of tonic water, which I did. Peso downed them straight away, headed back to the auto-rickshaw and the three of them sped off.

A few hours later, he returned in his small, hatchback car (which had somehow got us from Bombay to Goa). He told us that he'd been driving under the influence and had shunted a moped ridden by an English couple off the road. Fortunately, they landed in a builder's sandpit, escaping with a few scratches and bruises. But understandably, they were incensed and the police soon turned up. Peso was obviously a rebel and, to a large extent, it's the law of the jungle on Indian roads. But there was one rule that virtually everyone obeys: "Stay at the scene of an accident."

(The Indian Highway Code is based on the British version but to "stay at the scene of an accident", they've added "unless you are unable to do so on account of mob fury". And they've added it for good reason. But that's another story.)

Realising he was in a pickle, Peso's criminal mind kicked in and, as he was led away, he persuaded the cops that he had good reason to let his family know what had happened. They believed him and an officer accompanied him in the auto-rickshaw. Peso deliberately got them lost for a few hours on the way to our villa. He was buying time to sober up. And, of course, when he finally did arrive, he downed the tonic water to thin out the alcohol, and whatever else, in his blood. Back at the police station, he awaited the formalities while wearing a T-shirt which he'd had made at Harrods a few years earlier. It was a picture of himself with the words "Wanted, $10,000" emblazoned across it.

After a while sitting on a bench in the station, one of the police officers stood up, pointed at Peso and shrieked: "Look! He's vanted! [wanted!]"

Yeah, great detective work. Eat your heart out, Columbo. I was on the floor when Peso told me this. Anyway, his sobriety test involved a nurse looking into his eyes! She told the officers: "He's perfectly sober."

The nurse was right, thanks to that criminal mind. I kinda got a kick out of what he'd done, although I'm sure I'd have felt differently about it if something serious had happened to the couple. I mean, he once nearly ran *me* down when he was drunk.

One of *his* favourite stories, which demonstrates the sheer breadth of his experiences, is about shagging a goat herder girl in the Indian countryside. A goat managed to get inside her hut and, while they were hard at it, the animal licked his anus! The herder girl burst out laughing. As interesting as my life has been, his was far more interesting. He used to say: "I could write volumes."

It's true in a way but he didn't have an authentic voice. His ego was so big that he was the story, not the storyteller. I would have happily ghostwritten his autobiography *if* he'd been open and honest about his life. How he felt. The times when he wasn't the hero. And so on. The stupid thing is that his real story was far more interesting and multi-layered than the one he was trying to present.

Peso was incredibly materialistic and selfish. The time he saw me when I was five, he gave me a little, cotton-strapped, red Timex watch. It was cute but he went on and on about it, even when I was an adult: "Hey Siddy, remember that watch I bought you?"

It probably only cost him £5 and this was a man who had two servants and a cook. And he would regularly travel to Singapore to get the latest technology, such as state-of-the-art video cameras, radios and sound systems.

When I was around 13, he took me ice skating in Queensway, central London, the area he hung around in when he was over. I was quite excited about it beforehand but at some point, it dawned on me that he wasn't going to partake. So I just ended up skating badly, alone on an empty rink with him watching from behind the glass with a stupid grin on his face, clutching shopping bags full of things he had bought for himself. Not a great father-son bonding session. He only ever took me once but he used to go on about that, too.

"Remember when I used to take you ice skating in Queensway, Siddy?"

He was a crook. I could write a chapter about all the times he duped *me* alone. These schemes were dubbed "Peso moves". Everyone who knew him could see what he was up to but you had to go along with it or he'd become a tyrant and a bully.

I used to have to pay for my own plane ticket to see him in India even as a humble projectionist earning £130 a week. I was arranging my flights with a local travel agents in Herne Hill when I was 19 and was so excited. They were great about it, excited for me. The problem was that the cheque I wrote for them bounced. It wasn't my fault, NatWest had withdrawn my overdraft facility without warning. It was such a shitty thing to do. It was so humiliating with the travel agents. They pitied me. NatWest eventually restored my overdraft but I had to do loads of running around and the travel agents kindly absorbed the £30 cost incurred to them for the bounced cheque. In the middle of all this, I had thoughts for Peso: "You're rich and I live in Brixton, why are you putting me through this? Don't you want to see me? Don't you want me to be happy? Don't you love me?"

These sort of ordeals don't do much for your self-esteem when you're growing up.

My mum, understandably, left him when I was a baby. They had been living in Rotterdam because he couldn't get back into Britain after being jailed and deported. The British Government had recommended to the Indian Government that he never be issued with a passport again. But things went pear-shaped and my mum headed back to

England — while Peso spent the rest of his life arguing the toss over the mechanics of the break-up. I found this tedious because I knew my mum did the right thing. I knew that because I knew him.

He paid practically nothing towards my upbringing. He would pay for dinner and drinks because he was enjoying them at the same time but that was it. His real name was "Pratap" but his obsession with money made it appropriate that "Peso" is also a form of currency in some countries. He got the nickname during his schooldays. It was something to do with his initials, as in PS. I did ask him about it once but that was all I could extract.

One thing I have to say for him, though, is that he wasn't a "coconut [brown on the outside but white on the inside]". The absurd thing is that he wanted to be white. He wanted the respect afforded to white people, from white people. He took great satisfaction in managing to get into an exclusive Bombay beach club which was only for foreigners. Perversely, even though being fair (short of actually being white) is generally (and shamefully) regarded as desirable in India, he would actively work on his tan on beach holidays.

Pick the complex ironies out of that. As Ice-T would put it: "He had his shit twisted."

My wannabe white dad presumed I wasn't into my Indian heritage so was quite tickled when I told him I got into loads of fights in my teens over being called a "Paki".

On the rare occasion he did go out of his way to do something nice for me, he usually got it wrong. So wrong. I was staying with him in Bombay in my early 20s and he took it upon himself to get me bacon and sausages for breakfast. I appreciated the gesture but I love Indian food and would anyway rarely eat bacon and sausages for breakfast in London. The worst thing though was that the meat was disgusting. Pigs literally eat shit out there and they're generally regarded by Indians as dirty animals. Relatives presenting Western food to me happens quite often when I visit Bombay. It's frustrating but I can't say anything after they've gone to all the trouble.

Peso was an educated man with a degree in chemistry but he could come out with the daftest things. And sometimes I saw him express himself in an Indian way which surprised...and amused. For instance, after his St John's Wood-based uncle died, Peso had to go to a bank around the corner from Piccadilly Circus. The plan was that we would meet up there. When I arrived, he was at the counter talking to a cashier on the other side of the window. When he'd finished, he started laying into me for wearing a leather jacket to the bank. He was quite angry about it and said I looked like a "football hooligan".

The idea of wearing a suit and tie to the bank would never have occurred to me, unless it was a proper meeting with the manager, I suppose. But in his Indian mind, you dress up for the bank in a suit and tie, even if you're just making a withdrawal. I thought it was quite sweet. But sweet is the last thing he would have wanted to be regarded as, so I kept my mouth shut.

One thing he said was just outright stupid and I felt quite embarrassed. We were walking past world-famous toy store Hamley's on Regent Street and they had this window display of a "robot" in a kitchen. Peso asked the security guard if it was a real robot. This was something made out of cardboard boxes and tin foil. I didn't say anything as I cringed. This somehow played into his coconut aspirations. He always wanted the latest gadgetry and, ironically, did not want people to think Indians are backward.

At other times, he was unintentionally funny in ways which didn't make me squirm. I was once talking to him about why he felt ashamed of Indians. The example he gave was about a flight over from Bombay when all the passengers were given paper slippers. The next day he was walking down Oxford Street and spotted one of the other Indian passengers who was on the flight and actually wearing the paper slippers! *That's* why Peso was ashamed of Indians. I think that's funny.

Peso was the type of criminal who didn't even adhere to the "honour among thieves" code. When you're close to someone like that you realise that it's a state of mind. A compulsion. But back before I was born, he was *framed* in London, admittedly for something he was doing. Peso maintained his bitterness about it over the years. From what I understand, he was using white women as drug mules. Attractive white women. The police knew what he was doing but they couldn't nail him. For Peso, this was just a big game. He thought there was a level of mutual respect with the cops as they played cat and mouse. There wasn't. In the end, they just put a note through his letterbox which read: "2lbs to arrive at 2pm."

Then they broke down the front door of his flat. The thing which surely wound up the officers even more was that Peso had plastered his kitchen walls with unpaid parking tickets. It's true to say he had contempt for the law, as is often the way with rich Indians. But they tend to get away with it "back home" by buying their way out of certain situations. It came to be that he was convicted and jailed on the flimsiest of evidence, the planted note. That's his side of the story.

I once asked him what he thought of the English. He put a few moments' thought into it, which wasn't his usual MO, and then said wryly: "They like their games."

I may never have come to be if he hadn't been jailed. He told me my mum was his "number three" girlfriend when he was locked up. But she kept coming back to see him and brought him cakes she'd made. So, by the time he got out, she was his "number one". They had met when he was running a stall in Petticoat Lane Market. She would have been about 20 and he was in his mid-20s. I think he was selling hats. They were an incredibly good-looking couple in their wedding photos. But I don't know what they had in common. My mum had a thing about dark men and my dad probably thought she was ladylike with her posh accent, as well as being beautiful. I asked him what they had going on between them in one of the last conversations we ever had. He said: "Our faces kinda fitted."

Not a great basis for a lasting relationship. Having said that, my mum was definitely the love of Peso's life. I'm not sure whether the reverse is true.

One of the cooler moments with Peso happened when he was setting up a drug-smuggling operation with me there in Bombay aged 19. He had invited a blond American in his mid-30s for lunch at his flat. As Peso sat there like a maharaja at the head of the table, eating Hindu-style, exclusively with his right hand, the stage was his. Apart from proclamations by him between mouthfuls of food, their conversation was minimal. The yank said next to nothing, perhaps because I was there and more likely because he was focused on the job in hand. He was dressed all in black, combat-style clothes. He had the air of a military man. I knew the nature of their business but it took me a little while to figure out what was going on. It all made sense when Peso said: "Let's get him out of bed to do some work."

It was a drugs mule he was referring to. It was all so coded. I wasn't shocked and I never judged Peso for his drug-smuggling activities because it was just pot and I was a pothead. But he applied his criminal mindset to all areas of his life. There were times when he would have sold his own mother down the river. In some ways, he did. Peso did deal coke to his mates but again, I didn't judge him. They were all super-rich arseholes, not crack whores. He sent me out to do some debt-collecting once. I think he was trying to teach me a lesson but it so wasn't me. I didn't want to be anything like him, with his life.

He had a set of tiny metal weighing scales, encased in a velvet-lined box, in his bedside table drawer. And a gun.

Peso was an out and out alpha male. Real macho. And he was pretty much fearless, which I respected. The time I was most proud of him was when I was in my mid-teens and he took me to see England play a friendly against Russia. For me to go to watch live football at Wembley with *my dad* was almost like a dream come true. So excited to be able to tell my mates: "*My dad* took me to watch England at Wembley."

The stadium was only a third full and although beer was being sold on the concourse, the tops were taken off the plastic bottles because booze wasn't allowed in the viewing areas of the stadium. But Peso being Peso (the alcoholic) wasn't having it. He told me to grip my open bottle under my armpit so we could sneak past the stewards into the seating areas. I refused. I didn't want to get ejected and, frankly, I thought I'd end up getting covered in beer. So he snatched mine off me and took both. Peso was always a big guy, a six-footer, like me, and he got fatter and fatter over the years, like me, so he looked even more like a gorilla with one bottle under each armpit. But he did it and we took our seats.

After about ten minutes, bearing in mind the game was so poorly attended, three, white, male England fans in their late 20s pitched up in the seats directly behind us. One started to subtly put his shoes onto Peso's leather jacket, which he was wearing. A realisation of the potential for trouble slowly dawned on me. I turned and looked at Peso. He was aware what was happening and I could see his blood steadily coming to the boil.

Then — suddenly — Peso rose halfway to his feet, turned around and just glared at the three of them while holding the back of his seat. They were totally unprepared for this course of events. I didn't want any trouble but it was a fight or flight physical moment for me and I guess, as the son of Peso, it wasn't going to be flight. They immediately put their feet down and it all went quiet. About ten seconds later, they started leaving. One of them had a parting shot: "It stinks round here."

Cowards.

My most ambitious attempt to get closer to Peso was in my early 20s. I flew to Bombay with the intention of spending time with him, maybe even living with him for a while. But he was an abysmal host. The madness of the way he lived his life was quite evident from the point I entered the flat he shared with my grandmother on Marine Drive. Since Partition, they had the flat with the exclusive address but there was a man who had a studio flat within it. After many, many years, they bought him out. The irony was that it cost them so much they had to move into the studio flat and rent out the rest of the space, for a while.

The worst thing for me was that, even though he had plenty of notice about my arrival, he hadn't organised any sort of bed for me, so I had to sleep on the *marble* floor, like a dog. No mattress. Not a wink. Thankfully, we were only due to hang around for a few days before heading to the family's house in the nearby city of Pune, which is dubbed a "hill station" because of its high altitude (giving relief from the searing heat during the summer months). It was the season at the racetrack there.

Peso was a serious alcoholic for most of the time I knew him. And he could be vicious when he was fully loaded. Drink-driving was (and presumably still is) quite common in India. Peso did it every day. He actually took drink-driving to a new level and it's quite funny in a way. Before we started out on our road trip, he filled a cooler box with huge bottles of Indian beer. It was placed somewhere in between the driver's seat and passenger seat of his 4x4. He happily swigged beers as he drove. I was drinking as well and thought it was pretty cool. God bless India!

When we were driving up into the mountains on the way, there was this massive working bull elephant on a quiet part of the journey. We stopped, in the clouds, to admire him and his tusks, which must have each been at least 4ft long. He slowly made his way from his handler to Peso's 4x4, put his trunk through my open window and tickled me under the armpits with it. I mean, the tickling did make me laugh. God bless India! It was a nice moment with Peso as well because he knew it was an "only in India" moment I was experiencing. Part of him wanted to share the joys of his homeland with me. He never realised I appreciated it as much as I did. Thinking about that scene always makes me want to go back — and miss the part of Peso I loved.

The Pune house, which was in a gated community, was a bit rundown but perfectly liveable. One day, Peso went off on his own for a few hours and one of the local cleaning girls caught sight of me and started laughing. It was probably the first time she had seen a 'white' man. She started summoning all her housekeeping friends, about a dozen of them. Men, women and kids of all ages. It was a hoot. I ended up giving them all bananas. It was like a little banana party. But then Peso's car turned the corner and they fled like an air raid siren had sounded.

The real problem though was that we would spend our days in a windowless bar at the racetrack and he would get increasingly legless on whisky. It was okay for me to start with on the beers but after about three days of this, I realised that I was getting hooked, so I stopped drinking. Then I realised that I could only be around him when I was drunk. Peso picked up on this and started bullying me on the ride back to the house. He was deliberately driving erratically and I put my seatbelt on for the first time on the trip. In reference to that, he bellowed: "We leave things like that to God in India!"

Then he started laying into me — about God knows what — as his driving got more and more reckless to intimidate me. Eventually, I said: "What's your problem? What do you want me to be, an obnoxious alcoholic?"

Predictably, that totally enraged him. When we got back to the house, I told him I was leaving. I went upstairs to get my things together and I was pretty cool about it. When I came down with my packed rucksack ten minutes later, he said: "I'll give you one last chance to apologise."

I said: "I'm not going to."

As I walked away from the house, I took one fleeting glance back and he was standing at the front garden gate. The last thing I heard was him shouting: "Okay, fuck off."

It was late at night and I made my way out of the gated community on foot and hailed an auto-rickshaw. The driver was trying me to sell me dope and hookers, which put my head in even more of a spin. I felt that if I had apologised to Peso then it would set a terrible pattern. An even worse pattern. I was quite focused as I found a coach to take me back to Bombay. They all have TVs blaring out Bollywood movies 24/7 and it does my head in, especially at night. But I suppose it keeps the drivers awake as we snake through the mountains. When I arrived back in Bombay, I headed to the family home on Marine Drive but my grandmother wouldn't let me in.

She said through the letterbox: "If he can't accept you then neither can I."

It was a horrible moment. But I quickly found a reasonable hotel and, somehow, ended up with some weed. I didn't have any rolling papers but I didn't want to leave the room as I absorbed everything that had happened over the previous few days. Wearing only my boxers, I stood in the bathroom and looked at myself in a large mirror. I could see Peso in my face and I felt a sudden surge of emotions running through my veins, like: "Does this mean I am gonna hate myself as well as him?"

He was my Achilles' heel. The next day, I made my way back to the financial district near Marine Drive to amend my ticket and organise my flight home. It was all pretty straightforward in the travel agents, especially by Indian standards. I don't know why but I told the guy behind the counter: "I fell out with my dad so I have to go home."

He said: "Ohhh nooa."

As I turned away, I could feel myself welling up. There was something so genuine in that man's voice. I didn't realise I had tears inside me over this episode until then. I walked over the road to the promenade and, not for the only time in my life, sat down on a bench, leaned forward, head in hands and cried my eyes out for ten minutes. I felt so good afterwards, like I let the pain out. Every moment around Peso was about containing him. I had to put my own needs aside whenever I was with him and that takes its toll, sooner or later. He gave me a lot of emotional problems.

I have what may seem like a petty example of his selfishness but it is symbolic. Many years later, I was having dinner with him and my aunt in an excellent Chinese restaurant in the Cricket Club of India, which is a posh, members-only institution just off Marine Drive. There are so many little things I had in common with Peso that were not learned and one of those was our mutual love of a decent creme caramel.

As always, he was quite loaded and we both wanted the same dessert but there was only one creme caramel left. He insisted on having it because it went well with his brandy. There is something telling in this. I was a grown man but I was still *his child*. My daughter is only seven at the time of writing and I would put myself second to her on just about anything. I would always let her have the pick, aged seven, 17, 27, 37 and 47. I'll be 103 when she's 57, so I think I'll deserve the creme caramel by then. We'll see.

I have to say though that Peso did come through for me at my wedding in 2001, against all expectations. He provided me with an incredibly classy Indian outfit. It was nicely understated and beautifully tailored, perfect fit as well, even though I hadn't been measured up. He was the star of the show that day and he lapped up every moment.

During the three-hour ceremony, there was a lot of music in the Sikh temple (Gurdwara). It was something I enjoyed a lot as a regular visitor at my ex in-laws' Gurdwara in East Ham, east London. But Peso didn't know the score and managed to drop one giant bollock. The musicians played a particularly inspirational piece and at the end he started clapping and hollering as the hundreds of guests looked on in silence…and horror. Devotional Sikh music is not there to be clapped. It not a fucking gig.

A few days later, he visited me at my flat in Brixton and presented me with "the world's best fake Swiss Army knife". He put it down on the coffee table and told me: "Don't pick it up until I've gone."

But Peso obviously wasn't a disciplined sort of person and after five minutes he was like: "Go on, play with it."

He wanted to see me with the knife. But I declined, stating that his original thought process was correct. It felt like a rite of passage and I remembered a story he told me about how his father had slit the throat of a burglar back in Sindh. Before Peso flew back to India and I was about to go off on holiday, we spoke on the phone and, for the only time I can remember, he told me in earnest: "I love you."

He almost whispered it. I thought things were gonna get better with him after that. Sadly, they didn't. A few years later, me and my now ex were renovating a bungalow in a conservation area of Goodmayes, east London, and he visited us. Peso wanted to take a picture of us outside next door because our house wasn't quite finished. Do I have to explain the wrongheadedness of this? It said a lot about the way he thought. Things like that were no big deal, the alcoholism was the relationship killer.

One of the things he did in the last few years before I cut contact with him was the most innocent swizz imaginable. His mum was sick in a private, Bombay hospital for many months. Peso put a stethoscope on his dashboard and when he turned up in his 4x4, the parking attendants waved him through, with big smiles, to the doctors' parking area. This went on for quite a while. And they didn't think he was just a doctor, they seemed to be under the impression he was the top doctor in the whole hospital, such was Peso's feel for street theatre. But they finally cottoned on, when I was with him, and with a smirk, he pleaded his innocence: "I never said I was a doctor!"

After the attendants realised, they would look at him daggers as he made his way through to the paid visitors' section, giving him backchat, which further amused him. And me.

I cut off ties with Peso around six years before he died. Getting him out of my life was an act of self preservation as I recovered mentally from being sectioned several times. Also, I was unable to handle him the way I was before I met my now ex. They fought like cat and dog. Arguing with drunks, what can I say about that?

A few years after I told him I'd had enough, he sent me a handful of photos of himself. I'm sure a lot of people would consider that quite touching. I wasn't one of them. I wanted him, for once in his life, to put it on the line and act like a real parent. A real father. To overcome his mammoth ego and find the words to make me feel that I wasn't just one of the last remaining members of his ever-dwindling audience. I suspected that he had Narcissistic Personality Disorder, which is largely regarded as untreatable. He had a catchphrase before handing out some unsolicited advice: "Siddy, always remember in life…"

Then would come the unwanted nugget of 'wisdom'. I did not want his life. And there was no limit to his delusions. He once took me to an awful Italian restaurant in Bombay and got so drunk that he proclaimed, in all seriousness, that he was going to be the next prime minister of India.

I didn't hate him but over the years, the negative impact of his visits to London became greater and greater. The build-up, the reality, the aftermath. I did what I had to do and I don't regret it. I knew his health was declining over the next few years because his sister would fill me in. He eventually became bed-bound and it was only going one way.

In September 2016, my aunt asked if I could come over because she "didn't want to make the big decisions" on her own. She arranged my flights to Bombay, days before I was put "at risk" of redundancy at The Sun. Holding back tears, I recorded a video for him, saying I was on my way and I believe, via my aunt, that, even though he was delirious, he understood at some level that I'd made contact.

That video was the only time I ever addressed Peso as "dad".

Sleep deprivation is just about the worst thing you can do if you have bipolar but I stayed up all night listening to music before my flight. A strange thing happened on the way out. Although my Indian family are Hindus, they follow Sikh teachings. One of the articles of faith is a "kara", a bangle worn around the right wrist. I was given a gold one by my in-laws on the day I married. Eventually, I took it off because I didn't want to get mugged for it and bought a steel replacement.

I always wore it but was asked to take it off at Heathrow security to be put through the scanner. With other things on my mind, I forgot about the kara on the other side. I went back for it a minute later but it was gone. Someone must have taken it. When I returned from Bombay, I was wearing my late father's silver kara, which he'd originally spirited away from my mum when they were together before I was even born. So it's like one of the few things that is both my mum's and my dad's. Like me. It's as if something deep in my unconscious mind knew I would soon have a replacement.

Peso had been stretchered out of his flat on Marine Drive to hospital an hour before I arrived there. I got to see him a few times while he was unconscious on a life support system. A few days after my arrival, his heart packed up. His sister and I were very supportive of each other over the next few days. A philosophical friend of hers said of Peso: "He lived life on his own terms."

That was the best thing anybody could say about him, especially because it was true. I would say "he wasn't a good man but he had good in him". He did. I do believe in the adage that sons pay for the crimes of their fathers and even though he cut me out of his will, I don't bear a grudge. It makes it easier to forgive Peso knowing that he didn't realise what a destructive person he was. He never got a break from himself, not a moment's peace.

"Forgive them for they know not what they do."

I wept every day for a year after he died and then I pretty much stopped. I did get to know my father but he didn't *really* know me and that is a source of great sadness. Peso didn't *really* know anybody, not even himself. *Especially* not himself. Always projecting outwards with no reflection. He was an extremely damaged person.

He put me through a lot of shit. But we did love each other. The early years when he came over to London for a few weeks during the summer and we'd do beers and pizza, we'd spend loads of time together and it was mostly good fun. The last evening before he left was always hard and emotional. There was a point in the bowels of Oxford Circus Tube station where we would part, him heading north on the Bakerloo Line to his uncle's pad in St John's Wood and me southbound on the Victoria Line to my little flat on Brixton's Frontline. At least one metaphor in that geographical juxtaposition for anyone who knows London.

We would have a little hug and a kiss. He had a certain smell. Not a good smell or a bad smell but a "Peso smell". Like something out of March of the Penguins that helped parents find their mate or chick. A "that's my daddy" smell. Then we would part. I would have a stiff upper lip as we peeled away from each other. But I quickly welled up when he was out of sight, though I never broke down and wept. My thought was always: "When will I see my dad again?"

I still get a lump in my throat when I pass through that spot in Oxford Circus station. The world is a less colourful place without Peso.

My dad.

16. The silent majority

'That's white progress'

I've only ever heard white people say: "We're all the same."

I believe each and every person on this planet is unique. Even Ant & Dec (as it turns out). I should start off by saying that, obviously, there are many different types of white people across the globe. To be honest, *my* racial complex about white people is rooted in *my* white, English family. Even though I grew up on The Frontline, I now know what it's like to have "white privilege", most of all because I largely ended up losing it before even being aware I'd had it. A painful process.

Snoop Dogg says: "I don't trip to get a chip off a nigga's shoulder."

Yes, I have a chip on my shoulder. It's there for a reason. So don't tell me who I am and why I am the way I am. As reggae revolutionary Bob Marley sang:

We refuse to be
What you wanted us to be
We are what we are
That's the way it's going to be

It's hard to separate class and race in Britain. Looking back, my stepdad's white, working class parents instilled a lot of the values I hold dear to this day. They were Scottish and lived in the heart of Leicester's Asian community. It was great for me because I loved shopping on my own round the corner for Indian comics as a young boy on the city's famous, Hindu "Golden Mile".

We loved visiting them in their tiny terraced home in a quiet cul-de-sac. Before retiring, Granny was a district nurse. She'd be chain-smoking and supping whisky throughout most days in their living room. Granny would always make a wonderful trifle loaded with far too much sherry for our visits. I was its biggest fan. Her recipe is still in circulation many years after she passed away and someone in my extended family usually has a crack at it for Christmas Day.

We'd stay with them for a few nights and there was so much laughter and fun. Grandad was very droll and happy. And they were in love with each other for the entire time I knew them. Quite remarkable. Once, Grandad had a glass of whisky in one hand, a cigar in the other and proclaimed: "It's terrible what us working classes have to put up with."

As well as being down to earth, they were smart. Classy in their own way. The way they conducted themselves. And they were good to me. Not that she was doing it specifically for my sake but Granny used to make samosas and they were delicious. There was some sort of symmetry in that for me.

We used to drive up there before Christmas to pick up presents from them. The car would be bulging on the way back. The boot looked a bit like the back of Father Christmas's sleigh and all their gifts for us were marked: "From Santa."

None of what they gave us was particularly expensive but just fed into the whole sparkle of the festive season. They would give the kids a large bag of assorted sweets and Christmas wasn't officially over for me until mid-January when I'd finished the last of them, the (green, boiled) ones I liked least.

I felt so relaxed up in Leicester. I thought it was the best place in the world and should be the capital city of Britain. But I suppose my warm feelings about it were largely down to Rob's parents. One time when we were there, it was coming up to my mum's birthday. She was upstairs and I was downstairs with Granny, who politely instructed me: "Go and ask your mum what she wants for her birthday."

I duly obliged and she said she wanted an iron. I went downstairs and told Granny: "She wants a SodaStream."

That's the Peso in me.

Anyone who knows my mum would know that a contraption which carbonates sugary drinks is the last thing in the world she would want, short of a nuclear warhead or, worse still, a KFC box meal. But everyone thought it was so funny that Granny sent my mum a cheque with a little note which read: "For the SodaStream."

To my mum's credit, she did actually buy one with the money.

The whole experience was a huge contrast to visiting my English, upper middle class grandmother's huge mansion in a Hampshire village. My English grandad, who had bipolar and looked a bit like me, died of a heart attack when I was very young. But my grandmother married again and her second marriage was said to be a lot happier than her first.

It always struck me that upper middle class English people tend to have cold homes, like it's some sort of metaphor. It's a constant source of fascination to me how the English (strictly speaking, British, I know but I always think, "English") ended up ruling a quarter of the planet. Whatever the rights and wrongs of the British Empire, that obviously required a lot of intelligence. My 'inside knowledge' about the English would say the key to it is about looking outwards rather than inwards. I mean, trying to impose certain ways of being on other people. Of conquest. My now ex made an observation about the subtext of every Daily Mail headline: "We're so wonderful, so why aren't we happy?"

She used to work for them and, for the eagle-eyed hacks among you, note that it's even a Mail-style question mark headline.

It's interesting for me to get a view of white people from non-whites. I do often tend to have this affinity with black and Asian people. A few days before the time of writing, I was having a fag while waiting for a night bus home at 2am on a Sunday morning in Brixton. This white girl who was with a group of black girls asked for a ciggie and I gave her one. Then this big, young black guy in a hoodie coat came up to me and asked for one as well. The dialogue went something like this:

Him: "Can I have a smoke?"

Me: "Sorry, I only give one away a day."

Him: "A black man *like me?*"

Me: "What's black got to do with it?"

Thinking back to the skateboard park in Kennington when I was seven, me again: "I'm black, in my own way."

His face lit up with a smile. Then he raised his arm and we did a fist bump. I still didn't give him a fag, though. Blackness is so overanalysed and culturally raped and yet there seems to be little genuine enquiry about how black people regard white people.

I got back in touch with Ralph in the early Noughties after one of our old (white) school friends died. Ralph said: "My aunt told me that white people won't be around for me when I grow up. She gave that to me."

I suppose I imagine I'd be a lot angrier if I was black. I'm certainly a lot angrier than Ralph. I mean, I've come across plenty of angry black people in my life. But the vast majority don't seem to get too caught up in racism issues and politics. They are aware of it but seem determined not to let their disadvantages stop them enjoying themselves. Most of the staff at my local Sainsbury's store in West Norwood are black and I once asked one: "Why are you all so happy?"

She said: "We make each other happy."

That's in contrast to a white relative of mine, who said: "Black people cause all the problems on the buses round here."

I don't think that's true, apart from the 14-year-old black schoolgirls who are pretty boisterous. I don't want them to scrutinise me, it would be embarrassing but I actually find it quite uplifting that they are so confident and animated. Like they are going to enjoy the journey of life no matter what. Something vital and vibrant in the human spirit.

West Norwood is like 'Brixton Lite'. The same multi-cultural feel — racial harmony — but without a lot of the rough and tumble. That suits me where I am in my life. It feels like home now, although The Frontline will always be my spiritual home.

...

When I was researching this chapter, I came across a US article about explaining white privilege to a broke white man. The key points were:

- "I can turn on the television or open to the front page of the paper and see people of my race widely represented."
- "When I am told about our national heritage or about 'civilisation', I am shown that people of my colour made it what it is."

- "If a traffic cop pulls me over or if the IRS (Inland Revenue Service) audits my tax return, I can be sure I haven't been singled out because of my race."
- "I can if I wish arrange to be in the company of people of my race most of the time."

I find that the vast majority of people of colour are proud of their backgrounds. White people in Britain are the "host" population and have the dominant culture. They are the "norm", the "default". That's not a *problem* in itself but it manifests itself in white people being more concerned about asserting their individuality rather than defining their identity through their racial make-up. Of course, some white people do assert their racial identity and many of those, unfortunately, tend to assert it in a racist way.

Brian once wistfully told me: "When you're white, you have nothing."

I said to him: "But you're *Irish*."

I found it extraordinary that he was having such problems with his identity. I still don't know what to make of it but looking back, he was always trying to mark himself out as different, while I was, at the time, always doing my best to fit in. Somewhere. Turns out it was the funky part of south London all along.

I'm fascinated by the concept of Irish people, among others, being the closest that white people get to being "black". Of course, in the past, before race hate legislation came into force, landlords in English towns put up signs in their windows saying things such as: "No blacks. No Irish. No dogs."

I went through a period at The Sun in the Wapping days when I went to a pub where none of my colleagues would go, The Pepper Pot. It was quiet and they had regulars, many of them Asian. It was nice. But there was this old, white man who, always wearing a suit and a trilby hat, used to sit there every night on his own nursing a pint of Guinness. Probably being a bit "high" at the time, I decided to pull up a chair and talk to him. He was in his 80s and told me he'd come over from Ireland because of the crippling poverty in the Fifties at a time when the Irish would mainly travel in the holds of ferries.

Echoes of slavery.

. . .

Even Nad says I "racialise everything". But I was recently having a curry with one of my mum's (white) ex-boyfriends, who lived on The Frontline for a period when I did. He said that he used to eavesdrop on black men and noted how race was often introduced into the conversation when someone was telling a tale: "Yeah, white man."

It wasn't meant as a good thing/bad thing, just a thing. Maybe I picked up on that on some level. I firmly believe that any white adult who looks at a black man, sees a black man. This is not necessarily a bad thing. I've just always been fiercely adamant that I'm half Indian. Proud. I want people to see that I'm not white, despite a skin tone which varies greatly depending on the prevailing weather conditions. There was a time when The Sun was taking on its first black sub-editor and Arrogant Twat took umbrage to me making reference to this guy's race.

He asked me: "Is that what you see, a black man?"

I said: "Yes!"

Arrogant Twat said: "Well, I just see a man."

I'm sorry but bullshit. Maybe I am the problem but again, I come back to Why I'm No Longer Talking To

White People About Race author Reni Eddo-Lodge, who wrote: "Colour-blindness is a childish, stunted analysis of racism. It starts and ends at 'discriminating against a person because of the colour of their skin is bad', without any accounting for the ways structural power works in these exchanges. This definition of racism is often used to silence people of colour when we attempt to articulate the racism we face. When we point this out, we are accused of being racist against white people."

When I was at The Sun during my second incarnation there, around 2013, an elderly, white sub was being given trial shifts as a casual. He was a bit eccentric and brash, though seemed harmless enough. But he was having a loud conversation with the guy sitting next to him and blurted out: "Beer's cheaper in my local Paki shop."

Imagine if he'd said: "Beer's cheaper in my local nigger shop."

I was seething, not just with him but with all the white men he was surrounded by, who probably felt a bit awkward but didn't have the balls to speak up and say that type of language is not acceptable in a modern newsroom. In the old days, I'd have confronted him. But instead, I spoke to the guy who did the rota and the racist didn't get another shift. I wouldn't have gone down that road if just *one* of his white brothers had ticked him off.

The silent majority.

I didn't like it that he felt comfortable using racial expletives just because he thought he was surrounded exclusively by white guys.

...

Only rivalled by the Irish, the one thing I love about the English is the sense of humour. To me, Peter Cook is the funniest man who ever lived. Me and Brian used to get stoned and listen to the Derek and Clive records he made with Dudley Moore in the Seventies. Cook used to push things way beyond the bounds of acceptability and I think he only got away with it because it was like he lived inside the characters he was portraying.

There's one bit which had us on the floor and a lot of you won't find it funny (we were stoned when we heard it the first time). His character was talking about how he'd knocked down an old lady in his car, got out and had a look and...

"Naturally, I bent down to, er...rape her."

I'm usually against rape jokes but the use of the word "*naturally*"! No, not fucking "*naturally*"! That is Cook's genius in its most extreme form. Another line of his I like: "The thing about me and Dudley is that one of us Jewish. I'm not sure which one yet."

He also sang a song with the lyrics: "I'm a nigger and I fucked a white chick."

I still don't know what to make of that. Is it about saying that's a black male mentality or is it about white men's deep fears about big-dicked black men? I doubt he himself knew, such was the creative highwire he walked.

I do love the gallows humour trait in the English, it's definitely in me. It's a survival mechanism. I'd say that I have an "over-developed" sense of humour. I've been caught in some pretty extreme circumstances and being able to see the funny side of things has kept me together at times.

Irish humour is slightly different but brilliant in its own way. Urban myth has it that the daddy of psychoanalysis, Sigmund Freud, said they were the only people in the world who could not be psychoanalysed. I find that funny in itself. While a lot of English humour is built on "taking the piss", the Irish take it to another level. Broadly speaking, an Irish person will slag off their best friend, to their face, more often and more extremely than anyone else. It's a relentless assault on the ego. I was having a deep conversation with an Irish friend a few years ago in a pub and, at one point, she said: "This is not a very Irish conversation."

I said: "I'm not Irish!"

As Brian was such a big part of my life, I learned a lot about the Irish through him. We used to watch sitcom Father Ted together and it was a scream. He'd say things about the various characters such as: "There really are people in Ireland like that."

But I have met Irish people who hate the show because they feel it played up to the stereotype of their countrymen being stupid. It would be stupid if Irish people were so insecure about their own culture and society that they couldn't see the funny side of it or not want 'outsiders' to get an insight.

There are fucking idiots everywhere in the world.

I remember Brian's younger brother being puzzled about why the show was so popular outside of Ireland because the humour is so Irish. But it's still incredibly popular in the UK despite the last episode being broadcast for the first time over 20 years ago. There were only 25 episodes of Father Ted ever made and I must have seen each one at least 20 times. That living room set becomes an extension of my own living room when I'm watching it. And the characters are like old friends. It's my second favourite sitcom of all time, after Seinfeld (Jewish humour is also pretty fucking good).

My favourite black comedian is Chris Rock. In relation to Barry Obama becoming US President in 2008, the funnyman said in 2014:

"When we talk about race relations in America or racial progress, it's all nonsense. There are no race relations. White people were crazy. Now they're not as crazy. To say that black people have made progress would be to say they deserve what happened to them before…

"So, to say Obama is progress is saying that he's the first black person that is qualified to be president. That's not black progress. That's white progress. There's been black people qualified to be president for hundreds of years. If you saw Tina Turner and Ike having a lovely breakfast over there, would you say their relationship's improved? Some people would. But a smart person would go, 'Oh, he stopped punching her in the face.'

"It's not up to her. Ike and Tina Turner's relationship has nothing to do with Tina Turner. Nothing. It just doesn't. The question is, you know, my kids are smart, educated, beautiful, polite children. There have been smart, educated, beautiful, polite black children for hundreds of years. The advantage that my children have is that my children are encountering the nicest white people that America has ever produced. Let's hope America keeps producing nicer white people."

What elevates Rock even beyond that sort of insight is that he's not afraid to tackle black people as well as white people. In one set, to a seemingly exclusively black audience, he pronounced: "I love black people…but I'm tired of the niggas!"

It made me think about when I was getting a subwoofer installed into my car near The Frontline. The Jamaican migrant fitter told me: "Now you need a car alarm — because of the niggas."

On Barry, I think it's great that so many white Americans voted for a black/mixed race president. Progress. But I don't like the man. He gave a lot of people false hope that there would be tangible change, although I was never one of them. His politics aren't particularly black. He is an Establishment figure. Despite being a Democrat, he failed to close Camp Delta in Guantanamo Bay and the Ferguson riots happened on his watch. Crucially, his net worth was around £30million in 2018. He knows not to bite the hand that feeds him.

To compound the sense of betrayal was his eulogy at the 2018 funeral of Republican nominee for US President in 2008, John McCain. It was an election he lost to Barry. The former Vietnam prisoner of war died age 82. He once said: "I hate the gooks. I will hate them as long as I live."

Now you're dead. Good.

McCain also supported the rescinding of Martin Luther King Day, kept white supremacists on his payroll and helped lobbyists for dictators and terrorists.

He fought to keep the Confederate battle flag flying over South Carolina. And his religion-inspired bellicosity called for the US to wage war for the sake of "imparting our values upon humanity". But despite all of that, Barry said in his eulogy to McCain: "While John and I disagreed on all kinds of foreign policy issues, we stood together on America's role as the one indispensable nation, believing that with great power and great blessings, comes great responsibility."

He added: "When all was said and done, we were on the same team. We never doubted we were on the same team."

Well, I'm definitely not on their poxy team. At least warmonger McCain didn't pretend to be something he wasn't. Enjoy your many millions, Barry, because, like Blair, that's all you've got. Barry may want to contemplate Ice-T lyrics from 1991 track Straight Up Nigga:

I don't celebrate bullshit Thanksgiving
Sit up like some fool and eat turkey
That's the day your forefathers jerked me
Shipped us all over here in locks and chains
Split us up, twisted up a nigga's brain

If Barry's doing eulogies for the likes of white supremacist McCain, I'm sure he is sitting up like some fool and eating turkey on Thanksgiving. So whose brain is more "twisted", Ice-T's or Barry's?

Donald Trump is worse on the face of things but I find it ironic that he's probably the biggest threat to the US at the time of writing. He has turned the yanks into the laughing stock of the world for voting him in.

Good jaaarb.

...

I can get embarrassed by the subject of money and I reckon that's the English in me. It cripples me when it comes to business. But Peso was totally consumed by money and that destroyed part of his soul, so maybe it wasn't such a bad thing that I'm not more that way inclined. Maybe his mindset plays into my complex. I believe everyone has a dysfunctional relationship with money, it's just a question of degree.

Of course, I share characteristics with my white mum. But my whiteness has been broken down bit by bit over the course of my life. That certainly wasn't something

I could have predicted or expected. It's just a result of my experiences and how they have shaped me. As I said, I'm "politically black". This has not felt like a *choice*.

I feel white people are generally more into constructing "narratives" to build their truth and that does cover much of the Western world. I vaguely recall stories about the US military staging and filming dramatised versions of operations, like Hollywood movies. Propaganda. What's more "narrative" than that? The US produces a lot of great entertainment but it seems to me that the lines between fact and fiction are more blurred there than pretty much anywhere else in the world. It's more subtle in the UK. And I reckon those living under dictatorships pretty much know the score.

...

One of the most unexpected examples of encountering racism personally came when I was renovating the conservation area bungalow in Goodmayes, near Ilford, east London, with my now ex. We had totally gutted the place. The bathroom was a major task and we were looking for components. We stumbled on a huge plumbing store in Ilford, which has a large Asian population. Naturally, we went in to investigate. It looked good, well stocked.

There were four white staff on duty. We were the only people browsing and thought they would eventually approach us. But they didn't, even after we'd spent ten minutes having a look around. The three male workers had their backs to us. The woman, in her early 30s, was just scowling at us. We left straight away. Did they honestly just want to sell to white people? Bizarre in an Asian area. Maybe it was because we were a mixed race couple.

The thing is, so many white people complain about being overrun by immigrants in certain areas. Driven out. The truth is that it's mostly about the phenomenon of "white flight", when white people leave an area to get away from immigrants, or foreigners in general. In east London, the pattern is that they move out to Essex. West Ham United is a club which used to be based in the middle of an Asian area, East Ham but despite its (old) location, it's known as a club with an almost exclusively white following. So many Hammers made the trek from Essex for home games, before the club moved to the London Stadium in Stratford, east London, in 2016.

. . .

Flashback to 1993 on the kibbutz when I was 21...

I met Brian and we hit it off straight away, he was a happy-go-lucky, cheeky-chappy Irish lad. We used to clean the pub in exchange for a few beers. And we found a way with a broom handle to secure ourselves "a few" extra. But in the first week I met him, I was reading a story in The Jerusalem Post about how 250 people had died in an Indian train crash. Brian joked: "Ah, they're only Indians."

I didn't say anything but I was not amused. How would he react if 250 Irish people had died in a train crash and I'd joked: "Ah, they're only Irish"?

Badly, I guess. Probably with repeated punches to my head. But what really grated was that he then proceeded to give me a five-minute lecture on my sense of humour. I suppose I shrugged off the sides of him I didn't like over the years because I got a buzz out of the sides of him I did like.

Looking back, I feel my instincts were right about the story, although I was not equipped to vocalise those instincts at that age. Don't get me wrong, as I've said, I have a pretty dark sense of humour. But it didn't take me long to realise after my journalism career began in earnest that there's a "currency of lives" in the British press: 1 Brit = 3 Irish = 5 Yanks = 250 Indians and so on. I'm not stupid, I understand the need for this type of formula. I am not advocating that every Indian death is given as much weight in a British publication as a British death. The problem, for me, is that the UK media operates in such a way as to make an Indian life seem *worth less* than a Brit's life in readers' minds. People's minds. Net result, as a young, Pakistani-born woman put it to me: "They think they're better than us."

Maybe my friendship with Brian was never destined to last. It's a shame because we were close for huge sections of our lives. He was charismatic and funny. But he retained those same, original instincts over the years.

As Why I'm No Longer Talking to White People about Race author Reni Eddo-Lodge puts it: "It must be a strange life, always having permission to speak and feeling indignant when you're finally asked to listen."

17. Wedding cake

'Mixed race people don't belong to either race'

Deep down, I don't see myself as half English/half Indian, half white/half brown, mixed race/Anglo-Indian and so forth. I'm just a person who sees the world through the prism of my own experiences, as does everyone in their own way. But I definitely am "politically black". It's about where you stand, as Bob Marley put it: "In The Struggle."

He is one of the great black icons but his father was white — and he got a lot of stick for being mixed race while he was growing up in Jamaica.

I don't divide people into "good" and "bad" depending on their racial background. But despite being a huge generalisation, there are shared traits within the races. I know that — feel that — from my own experiences and recognising my "inner Peso". I used to beat myself up about having aspects of him in me. Now I leave it to others.

Progress.

Such an irony that on the one hand I've got people comparing me to Peso and on the other I've got people telling me that I'm white.

My experience of being mixed race is that it's like being a bridge between the races — bridges get trampled on. I've had it from all sides, people telling me what I am and what I am not but again, largely not from black people.

And if you think I'm preoccupied with racism, you're right. I am. Try being on the wrong end of it from relatives, sometimes your own flesh and blood. My interpretation is that white people who tell me that I am white don't want me to be white, they want me to *want* to be white. Maybe I look white. But I am not white. I have many facets and after all the racist shit I've endured in my life, please let me define my own racial identity. I'm gonna do it anyway.

Some see the mixed race aspect of me straight away, it's quite random. Early on at Pimlico, I struck up a friendship with one of the PE teachers, a white, Scottish guy. As a football fanatic, I was in awe of him for being on Celtic Football Club's books as a youngster. So we used to chat and, somehow, probably because of my full name, it occurred to Mr Steel that I wasn't white. I told him my dad was Indian and he said: "I knew there was something I liked about you."

He recognised I was a bit different. He used to get sent Christmas cards by Celtic and one year he gave the card to me. Mr Steel was nice, especially bearing in mind that I wasn't a great sportsman, and there were plenty of those at Pimlico.

. . .

I did grow up in a white family. And my dad wasn't really an immigrant. He spent the vast majority of his life in Bombay. He didn't play a big part in bringing me up day to day but the apple doesn't fall far from the tree and his genes are dominant in me. So, even though I have relatively fair skin and a Cockney accent, how can I possibly be white? My racial background came up when I was having a blood test recently and I told the Gujarati nurse that my mum is English and my dad was a Sindhi. She said: "That's a good combination, mild *and* spicy."

That's me.

I was aware of being "half Indian" from a very tender age. I had Indian clothes sent over by relatives from when I was a toddler and I was proud to wear them. A lot of people think I look Greek or Italian. In Lebanon, they thought I was Lebanese. In Israel, they thought

I was Israeli. It's like I belong halfway between London
and Bombay. I actually feel it but I can't fathom out how
it works: Is it because they think I'm from there or is it
because I see so many people around who look like me
that my behaviour changes? I genuinely don't know.

...

Over the years, I've developed a bit of a complex when
it comes to ordering Indian subcontinent food. Peso used
to take me to this great Pakistani restaurant in Bayswater,
central London, called Khan's. It's still going. One of the
few useful things he ever taught me was how to order food
from that region, how to combine the dishes and how to
eat exclusively with my right hand, like Hindus.

But there was a time when my mum would have me,
(her by then ex-husband) Rob, my half brother and my
half sister round for a treat of Indian takeaway. I found
the way they ordered so frustrating. It was like a Western
democracy. Each person would select a dish and we'd
have naans and rice as well. It ate at me that they never
once asked my opinion, especially as I had quite a bit of
expertise to bring to the table. It was also an issue for me
that I wasn't able to demonstrate that Peso wasn't all bad.
That he'd taught me something. He still is portrayed by
many as this two-dimensional character. He wasn't.

I would never have dictated but I could have *suggested*.
These days, when I'm ordering Indian food with most
people I want to break bread with, I make *suggestions*
and my expertise is usually valued. Obviously, if someone
doesn't like spinach, I'm not going to order a dish with
spinach. And what to order varies from establishment to
establishment. Some do certain dishes better than others.

All of this may seem petty, it's no big deal in the greater scheme of things. But it's symbolic to me.

It is another great source of frustration of mine that mixed race people don't get much of a voice in the media when it comes to race relations: We have a unique insight into different worlds. Maybe I'm not fully trusted by any one set of people across the racial spectrum but that doesn't preoccupy me. To be clear, there are things I like and dislike from both sides of my cultural heritage.

Many years ago at The Sun, there was a story about how mixed race people would be the biggest racial minority in Britain by 2025. Filed by a senior writer, it was presented as a calamity. The interesting thing is that someone (I can't remember who) gave it to a mixed race person to edit. Me. In a subtle way, I neutralised the tone of the story and reduced it to the bare facts. That's a good example of how to make a direct impact on the wider discourse in our society. There's no doubt in my mind that whoever gave me that story was on my side. The reason I don't remember who it was is simply because I didn't realise the personal significance of the story when I was given the filename to work on. Once I got stuck into the story, I became totally focused.

I didn't present the statistic about 2025 as a good thing or a bad thing, I just wrote the story in such a way that the readers could draw their own conclusions. It's a balancing act in the media if you are trying to have an impact on a consistent basis.

A few months later, I was having a curry night with a multi-racial group of friends and family I played football with and I was telling them about the tickle I'd given to the story. This thick, white boy, who always wore an England shirt, made a remark about "not everyone being pro-mixed race people". This weird, ugly expression came over his reddening face. I could feel the anger bubbling up inside me and I wanted to punch his lights out. I knew he was saying he was against mixed race people and it made me feel like he didn't want me to *exist*. I came close to walking out or having it out with him. But that would have been self-defeating, in the long run.

I just wanted him to come out and say what he wanted to say and face the consequences — or shut the fuck up and keep his racist views to himself. I find that kind of passive aggressive behaviour to be a big part of the English psyche. My mum comes from an upper middle class, English background and the whole world of manners and etiquette is a minefield. I find it tedious. Life's too short for that shit.

I don't recall how it came up but a (very!) white, posh colleague at The Sun once asked me: "What's wrong with being a coconut [brown on the inside and white on the inside]?"

She was quite a high-profile Tory activist and I respected her for the way she used me as a sounding board for her political ideas. I hate her Thatcherite leanings but she was genuinely all ears. And she was a nice person, despite the effect privilege had on her. My understanding was that she felt that it was insulting to white people that people from other racial backgrounds don't want to be white. I told her that it's "about trying to be something that you are not". Coconuts are not trusted by people of colour. And I believe coconuts will never be fully and truly trusted by white people.

Many years ago, when I was working in the ethnic minority press, a Bangladeshi colleague said that I was "a wedding cake. White on the outside, brown on the inside".

I think that's true. Growing up in a white family, I largely know how to tune into white people's frequency. But it gets to me not being met anywhere near halfway and

I can get frustrated at not being able to express myself in the way I want to. And that's not just about white people.

I struggle to comprehend how differently people react to me and treat me in different circumstances. I am a "chameleon", as a consultant psychiatrist described me many years ago, in the varying racial contexts I find myself. But deep down, I know myself. I know who I am, what I am and why I am the way I am.

Black comedy legend Richard Prior gave up his first career as a stand-up comedian in his early days. He was doing his then 'vanilla' act in Las Vegas and spotted members of the Rat Pack, such as Dean Martin, in the audience. He decided there and then that it just wasn't him, even though he was being extremely well paid. Years later, he said: "It's been a struggle for me because I had a chance to be white and I refused."

I relate to that. Prior went on to push the boundaries as a politically black figurehead. And for his faults, he made a difference to many lives. He had an impact on the discourse of culture and politics in America and beyond. He certainly had an impact on me.

...

As I touched on in the previous chapter, my immediate white, English family hated going to Hampshire to see my English grandmother in her mansion but one year, when I was 15, we had to go there for Christmas. Things did not go well and I had a bust-up with my uncle over my attitude towards his racist mother. It was a whole big scene (that's the short story). I was staying with him but ended up in my aunt's house, where the rest of my immediate family were staying. I was already in tears when my mum informed me that my grandmother told her: "Mixed race people don't belong to either race."

Firstly, such a thought had never occurred to me, up to that point. Thankfully, I went to multi-cultural schools and there were plenty of mixed race kids around way before the whole concept of race and racism was imposed on us. But those words still haunt me. That my own grandmother would say it about her own flesh and blood. What hurt me more was my mum relaying this to me.

Then, years later, during the late Nineties, something weird happened…

I was being driven around Tel Aviv by my Israeli girlfriend and, out of nowhere, I told her that I wanted to know my English grandmother. I flew back the next day and the next day after that, my mum told me that her mother "wants to know her grandson". It's one of those things that happen to me every now and then and, these days, I just accept it, which is quite Indian.

We all travelled down to Hampshire and…it was okay. I was the star of the show and my grandmother was the co-star. Evidently, she'd been following my career and said: "I think you're very good at what you do."

It was poignant closure.

...

Some of my now former partner's relatives were against our marriage, despite the teachings of Sikhism — racial and sexual equality. The reality is quite different. The Sikhs who have created their own castes, propagate sexism and pander to prejudices are total hypocrites. Some said the marriage wouldn't last. It didn't but not for the reasons they predicted. I worked so hard to integrate and I ended up being very close to my now ex's immediate family. I miss some of them, deeply.

But there was one particularly hurtful episode. My now ex has a cousin who has done well for himself and he has a mansion with a swimming pool and tennis court in a fancy part of Essex. One evening we were invited over for a barbecue. I was playing water polo in the pool and my now ex's cousin's two teenage sons were saying they didn't want to be on the same side as a "gora", essentially a putdown term for white people.

After all I'd done in my life — pulling myself up by the bootstraps as a Brixton boy, to becoming a successful journalist, to becoming accepted and respected in that Sikh community, jumping through hoop after hoop — two little pricks who had everything laid on a plate for them felt superior to me. They are grown up now but they wouldn't last two minutes in my world. The reason it got to me so much was that I couldn't say anything back because they were kids (but old enough to know what they were saying). A bit like the boy in the playground when I was aged 15 and getting stoned with my mates.

I hate being a pinball between the races. That's part of why I have a small but select circle of friends, because I don't always want to go through the whole process of explaining myself to potential new mates. I was kinda hoping this book might serve that purpose.

When I was at The Screws, there was a messenger boy who was a quarter Indian. All the other, exclusively white, messenger boys used to take the piss out of him for it. I only know this because I was ear-wigging their conversation about his Indian blood and he said: "I hate this."

I never wanted to bury my roots because, from a tender age, my unconscious mind knew that would have destroyed me. This brings me back to Brian. I have mixed feelings about him, he played a big part in my life. We shared my tiny, one-bedroom flat on The Frontline for about half the Nineties in total. We made sacrifices for each other. We were both mostly patient and understanding. And we enjoyed each others' company. We got stoned *a lot* and it was great.

But one night, we decided to get ourselves together and go for a pint in central Brixton. He had met an Indian woman in Goa and had decided he wanted to spend the rest of his life with her. I was the one who had directed him towards India and, specifically, Goa. But at some point in the pub, things got nasty when it came to the topic of kids. I was saying that having an Indian name helped me because I didn't want anyone to think I was hiding my ethnicity. It meant I was always on the front foot. Somehow, this degenerated into a row. He just kept saying: "But that's you, Sid."

I wasn't laying down the law, I was just giving my perspective, telling it the way I saw it, the way he spoke his mind. I did it because I cared about him. But Brian has always had all the answers and didn't want to know. I was recently watching comedian Stewart Lee on TV and he was doing this whole mock bit about how his routine was falling apart, rhetorically asking the audience something like: "Who knows most about stand-up comedy, me or you?"

He added: "It's me, right?"

I should have asked Brian: "Who knows most about being mixed race, me or you?"

Then added: "It's me, right?"

I felt like he was invalidating my whole experience of being mixed race. For a change, we went our separate ways as we left the pub. I headed to the gardens which surround the massive church which threatens to dominate the whole of central Brixton. Like when I cried over Peso, I sat down on a bench, put my head in my hands and bawled my eyes out for ten minutes. But the thing about me is that I've always had to rely on myself, so even when someone has outraged me, I have to make the best of things. We got back to normal after a few days. But deep down, it did change my feelings about Brian.

. . .

I'm not a fan of the royal family. Their presence plays a major part in reinforcing the British class system. But I believe the addition of mixed race Meghan Markle is, on balance, a good thing. However, am I the only one who noticed that Prince Harry's racially-charged antics over the years were conveniently forgotten when the engagement was announced? Antics such as wearing a Nazi uniform to a fancy dress party and describing one of his army colleagues as a "Paki".

But totally randomly, the thing which stuck out for me that week was comments by comedian Josh Widdicombe on Channel 4 show The Last Leg. He was talking about his frustration that people were even talking about Meghan's racial background in this day and age and seemed genuinely seething.

Now, he's a nice white boy who grew up in Devon and I like him and his sitcom. But I have to say such attitudes are part of the problem. It *is* a big deal and should be treated as such. It's almost like he was saying that racism is a thing of the past. It isn't. It's like a virus which is constantly morphing into new strains to defeat the latest antibiotics. And, as a mixed race person, I *want* people to talk about it. I didn't see one mixed race person being asked on TV for their take on the engagement. That shows how far we *haven't* come. Of course, I applaud Josh's good intentions. But the path to hell is paved with good intentions.

It's funny how these sort of things come out of the blue. For instance, David Dickinson became a major TV star in the early Noughties as the presenter of BBC show Bargain Hunt. There were loads of jokes about his "perma-tanned" appearance and he was a bit of a figure of fun. I didn't see his programme but he seemed like a nice, charismatic guy.

Anyway, one evening I was watching a BBC chat show and Dickinson was one of the guests. Host Terry Wogan alluded to his complexion and there were a few chuckles in the audience but the response stunned me. He told Wogan that his biological mother was Armenian and that was why he was dark skinned. He was then adopted by an English family. Clearly sick of all the ribbing, the normally affable Dickinson was in serious mood as he delivered his explanation. It was clear that all the ribbing about his "perma-tanned" appearance had deeply affected him.

...

In my early days at Eastern Eye (1995), I did an opinion piece about being mixed race. Before I wrote it, Nad reckoned I "could be a spokesman for mixed race people". This is it:

HEADLINE: Who do you love more?

"My mother is white and my father is Indian. People often ask me if I feel more Asian or white. If my reply seems angry then I'd ask you to understand that I am merely irritated at those who try and force me into a choice that I don't believe I should have to make.

"My answer may well be one that isn't necessarily convenient for either Asians or whites. I am not going to claim to represent mixed race people as a whole, I'm only an expert on the subject in as much as having experience of being mixed race.

"I know people of many weird and wonderful mixtures — Indian/German, Iraqi/Spanish, Moroccan/Italian — how can I speak on their behalf any more than a Bengali can speak on behalf of Pakistanis?

"I've been half Indian, half English all my life, I'm quite used to the idea and I've got a very strong personal identity.

"Being mixed race has put me in a unique position. I believe that I know more about the way a white person thinks than any Asian and more about the way an Asian person thinks than any white person.

"I'm constantly being told that I look white — therefore I am white. Does that mean that if I had darker skin then I'd be more Asian? I really don't believe that Asian identity is as weak as a shade of skin.

"I know mixed race people who are darker than me yet consider themselves white and I know Asians who wish they were white.

"I don't regard myself as white. To me, much of the idea behind 'white identity' is based, literally, on whiteness, not history or culture — a kind of misguided sense of racial purity — therefore how can I be white?

"I'm mot trying to dismiss any real culture, all I'm saying is that 'white', as a saying, is merely a convenient term of reference, not an actual cultural identity in itself, though some try to use 'white' as a racist tool.

"Some Asians have informed me that I don't know what it's like to be on the receiving end of racism. The thing they don't consider is that white people often put their foot in it by talking about those "f******* P***s" — it's a tiring situation and one which I invariably feel compelled to react to.

"The last time somebody spoke about "f****** P***s" I was in a car with four white guys who knew me just as "Siddy". I told the man in question that "I'm half Indian and you're lucky I don't break your jaw". He apologised but needless to say, the atmosphere for the rest of the journey was uneasy.

"You may think I was wrong to react so angrily to what was a mistake. But was I supposed to say "it's okay, you didn't know"? Or was I supposed to just keep quiet?

"In public or in private, that man was a racist and none of the other white men said, 'I'm not a racist and I don't want to listen to abusive, racist language.'

"I was on my own. I find this kind of 'secret racism' the most worrying of all.

"That experience of unwitting infiltration, like in the car, has made it very hard to identify who's a racist.

"I now make a point of letting people know, quite quickly, that I'm half Indian. I get one of three reactions: Indifference, curiosity or disdainful shock. If I get the last of those reactions then I know that I don't really want to have anything to do with that person.

"I think I can learn more from that little test than all the discussion in the world.

"I have been to India twice and I absolutely loved it. My relatives were pleased to see me, being accepted wasn't an issue. The level at which I was accepted didn't really seem like something that should trouble me, after all, I've grown up in Britain, I'm not trying to pretend otherwise.

"That contrasts with a lot of people who go 'back home' and I find that their relatives are jealous of their often richer

Western counterparts and see them as outsiders. So my experience of India has been relatively positive.

"A major regret is that I can't speak Hindi but then my father is from and again lives in Bombay, where English is universally spoken and is certainly the most spoken language amongst his family and friends.

"I would like to speak Hindi because it's part of the culture and I'd like to live in India at some point in my life, not only is it the land of my father but it's a fascinating country, full stop.

"One of the conclusions I came to when I returned from India was how Asian communities in Britain seem to have an almost exaggerated sense of their own cultural identity. I can understand that protectionist attitude but I would still prefer to learn about Indian culture in India, not Bethnal Green or Bradford.

"I can't help wondering if a chain reaction of sneering has occurred — maybe British Asians, who are judged by their families 'back home', should be telling those 'back home' that they are Asian as well as British rather than judging me the way their relatives judge them.

"With the shared history of Britain and India, I have asked questions about both sets of heritage. Remember, I don't have the option of wallowing in my own ignorance, of believing that everything MY people do is right, of believing that only MY people are good, that only MY people can be trusted. Of being insular.

"I don't want to be the 'he's all right even if he's half Indian' amongst whites or 'he's all right even if he is half white' amongst Asians.

"I don't believe that I should have to choose between being Asian and being white. What sort of person would ask: 'Who do you love more, your mother or your father?'"

Nad read it and said: "It's well written but there's no way we can publish it."

Looking back, I was finding out a lot of stuff about myself. I was angry, aggressive and smoked too much dope. That's the Brixton in me. But I didn't see myself that way at the time. I thought I was soft and amiable. It makes me wonder about the people I've been scared of over the years: What was really going on inside them?

. . .

When it came to what to write on the front cover of this book, I got stuck on: "Stories of a *mixed race* boy raised on Brixton's Frontline."

The thing is, I didn't want people to make the assumption that I am half black/half white, which would be the obvious conclusion. So I changed it to "Anglo-Indian". But that means something quite specific in India and it isn't me. There's a dwindling "Anglo-Indian" community over there linked to the Raj era. But if James Brown can reclaim "black" and Snoop Dogg can "bring the Afro back", then I am having "Anglo-Indian".

It's mine.

Part V: Obey

18. War of ideas

'We're the Greeks and they're the Romans'

My mum took me to see my great aunt in Hampshire when I was two. She wasn't one of those who rejected me because of my mixed race background. But she was incredibly posh. My mum tells the story of how Aunt Jassie said: "What a delightful child…but where did he get that frightful accent?"

I piped up: "Lundun uh corse!"

Not a bad comeback for a little tyke. It's nice, looking back, that Aunt Jassie's only problem with me was my accent.

I was initially brought up single-handedly by my mum in a Brixton squat. One day, when I was around five, this older, white boy came up to me and shrieked in my face: "You dirty squatter!"

I wasn't upset, just a bit confused, so when I went home I asked my mum: "Am I a dirty squatter?"

Seeing the funny side, she smiled and said: "Yes!"

I shrugged my shoulders and said: "Okay."

I didn't even know what it meant, although I realised at the time that it obviously wasn't a compliment. One of my earliest memories of living in a squat was having my weekly, kettle-filled (because we didn't have hot running water), tin bath in the living room — like a cowboy. I actually loved it. There was something so cosy and intimate about the whole scene. I fondly remember being snuggled up by the fire in a towel afterwards.

I had a lot of freedom back in those days. Tunnelling under the fence in our back garden into Brockwell Park with my bare hands was fun. Me and a friend used water to turn the earth into mud, which made it easier. And, unsupervised, we bent bamboo sticks in a hot bath to make make archery bows with string, using twigs as arrows.

My mum also has pictures of me and a few friends playing a game when we were about six that the three who took part called "Naked Angels". It involved taking all our clothes off and running across the road and back again — a paedophile's dream come true. But Karl and Cassie insisted I was cheating because I wore socks. On my feet, I might add.

The area could be tough, though. There was this scary, scary kid in those Brailsford Road, Brixton, days. He was a few years older than me. I'm not sure what his racial make-up was but he looked quite like Elvis Presley, a particularly handsome lad. He set fire to the house next door to us and I can vividly recall my panicked stepdad Rob and other squatters, fearing the blaze would spread to our house, running to and fro in the back gardens with buckets of water, ahead of the fire brigade's arrival.

I spotted that boy working as a security guard at Brixton's Morley's department store several years later. Then a picture of him posing with his sporty Ford Escort XR3i car popped up on the local TV news because he'd been missing for several months. It turned out that he was pimping his girlfriend and her mother, effectively using them as sex slaves. They eventually murdered him, cut him into bits, put the remains into a wooden box and dumped it in the Thames.

I wonder what happened to his XR3i.

But this is not a sob story, my squatter days were largely happy. It was normal for me. I did however appreciate central heating when it finally came into my life. I hated those gas fires. You'd be either too hot or too cold. Sometimes both at the same time, depending on your position in the room. I was once wearing a jacket with my back to the gas fire and, eventually, realised it was melting.

I also suffered bronchitis in the winters because of the poor heating. But as I say, mainly happy days. There was a real community spirit because "squats" usually consisted of a clutch of houses, sometimes a whole street. And there was a political element to it. For many of the, mostly white, squatters it was a political statement: "Property is theft."

And many, many of the people from those communities ended up doing well in creative industries, particularly music, film and computer software.

So, I count it as a privilege that I wasn't limited in my own mind. Although I didn't have a direct example to follow as a journalist, being surrounded by people like that gave me the confidence to believe I could succeed in my chosen field as well. I mean, Rob was quite successful in the film and TV business but I was never in awe of him intellectually.

It grates that I went through that only for Brian many years later to accuse me of being middle class. *Accuse*. I have never stated otherwise. But I grew up poor. Dirt poor. Class is a complicated thing in Britain. As I said, I believe my middle class roots helped me to believe that I could achieve things. But I'm a self-made, self-educated man.

The irony in Britain is that many second generation immigrants onwards are exempt from "class classification". In my case, even though my parents came from upper middle class backgrounds in England and India respectively, I have a south London accent, which means I am perceived by most to be working class, especially if people don't know much about my personal history. I don't take that as a compliment or an insult.

Conversely, Nad, a second generation Pakistani Muslim, was raised in the Handsworth ghetto of Birmingham, and has far greater social mobility than me because the majority, white, native population don't have a marker for how he would be pigeonholed in Pakistan. I'm happy for Nad. But it is worthy of note that he said I have the "working class touch" when it comes to my job. I grew up on a middle class diet and I hated it. Despite its Indian origins, kedgeree was the dish I dreaded most. I just wanted chips, like my mates: The silver lining of being poor (for them).

My English background has made me quite aware that Britain is still, ultimately, ruled by the ruling classes. The ones with the right credentials and backgrounds are chosen for power, in everything from corporations to politics, particularly, regarding the latter, in the Tory Party. Famous broadcast journalist Jeremy Paxman, in his book, The English, reveals that this particular type of men are known as "The Breed". And he was told by a high-ranking Establishment figure about the English and the Americans: "We're the Greeks and they're the Romans."

I was close at one point of my life to a guy who is now quite high up in the UK political system. He was Cambridge-educated and seemed quite baffled as to how I was never intellectually bullied by him. He said: "Imagine what you'd be like if you had been well educated."

Flattering though I found that sentiment, my take on matters is *because* I didn't subscribe to The System. I can't remember if I told him that. A wise old man, an immigrant, once told me: "This country still controls the world…and they need to control their own people to do it."

I do not fully know what to make of that but London, the cradle of capitalism, is still the most important city in the world, I believe. It's the world's capital city. It sets the standard, leads the way in many senses. Remember that most Brits suffered terrible conditions during centuries when the UK state ruled the waves. It's a constant battle to divide and rule Britain's own population. Racism is a crucial dynamic in this. The US takes this to a whole different level and it scares the shit out of me (Trump is their president at the time of writing. Fascism is on the march again).

Many years ago, not long after the Iraq War began, an older, white colleague — who I had a lot of respect for — said that I would have to "choose which side you are on in this war". I told him: "I don't."

I am ruled by my conscience, not the laws and acts of hateful men.

The irony for me was that years after he left, I was deliberately and consistently given sensitive Muslim stories to edit at The Sun. Not every middlebencher made a show of giving them to me but one of them told me several times: "You won't be silly with this."

For me, it was a validation of my decision to change The System from within, even knowing I'm not going to garner any praise from either side of the political divide. But again, I am ruled — and guided — by my conscience. I have to say I think I'm in a minority on this within the media industry.

In 2015, then Sun columnist and professional hatemonger Kelvin MacKenzie ranted: "The old saying that not all Muslims are terrorists, but all terrorists are Muslims has never been truer."

What an absolute crock of shit.

It flies in the face of reality and facts. I'm almost loath to dignify it with a response. I wonder whether in his Eighties heyday as Editor of The Sun he would have ranted: "The old saying that not all Irish Catholics are terrorists, but all terrorists are Irish Catholics has never been truer."

He also managed to distort the findings of a recent poll, which actually showed that most British Muslims identify themselves as British, to suggesting that anyone who recognised the reasons for the Charlie Hebdo attack automatically supported the terrorists. I understand the principle which drove the attack, does that mean I supported it? No, it doesn't. It's all tied up in iconography. A physical depiction of Mohammed suggests the way he looked, so the more you look like the icon, the danger is that you will be seen as being closer to God. And vice-versa.

MacKenzie was suspended as a Sun columnist in 2017 for comparing a mixed race Everton and England player to a gorilla. The longstanding ally of Rupert Murdoch wrote: "Perhaps unfairly, I have always judged Ross Barkley as one of our dimmest footballers.

"There is something about the lack of reflection in his eyes which makes me certain not only are the lights not on, there is definitely nobody at home.

"I get a similar feeling when seeing a gorilla at the zoo. The physique is magnificent but it's the eyes that tell the story."

Next to the article was a picture of Barkley, who now plays for Chelsea, and an image of a gorilla, with the caption: "Could Everton's Ross Barkley represent the missing link between man and beast?"

MacKenzie claimed he was unaware that the player has a Nigerian grandfather.

His contract with the paper was "terminated by mutual consent".

I was going to write about fellow hatemonger and newspaper columnist Katie Hopkins, who described African migrants as "cockroaches" in The Sun and Palestinians as "filthy rodents" on Twitter. But as I began to research her "work", I decided that I did not want to be exposed to the literary equivalent of a snuff movie. And I do not want to put you through that, either.

As far as getting my opinions is concerned, it's complicated but I used to read The Economist many years ago. I thought it was intelligent, well-written and educational. It is. I was even friends with their Lebanon correspondent during my time there. For me, it was the best publication to understand what is actually going on in the world, in a left field sort of way. But things changed in the lead-up to the Iraq War: They advocated the use of propaganda. It just made me think: "Why should I trust *you*?"

I haven't picked it up since.

Propaganda has evolved alongside many other things and we are led to believe that the Empire crumbled after WW2. But I believe it was only our perceptions that changed. Colonialism is alive and kicking today. My formal education involved being told that history falls into two categories: Pre-WW2 and post-WW2. There is an obsession with the Nazis but the British Empire had a far more destructive impact on the wider world. That the Nazis were ideological was the key to their failure. The British Empire's success over the centuries was built on its economic success. I suppose that is an ideology in its own way but you get the point.

And people are the greatest commodity, whether they are cheap or talented. The NHS, for instance, would fall apart without immigrants, from consultants to cleaners. I see this as what I call "inverted colonialism". It is no longer practical to enslave people in their own countries, so they are invited to Britain to do the jobs the native population is unwilling to do. Immigrants are then blamed for many of the ills of society. This has been going on for a long time. Gandhi was once asked his opinion on Western civilisation. His reply: "It would be a good idea."

English comedian Ricky Gervais said of that: "Sarky git."

Two witty men. I can relate to both.

Being mixed race makes me challenge things more than most and I came across a great example of an insidious form of propaganda that I find more dangerous than outright racism or Islamophobia…or Ricky Gervais. It manifests itself on US TV shows such as Sky-CBS police drama Blue Bloods, starring he of the all-conquering, Village People-style moustache, Tom Selleck.

It's billed as a "gritty cop drama". Gritty my arse. It's about a white family who all work within the justice system. Selleck plays the NYPD Police Commissioner, his dad, who lives with him, used to hold the post, two of the boss's sons are cops and their sister is a district attorney. The observant Catholic Reagans (a reference to Ronald Reagan, surely) gather every week for Sunday lunch with all the grandkids to discuss their moral dilemmas and put the world to rights. It's Christmas every Sunday at the Reagans.

As Ice-T shrieks in one track: "SHIT AIN'T LIKE THAT!"

The show is actually a cross between Eighties US dramas Hill Street Blues (a genuinely gritty cop drama) and The Waltons (a sentimental series about a tight-knit pre-WW2 family). Blue Bloods is a lavish production, filmed on location in New York City, and that's part of the attraction. Here comes the problem: The family constantly bends the rules for friends, family and political allies. Lots of nods and winks. The viewers are being conditioned to accept it. That they and their friends get 'Justice Premium'. That's the way its narratives have been structured. Don't get me started on the racial stereotypes, it's off the scale. A whole other book should be devoted to it and it's been extensively covered online.

At the same time, Blue Bloods is set in the world the way most of us wish it to be, with The Establishment having all of our best interests at heart, despite all the evidence to the contrary being rubbed in our faces in real life. And it's sort of like a modern day cowboys and Indians.

It is currently the most popular network television show on Friday nights in the US, though you may be forgiven for never having heard of it, because the median age of the (mainly white) viewers is over 60.

The show is sentimental and formulaic. Top detective Danny — played by New Kids on the Block star Donnie Wahlberg — bends the rules (sometimes breaking the law) to get a result more than any other but he always gets the job done. The only, occasional, concession is that it may take him two episodes to "crack the case". There's always collateral damage in Blue Bloods but as long as a Reagan isn't shot, it only garners a passing mention at dinner time in the patriarchs' mansion.

The scary thing personally is that, when I watch it, I buy into it. I wish things were that way. I wish I could live next to a Reagan or even *be* a Reagan, I'd never get burgled either way. And if I did, Donnie would track down the "perp". And if he didn't, maybe one of the patriarchs have a contact in a charity which can write me a nice cheque. For that hour I'm watching Blue Bloods, I'm the safest person in the world, with my pals who, ultimately, possess such moral riches. Sleep easy tonight, folks, the Waltons are looking after us.

G'night Jim-Bob.

19. Rise of the clones

'Keep people afraid and they'll consume'

There's a 1988 movie directed by John Carpenter called They Live, it's a cult classic. To some, it's a prophetic masterpiece. To others, it's a tiresome B-movie. It was actually number one at the US box office and stayed in the top ten for a few weeks after it was first released. It is still being shown in cinemas around the world. It's a precursor to 1999 blockbuster The Matrix which, admittedly, is a much more watchable movie.

The most important thing I took out of They Live was how the media is corralling us into building our own, personal prisons. Aside from the film's deeper meaning, there was an important scene for me personally in which a poor person is getting stoned because he wants to block out the reality of what is going on around him. I can relate to that. A lot of my dope smoking activity was about losing myself in an inner world.

But my experiences in and out of psychotic episodes have convinced me that my take on the outer world may be closer to reality than most fear. I go from wondering whether having bipolar means I'm totally immune from the controlling messages of our consumer-driven society… or that I'm totally susceptible and that's what drives me into secure mental health units. Either way, They Live has helped keep me off the weed. But not nearly as much as fatherhood.

Carpenter has always maintained that They Live is an assault on Reaganomics/Thatcherism, not a dig at Zionism, as it is accused of being from time to time. Either way, it helped push me over the edge. Maybe that's what I needed, so I could start building my reality from scratch.

In my mind, consumerism has taken over from religion as the new opium of the masses, certainly in the West. England's 2011 'consumerism riots' spread like wildfire across the country, triggered by the killing in highly-suspicious circumstances of Mark Duggan, who was black, by armed police officers in Tottenham, north London.

Rioting is where this book began.

In the build up to the Iraq War in 2002, rock star Marilyn Manson said: "It's a campaign of fear and consumption. Keep people afraid and they'll consume."

Our heads are kept spinning by countless offers, tariffs, energy supplier options, investment schemes, payday lenders, gambling outlets etc. Everyone needs a PA these days. But where do you find the best value for money PA? I'm sure there's a website for it.

My favourite stand-up comedian is "Champagne socialist" Stewart Lee. He pointed out in a routine that you need to phone up or go online to activate your guarantee for many electrical goods these days, when all you needed in the past was a receipt or a guarantee they would hand you at the point of purchase. Presumably, having to activate it is just to put people off. That's pretty fucking cynical. Sharp practice.

Don't get me wrong, I like to have nice things. Nice cars. Nice clothes. Nice homes. Champagne! I'm not sanctimonious, it's just that I've become increasingly aware of this pagan, consumer society's pitfalls. Of how we are going further and further in that direction, unchecked. I know I'm also a consumer but I'm not into futile gestures, so thanks for the nice things, just that it's not my dream.

It seems to me that people even buy their opinions these days. Maybe that's always been particular to the

English but the digital revolution seems to be accelerating this process and the handling on this juggernaut of a 'world society' seems to be getting ever more unwieldy. When it comes to opinions, I go back to Israel, which I have mixed feelings about. In Britain, reporters on national newspapers are generally sent out to get a particular story and write it in such a way to be in line with the paper's editorial policy.

On message.

But I had dinner with an Israeli journalist in London many years ago (because he was doing a story about Syrian dictator Bashar Hafez Assad's wife, who hails from Ealing, west London) and he said their journalists go renegade and just file what they want, without being told what story to work on or how to cover it. That's so Israeli, in my experience. Thinking for yourself is the most important lesson they taught me. So, for those of you who feel betrayed by my current political stance on Israel, remember who taught me to think for myself. I'm not sure how it varies from paper to paper there but that Israeli journalist couldn't believe how we do it and vice-versa.

Maybe their way is best. All I see in our media is, effectively, marketing. Marketing of opinions, ideas and products. I know for a fact that one national newspaper even lets its advertisers choose which stories their ads sit next to.

Malcolm X said: "If you don't stand for something, you'll fall for anything."

I do get concerned at the way consumers get blown around by the prevailing winds: Politically, morally and so forth. It's mind *fashion*.

Like why is everybody getting a fucking tattoo and why are so many men growing fucking beards these days? This is the culture of clones. The rise of the clones. This goes far beyond *fashion*. The way consumers are addicted to and distracted by their mobile phones and social media is disturbing. Disturbing because there's a generation coming through who have never known any different. They actually feel empowered by technology but it's all part of the deception, in my opinion.

I grew up on the threshold of the digital revolution. Our school had three "Acorn" computers when I started there. And I had a computer from the age of about 12, a Sinclair 48k Spectrum. Admittedly, I mainly used it as a games machine, although I did have a little dabble at basic programming. The point about my generation is that previous ones wanted to be down with the kids and future ones didn't know any different. We were at the crossroads.

One of the things I appreciate from my upbringing was that there was so much more freedom of expression. There's a lot more pressure to conform to the consumer-driven juggernaut now. Brian even had a go at me for ordering a Big Mac and Filet-o-fish, just the sandwiches, rather than as part of a meal with fries and a drink. He even invoked his 12 year old son to back him up. Brian jokingly compared me, in a story, to his late, Indian father-in-law.

Why can't I order what I want? Why do I have to order fries and a drink?

The story about his father-in-law is brilliant, though. He was in an Indian restaurant in his Kolkata hometown with his own family and Brian's parents but wasn't impressed with the menu. Things broke down so much that he ended up arguing the toss with all the waiters, who were crowding round, trying to appease him. It ended up with him ordering from Pizza Hut and eating it at the table of the Indian restaurant. Peso was more sophisticated than that but essentially, the same spirit.

The whole scene was just to *impress*.

David Beckham doesn't impress me. Not because he didn't have a left foot, was slow, couldn't dribble, couldn't head. Not because he gave a copy of his autobiography to Nelson Mandela for Christmas. Not because he sported corn rows when he met Mandela (later admitting he was embarrassed about that but I wonder whether it was the cultural appropriation aspect which he regretted or just that he thought he should have had a short back and sides when meeting the icon). Not because he cheated on his wife. No, I hate him for two other reasons. Firstly, because he said "I'm a nice guy" when he was probed on whether he'd been playing away. You can't have it both ways, son, although maybe you did…

The second — and main — reason I hate him is because of comments he made in the aftermath of England's 2011 'consumerism riots'. Multi-millionaire superstar Becks, who admittedly hails from humble beginnings in east London, told the Wall Street Journal (of all publications): "The problem is, there is a minority of youth today in England who are not scared of authority. If they steal something, they are not worried about the consequences.

"When I was a kid growing up, I respected elders, I respected the law. If I was on a bus and an elderly lady got on, I would stand up and let her sit down. That doesn't happen these days. We've got the Olympics next year and these pictures are being seen all around the world. It makes me feel physically sick."

What I want to know, Becks, is: Did you actually vomit? Because you make me want to hurl. When was the last time you got on a bus? You absolute prick. A seven-seater Range Rover doesn't count, by the way.

However politically-motivated the rioters were or weren't, looting has usually played a major part in these situations, even if the beef is valid, because the participants are usually poor. The opportunity to get your hands on a large-screen TV or the latest trainers is pretty fucking tempting when you've got nothing to lose.

As Ice-T rapped on New Jack Hustler (1991):

I had nothing and I wanted it
You had everything and you flaunted it
Turned the needy into the greedy
With cocaine, my success came speedy

This elephant in the West's room is the relentless, destructive march to an almost universal, materially-obsessed society, with most people not even participating in a genuine society, let alone contributing to it. Becks — reportedly worth nearly half a billion with Posh — can thank the tens of millions of mugs who shell out money they often can't afford to buy products because he's endorsed them. They were among the products being looted. Maybe he's just protecting his interests.

Having it both ways again, son. He doesn't even realise.

I was watching a documentary a few years ago about him doing a vintage motorbike tour somewhere in South America. He kept talking about how how great it was to be anonymous in those surroundings and how it was "all about the journey". When they stopped at roadside eateries, his mates would excitedly ask befuddled locals if they recognised Becks, who sat there with a big, stupid grin stretched across his face. It made me feel a bit more sympathetic towards him that he craved a normal, anonymous life. But what would have made me even more sympathetic, if he truly wants to be anonymous, is not to bring a fucking film crew around with him. As folk hero and EastEnders thespian Danny Dyer would say: "Twat."

Having said all of that, actually, I don't think Becks was a crap footballer. He was pretty good and he got England to the World Cup, after all.

I do, however, think he's a crap person.

The riches to be gleaned from football are astronomical these days, as Becks will testify. But I vaguely remember an informal agreement by top flight clubs during the Nineties to only change their home shirts every other season because kids always want the newest versions and parents were complaining about the spiralling costs. What happened to that pledge? Now we get three new kits every season: Home/away/third/cup/'mug'/whatfuckingever ones, presumably designed by drug-addled toddlers. This may seem trivial but it's not, it's symptomatic.

Maybe what is happening in the world right now is WW3 and consumerism is driving it. Arms is still the most lucrative trade in the world. Ice-T predicted decades ago that WW3 would be largely "fought out in people's minds". It seems to me that a lot of things are being "fought out in people's minds" at the moment. It is being billed as a "clash of civilisations". I wonder how far away from the truth Western narratives are getting. Swiss psychiatrist and psychoanalyst Carl Jung was obsessed with the East and he concluded: "India is reality."

I know what he was banging on about. Me and my Indian aunt went to the crematorium to see Peso turned to ashes. The only other people who came with us were a male cousin he hadn't seen for five years and that guy's wife. The funeral set-up in India is different there and a "condolence meeting", effectively a memorial, was held several days later and was reasonably well attended.

My aunt beautified his body with some flowers and stuff before he was cremated but there was this large group behind us and we were holding them up. The widow was all over the place, in utter despair, having to be kept standing by relatives. Shrieking and sobbing. I made an effort to move things along. She was in her early 30s, so I guess her husband was taken quite young.

That scene was real.

A more positive example I recall is being driven through the streets of Bombay in a taxi a few years ago and this girl, who must have been about seven, ran out into the road and did a fantastic little dance for us, jumping back out of the way just in time. She was wearing an immaculate and striking purple outfit, despite probably being a slum dweller. What really struck me was how happy she was. How happy she was dancing on the edge of death. Not that I'm a rich man by Western standards but I sense that this girl was happier in that moment than I've ever been or will ever be.

Living in the moment comes and goes for me but that situation is improving and I'm convinced it's the key difference between East and West.

One of the things that particularly bothers me in our society at the moment is the explosion of gambling culture. There are so many options, especially now the internet has taken over. It makes me laugh when I see the UK's "When the Fun Stops, Stop" ad campaign. Are we being led to believe that gambling firms want to stop us gambling? They are paying hundreds of millions from their profits taken from punters for adverts to get people to gamble *more*. And they are paying millions from their profits taken from punters for adverts to get people to gamble *less*. Maybe they've reinvested in ad firms. Now *that's* a safe bet.

I could write a chapter about some of the most distasteful, disturbing advertising strategies I've seen but there was a Ladbrokes one which bothered me the most. The TV ad portrays a group of friends, young men in their mid-20s, who all have different characteristics, such as "The Believer" or "The Chancer". These positive, trendy men are living "The Ladbrokes Life". A life where gambling is a key part in finding happiness and fulfilment as a human being. "They" want you to buy into this image and, ultimately, want you to lose to them. Lose your money to them.

Arseholes.

The explosion of extortionate interest payday loans is also utterly shameful. Legalised loan sharks. I recall "I'm a pretty straight sort of guy" Tony Blair pledging to get rid of them before he came to power as PM in 1997. Now you can't get through an ad break without several such firms offering loans at extortionate interest rates. How much is Blair worth these days? Reckoned to be £27million. Politicians and promises, eh?

Lend us a fiver, Tone. He'd probably charge interest (2,364% APR. Ts&Cs apply).

But there is a side to our society which disturbs me even more than that. I call it "deteriorating norms". I consider myself to have quite a dark sense of humour but every now and then these days, I come across something which leaves me speechless. One image in particular was circulating in people's Facebook and other social media accounts and is a Photoshopped version of the iconic picture of a nine-year-old, naked, napalmed, Vietnamese girl running down the road from the scene of a US airstrike.

The snap is commonly known as "Napalm Girl" and was first published in 1972. The Photoshopped version has a superimposed image of late BBC star and serial paedophile Jimmy Savile chasing after her, rubbing his hands with glee. That image sent a chill down my spine. The victim, Phan Thi Kim Phuc, is now a Canadian citizen and has two children. But she still suffers with her burns and has to be treated for them daily.

The original image was published in the year I was born. But my understanding was that it shook up the world at the time. The point being that it was — on that single occasion — permissible to print a picture which displayed the genitals of a nine-year-old girl because it was for the greater good.

Whoever Photoshopped it was doing it for the greater bad and everyone who shared it was facilitating a stain on the human race.

20. Back to Brixton

'They said you controlled me'

Like the first time, around a dozen cops were there when I was sectioned under The Mental Health Act (1983) for the third, and hopefully last, time. But thankfully, the scenario in 2009 was quite different. It wasn't ideal, though. Me and my now ex were living in a crummy little flat in West Norwood, south London, after leaving our dream home bungalow in Goodmayes, unable to pay the mortgage because I was in no fit state to work.

It was a horrible time. The flat was on a punishingly steep hill, which was murder to walk up and it was a busy road. The sounds and vibrations of buses and lorries driving up used to cut through me like a blunt sword. I was so depressed and slowly going mad with nothing else to do but watch repeats of lame US sitcom Friends. My now ex wanted to chill out after a long day at work, while I wanted a bit of company. Tensions were running high. And it all came to a head pretty quickly one day.

We were due to visit India but somehow things blew up. I put on my "wedding turban", started tearing up wads of Rupee notes and played NWA's Panic Zone on my turntable.

She panicked.

Police started arriving at the flat as I sat down to play Big Mutha Truckers on my Playstation 2. I was being quite talkative with them. I was chatting about pizzas with this young, slightly chubby, blonde, female officer. My now ex later informed me that it was a young, male copper's first day on the job and he told her: "But he's so nice."

Then psychiatrists started turning up to assess me. The flat began filling up with more and more cops but I wasn't bothered. I didn't know it at the time but my now ex told me that they had spent an hour quietly removing sharp implements from the open plan kitchen-living room space before pouncing on me. They evidentially had my 2008 arrest in mind. But it was all a bit of an anti-climax in the end. My mind wandered for a moment, an officer took two steps forward and put some specially-adapted handcuffs on me. I was gutted. Not that I was in the mood to fight, just that I knew this was the beginning of another shitty chapter of my life. And being cuffed makes you feel pretty fucking impotent. No cuts and bruises, though.

I was taken by ambulance with a big, black cop to Lambeth Hospital, which is for mental patients and is located a five-minute walk from Brixton town centre. I was placed in mixed-gender Lambeth Early Onset (LEO) ward, even though I was technically too old to be on it. I got lucky. It was actually pretty nice, as 'prisons' go. I spent the next two months in there and didn't sleep for the first half of that period of incarceration, scared that the evil spirits would enter me if I drifted off. My ankles were inspected by a doctor after a few weeks because, as I hadn't slept for so long, they were concerned about swelling in my lower legs.

The nights were spent with other patients and the late shift nurses. I remember this young, male, Scottish staffer saying to me: "I don't know how you do it, Siddy."

When I finally did sleep, it was only for eight hours and I felt fine after that.

There were some tricky moments on LEO, some tricky customers. But most of the time, it was okay. I couldn't have wished for a better ward to be on. I liked it being mixed and most of my interactions were with youngish women, though not all.

However, I did blow up one time in particular. It was a sunny day and I wanted to sit down and lap up some rays.

But one of the nurses told me I wasn't allowed to take a chair outside. I wanted to know why and, without any sort of explanation, I got increasingly enraged. She looked quite scared. Somehow, I ended up in a room inside the building with more and more staff entering. They were mostly black, male nurses. I later learned they were drafted in from other wards on the complex. Eventually, I was cornered by about a dozen of them. I boomed: "I can outtalk any one of you."

They pounced, eventually wrestled me to the ground and managed to inject some sort of tranquilliser into one of my buttock cheeks. If that sounds traumatic, wrong. Whatever was injected wiped away the painful part of the memory and all I can clearly recall is all of them standing there and me saying my piece.

But the maddest thing I did on LEO was a dance. The Shivdasanis are the special devotees of Hindu god Lord Shiva. Peso introduced this idea to me during my 20s. I thought it was utter bullshit to start with but somehow I started getting interested in Shiva. It turns out that, like me, he is very creative and very destructive. Anyway, I tried to do Shiva's "Cosmic Dance" in the outside area. I just went with the flow, it was very aggressive, like a war dance. It must have lasted about ten minutes. The staff sealed the doors. I was totally exhausted by the end of it. Nice to get it out of my system, though.

I was relatively happy on LEO. It was a nice living space. And after I'd settled down a bit, the staff sent student doctors to talk to me about bipolar in the computer room. I quite enjoyed it. I'd show them my montages of different images I'd googled.

My best friends were two young women. Our friendship was special because I felt that we had a collective sanity between the three of us. I was never expecting them to suddenly do or say something odd out of the blue. It was a camaraderie and there was no sexual component to our interactions. 'Jane' would ask me to get rid of this particularly annoying, lazy-minded staff member, who treated the place as his personal playground. He was gone inside 60 seconds. I just told him straight that he wasn't wanted. Sort of *acted* mad. The other girl, who has a similar racial mix as me, told us that the head psychiatrist diagnosed her as "acutely psychotic". I always used to say to that: "He means, 'A cutey psychotic.'"

She was into self-harming, scarred by the cuts she'd made to her inner forearms. Her life had been tough and she had no idea what she wanted from the rest of it, not helped by having a mental illness which could pull the rug from under her feet at any time. She was a lovely girl, though. Smart and interesting. And beautiful, although not in a conventional sense.

They brought in a specialist psychiatrist to speak to me at one stage. He was Icelandic and I fondly told him how I'd won over £1,000 on Miss Iceland winning Miss World in 2005. He was a nice guy and I didn't find him at all patronising. At some point, he said: "You're clearly highly intelligent, so what's going on here?"

I can't remember how I dealt with that. I suppose I was *experimenting* with my thought patterns. I used to do loads of things which were quite random. One time, I went round the whole outside area and picked up every last fag butt (hundreds) and threw them away. Another time, I made a cemetery out of Jenga pieces in the activity room. I did installations using bottles, sticks and stones outside. I arranged the dining room tables and chairs in a certain way in the middle of the night to help the "energy flow". It was kind of like my own version of Feng Shui.

But I didn't give it a name. I just had this sense that everything around us impacts the unconscious mind, so even the smallest adjustment could make a big difference.

I could go on and on about my installations, it preoccupied me for the most part of most days. That and table football, which some of the staff joined in with, including the head of the unit, who was a lovely and attractive young woman. The table itself wasn't as big as the ones you get in pubs but that made it intense. I was good. Fucking good. The Top Dog. I used to have my own table when I was a kid and my mum's brother used to play it with me for hours on end when he lived with us for a year or so from when I was about ten. It was the only time we ever got on.

The funny thing was that my childhood way of playing table football came back to me after all those years. My basic strategies: Keep your left hand on the goalie at all times, be 'Roy Keane' relentless at all times and play square balls from the wingers to the centre forward to hammer home. I particularly liked it when I would take on two players. But my biggest competition was from this cool, Ethiopian guy. He was more creative but I just about had the edge on him with my relentlessness, most of the time. He once saw me building formations with plastic, toy soldiers and said to me: "Let's play. Anything."

Funny thing is that Mr. T came to see me in LEO and he beat me at table football, narrowly. I don't know when was the last time he'd played but I think it was more of a psychological thing than anything else. He was like a big brother figure to me, so I didn't express myself in the way I did with the other patients, who would accept my mentality in a way that no sane person could.

There was a good relationship with the staff in LEO. But some fucked up things happened. The most extreme was when the whole unit was locked down one evening after a young, Afghani guy went on the rampage. It was like something you might see in a documentary about an oppressive US prison. He was a handsome lad and, although he did require a lot of one-on-one attention away from the rest of us, the thing that really stood out was that he always wore scrubs. This was the last resort for patients who didn't have any clothes. I had the idea of us all wearing scrubs as a show of solidarity. But I don't think I ever vocalised that sentiment.

Ever the revolutionary.

Me and my two female friends were trapped in the TV room for about two hours. You could hear smashing, shouting, screaming. I always wondered what his story was. Had he got caught up in military action in Afghanistan? Anyway, we just about took the incident in our stride. In the end, we just wanted to get out for our hot chocolate and go to bed.

LEO was an exception to this but I find it curious how badly some of these mental health units have been thought out. During that last period of incarceration, I went with a few others to a kitchen in a high security women's unit to make my famous chilli con carne and I was struck by what an oppressive living space it was. Women were lying on the floor. I think the architect who designed that unit needs to spend a few weeks there. Also, I felt like I was treated like a convict at times. Technically, I had committed a crime first time I was sectioned, in 2008. But the second time, in 2009, I hadn't. This state of affairs needs to be reviewed. Those places are *our homes* when we are incarcerated against our will.

There was a black kid who particularly got on my nerves. He was about ten years younger than me and was a "revolving door patient" when he wasn't in jail for mugging. He used to show off his little criminal tricks, such as opening locked doors without a key. And I'm sure he stole my Dr Dre The Chronic CD. He said jail was an easy life. He was devoid of any ambition, totally lazy-minded. But what I hated most about him was that he always had a hand down his pants. I used to tell him to "get your fucking hand out your pants, you prick".

He would respond: "You sound like my dad."

This guy wasn't even being sarcastic, I took the same, dim view of him as his dad. There was another black patient who turned up during my time there, 'Mickey'. He was in his early 30s and seemed to be getting round-the-clock attention. He came across as a sweet guy. I think he was. But his room was opposite mine and one night, before I went to bed, I could hear him say: "I just want to see him."

It was a bit bizarre the first time because he wanted to see *me*! Eventually, one of the nurses knocked on the door to ask if he could see me and I obliged. This became a little ritual. He would open the door, have a quick look and then go to bed. It happened about half a dozen times. If I was the Top Dog at table football, Mickey was the Top Dog at table tennis. He was incredibly skilful and it was a battle of wits between us, all about spin and craft. I did beat him but only once.

Looking back, my Israeli girlfriend in the Nineties had me pegged, as in having a mental illness, from the start. She was a genius and her mum was a leading psychiatrist. I looked pretty good when I was young, in good shape and with a nice tan. But whenever someone alluded to my looks around her, she would tell them: "I'm with him for his *mind*."

I'd say: "Thank you!"

She said she saw me in The Catcher in the Rye, which is about a youngster with mental health issues. I suppose I related to the lead character and his thought processes. It's remarkable that my Israeli ex still had such feelings for me even though she, essentially, thought I was mad.

It's hard when people think you're mad.

After my last spell in a secure mental health unit in 2009, I was a broken man. I wanted my old, less shitty life back, being institutionalised at The Sun. I had nothing to fill up my days, other than going back to repeats of Friends, a bit of cooking and cigarettes. Eventually, my care worker suggested I attend a nearby charity for people with mental illnesses, Mosaic Clubhouse. I can't say I liked it but it gave me a tiny sense of purpose and it was something to do.

Anyway, I did end up getting that newspaper life back at The Sun and, over the years, I got stronger and stronger mentally and professionally, to the point that I'd not only picked up where I'd left off but was exceeding that level. However, every now and then, I'd get a little reminder about being on the police radar. I was on the way over to Ireland to see Brian in 2016 when armed police picked me out at Gatwick Airport and one of them got on his phone. The only thing I heard him say was: "In 2008."

Clearly, they had my arrest at the back of their minds. I suppose I put up a hell of a fight before I ended up in Goodmayes Hospital.

If the nurse who got me walking again during that period of incarceration was the kindest person I've met in the NHS mental health system, the most wonderful was a tiny, elderly, African, female, psychiatric nurse. She handled me so well when I was in the danger zone in 2014, close to having a full-blown manic episode.

The psychiatrists used to let her do all the talking and they would just take notes. This is because she had such a respectful vibe that made me feel like she had some love for those in her care. Well, I can only speak from my experience. But she didn't make me feel like a freak or a damaged person. She treated me as an equal, while recognising that I was going through a tough time. I would say her attitude and professionalism helped keep me out of hospital to a large extent during that particularly difficult period.

I believe my knack for journalism is rooted in bipolar. I can be quite creative, especially at the point where I'm potentially about to slip into an episode. It's a balancing act when I want to give birth to an idea, this book is a case in point. I knew I was losing it a bit as I started to build a concept for it. But then I got it to a certain point creatively, when I knew where I was going with it, pulled back and said to myself: "Now slow the fuck down."

It's great that I managed to self-police in that way. Real progress.

There is a whole phenomenon of bipolar in creative fields, whether it be journalism, art, theatre, films or sport. Talented and famous examples include Paul Gascoigne, Frank Bruno, Mike Tyson, Carrie Fisher, Richard Dreyfuss, Vincent van Gogh, Mel Gibson, Kurt Cobain, Jimi Hendrix, Ernest Hemingway, Catherine Zeta-Jones, Vivien Leigh, Frank Sinatra, Sinead O'Connor, Jean-Claude Van Damme, Winston Churchill, Adam Ant, Beethoven, Russell Brand, Robert Burns, Mariah Carey, Francis Ford Coppola, Stephen Fry, Spike Milligan, Allison Moyet, Lou Reed, Rene Russo, Nina Simone, Britney Spears, Dusty Springfield, Ted Turner, Kanye West, Brian Wilson, Amy Winehouse and, last but not least, me.

Having spent most of my working life as a sub-editor, I'd say that bipolar makes me obsessive. I'd obsess over a headline for days after that edition of the paper had been printed. *Days*. I'd kick myself when I came up with a better one. But that process made me resolved to do better next time. I was once sitting next to a sub and I peeked at his story and made an alternative headline suggestion, just to get a conversation going about it. But he was like: "This is okay, isn't it?"

"Okay" doesn't cut it for me.

In the Nineties, I became obsessive about the Middle East after my kibbutz experience. I would consume book after book about the region and, effectively, created my own degree course. I awarded myself a 2:1. In the Noughties, when I had the idea of opening a pizzeria in Goa, I learned every aspect of creating an authentic Neapolitan version. I even did a pizza-making course in Naples itself.

Obsessive.

That was after I took voluntary redundancy from The Sun the first time in 2007. I took it again at The Sun towards the end of 2016, just over a year after I split up with my ex and, in the same week, my dad died. In 2018, I started holding journalism workshops at Mosaic Clubhouse. It had changed location from Streatham to Brixton and the new site was much better.

I enjoyed empowering people. I planned out each session in detail with notes and a homework task. The biggest challenge for me was that the ability levels and behaviour patterns ranged across the spectrum. But these people are mostly patient with each other and my strategy of being open about my mental illness seemed to put them at ease. I didn't patronise them and wasn't afraid to keep things moving. When I was firm, I did it in a respectful way.

Every now and then, I got a rewarding moment, whether it be by something submitted or just a good observation by one of the students during the sessions. It's nice to give something back and it was so good for me to have a sense of purpose, rather than just trying to survive in a vicious, toxic newsroom.

At the time of writing, I have found a job as a media consultant on a well-known news website. I'm trying to improve its readability using various methods. It's perfect for me because I can largely work from home and the hours are flexible. I'm tired of being on the treadmill, pumping out words like a machine. I don't ever want to go back to that, especially because the workload has increased so much for subs in the last 20 years.

I'm happy with the life I am building for myself and the best part is having the love of a child. Nothing else compares. I haven't smoked a joint for ten years at the time of writing and have no intention of doing so again. Maybe on my deathbed. My daughter needs me. I need me! But I dream about dope a lot, it was a big part of me for many, many years. I was a total pothead. A Melting Pothead. Snoop rapped about his love of weed in the track I Miss That Bitch (2002):

I was young when I hooked up with her
One hit and I couldn't stop trippin'
A long lasting relationship
Pass you around, and let my niggas take a hit
I used to break you down just to roll you up
You the real, you never will slow me up
And you was always on my mind
Say no more
I still miss you at times

All of a sudden you lost my interest
I packed it up and set about my business
You used to have a hold on me
Sometimes to the point that they said you controlled
me

I can totally relate to that. I miss that bitch so much. Shiva is said to have given us ganja to help us see different worlds. But I was a junkie, I can see that now. There were times when I was just living for that next hit. There's more to life and I realise it now. It's a great move forward. But the desire to get high will always be part of me.

The thing is that now I'm a drinker and am liable to get into trouble when I've had a few too many. But a lot less so than when I was young and immature. At least, unlike cannabis, alcohol seems to flush out of your system pretty quickly. A lot of people openly smoke cannabis in my area and I'm like the "Bisto Kid" (a boy in a TV ad who can smell a gravy brand from a distance), trying to inhale their fumes when I get the chance. It's a bit pathetic.

Epilogue

A friend who read the manuscript of Melting Pothead said I wasn't revealing much about my personality. That reminded me about something my first Editor told me: "Only mad people talk to newspapers."

Okay, I get the personal irony of "mad" but I have revealed as much about myself as I want. This is not — and was never meant to be — a warts and all autobiography. It's not an autobiography. I'm more a storyteller than a story.

Peso was a story.

I just chucked in loads of stuff that I hope you found thought-provoking. Also, entertaining in parts, even though I appreciate it's not always an easy read. There's no central point to this book, it just comes from a desire to express myself.

Being the product of a racial taboo has caused me problems. But I believe it has largely been about external forces invading my inner world, rather than me projecting outwards.

A big part of writing this book was about asserting my identity, so even those closest to me would understand me better. The lack of a decent father has weighed heavily on me. But if I'm down, I just curl up into a ball and shut out the world, rather than inflicting my misery on others.

The bad moods don't tend to last so long these days, now I have a better understanding of my condition. But the scale of ignorance I've encountered over mental illness is not something I was prepared for. I'm open about bipolar because — at the time of writing — I feel strong enough to represent myself and others who have faced similar challenges.

Journalism is in me. I've had questions from the time I could first talk. And I saw from a tender age how the media's portrayal of black people, in particular, was so different from what I knew to be true. I don't want to live in a ghetto yet, in my mind, I've never truly left it.

Despite this book's title, I haven't written much about dope. What do you want me to say, that I got wasted a lot? Got high. My destructive-creative soul was always in me, dope just played a part in bringing it out. I'm not going to write another book about how my life would have been if I'd never smoked a joint because I don't know. But it would have been different.

Someone recently suggested I say things just to get a reaction. I don't. I just speak my mind. A journalist once asked Nineties Indian Test cricketer Manoj Prabhakar: "Do you court controversy or does controversy court you?"

His reply: "We were made for each other."

A kindred spirit.